I0418277

Let the
WILDFLOWERS GROW

*One Mother's Journey through
Adoption, Attachment, and
Borderline Personality Disorder*

BRIGITTE M. BECKER

copyright © 2024 by Brigitte M. Becker

All rights reserved. No part of this publication may be reproduced, distributed, or transmitted in any form or by any means, including photocopying, recording, or other electronic or mechanical methods, without the prior written permission of the publisher, except in the case of brief quotations embodied in critical reviews and certain other noncommercial uses permitted by copyright law.

Although the author has made every effort to ensure that the information in this book was correct at press time, the author and publisher do not assume and hereby disclaim any liability to any party for any loss, damage, or disruption caused by errors or omissions, whether such errors or omissions result from negligence, accident, or any other cause.

To protect the privacy and confidentiality of key individuals and institutions, their names, locations, and identifying details have been changed.

ISBN: 979-8-9911330-0-5 (eBook)
ISBN: 979-8-9911330-1-2 (Paperback)
ISBN: 979-8-9911330-2-9 (Hardcover)
ISBN: 979-8-9911330-3-6 (Audio Book)

Independently published by Brigitte M. Becker

For signed copies, bulk orders, or requests for interviews or reprint rights, contact:
brigittebecker@letthewildflowersgrow.net

Cover designed by Brigitte M. Becker

Edited by Margaret A. Harrell, margaretharrell.com

To my daughter, who is on her own journey:
my heart's desire is that our paths will converge once again,
filled with love and warmth

Contents

Part 8 — 2020

Part 9 — 2021

Part 10 — 2022

Part 11 — 2023

Part 12 — 2024

Introduction

My favorite job in the whole world is being a mom. For me, raising children has been immensely rewarding, joyful, heartwarming. And, at times, challenging and extremely heartbreaking.

To find the heart of this story, let me take you back to one day in 2013 . . .

Walking down the street with my daughter, Anna, and our dog, Lily, taking Anna to elementary school, I wanted to pinch myself—to start skipping—I was so happy. There was this place in my heart where I had wanted more children. And Anna was just all of a sudden there, like a double rainbow appearing in the sky, this bright, young Ukrainian, transported across continents to Boston to live with us. Her presence completed our family in a beautiful way. I vowed I'd be there for her, always.

Right away, I met a whole new group of incredible parents, teachers, and students her age, which I added to our existing friends. The world opened up to my daughter too, with new friends, sports, birthday parties, fun holidays, and incredible expressions of giving and receiving love.

One thing I heartily appreciate about her is, she's so adventurous. I am also adventurous, and we did many fun things together those first months. I felt like she was so brave—not knowing what to expect on the other end, coming to the United States from faraway.

She was intrepid in trying new foods and quickly took a liking to yogurt, salmon, and sushi. She practiced good hygiene, but we had to remind her not to use too much toilet paper, now that she could "flush" it down the toilet instead of putting it in the trash. We laughed about a lot of things over the years, like when she told me she shaved. I asked her, "Your legs?" She said, "Everywhere!" I laughed so hard, and she started to laugh until we were both crying-laughing.

Just a couple of culture shocks—minor ones that made us erupt in laughter.

Having a variety of clean clothes, warm showers, and an abundance of tasty food was a luxury to her that she deserved.

What a sense of independence I saw in her. She didn't want to sit home. She was up for anything—and kind and giving in the process. When I asked her if she wanted to participate in a community service with strangers or to come along and volunteer with me, she didn't blink an eye. She eagerly joined her brother in getting muddy on the Slip 'n Slide and tossing their younger cousin around on old mattresses ready to be thrown away.

We right away discovered a lot in common. In fact, she practiced her English only with me, expressing our immediate bond. And she sang to me in Russian in the car or around the house—but not with anyone else. She loved it when I took pictures of her, though she felt self-conscious about her appearance and didn't think she was pretty. She was wrong. She was beautiful inside and out.

As I sit down to write this story, I struggle with what my journey was like and how our family was profoundly impacted by love, trauma, and mental illness. Yet there were so many fun, joyful, beautiful, blessed, and inspiring days, weeks, months, and years.

But then there was this: long stays in the hospital. One day, returning home from a hospital stay after a manic-type episode, she said to me, "I'm not going to be the person you want me to be anymore."

How did we get from that beginning to the hurting person who was standing in front of me?

Who is this? Have I lost her? I asked myself. Please no. What could I have done differently? And is it too late? Can things still change or was this inevitable?

What do you do when someone drives you too far, and it's your own daughter?

You are not behind the wheel. You are not driving. Then what? Any mom knows what to do—love them unconditionally.

BUT—*she's sick. Mentally.*

What road do you follow when someone you love, fearing to lose you, pushes you away—again . . . and again . . . and again?

But it's your own daughter.

What do you do when, faced with rejection, you are powerless to change the situation?

But it's your own daughter.

It's easy to trace the beginnings of this story, from my point of view. It began in Ukraine. 2013. An orphanage. At that time Russia had dark motives, unbeknownst to us. But that was neither here nor there, just one reminder of the turmoil and lack of stability her young life had already been fraught with.

A year later we found her on the internet, at eleven, in her new home with us, looking at her orphanage in the news; Russian soldiers had gone in and *tried to steal the children*—some of her friends included. She was worried about what was happening to the others, those left behind. Not the most usual or peaceful thoughts for a little girl to have. Rather, quite disturbing. But at least she knew she was safe with us, a family who loved her.

Even so, I saw signs of attachment issues as early, in fact, as the first and second day we met her in the orphanage. Knowing we were there to potentially adopt her, she seemed interested in us, but had an odd detachment, withdrawing a bit, keeping her distance—at times apparently more attentive to the other girls than us. Who wouldn't be protective of herself in such a situation though, hardly daring to dream we'd whisk her away? What no one had told me yet was that she'd refused adoption opportunities from local Ukrainians but twice visited a family in Italy. How that must have gotten her hopes up, only to plummet when they dropped the adoption plans.

By our third trip, however, when I spent eleven days alone with her, she allowed me to hold her hand, rub her back, and stroke her temple. I thought: *Okay. I got this. She likes me. We can do this.*

The interesting thing is that she already seemed to have a distinct need for control—I was confused. At the same time as my heart wanted to shout from the rooftops, I was drawn into a competitive chess game with lots of push and pull. The moves being hard to anticipate, I could only sit quietly and try to do my best to respond.

After coming to the United States, my daughter worked hard with a Russian-speaking psychologist who specialized in issues affecting adopted children; increasingly, Anna communicated openly and quite naturally—trusting us, telling us how she was struggling with ups and downs of emotion. I read books and articles, and my husband and I sought out the best help we could to support her.

At the beginning, Anna took advantage of any opportunity to participate in soccer, dancing, and cooking. She loved organizing and was very good at it. When we asked her to do chores, like washing the dishes, she did not complain at all. She did a lot of very sweet things for me and others, such as writing kind notes and making beautiful cards. She loved cutting up fruit and making fruit cups and parfaits. This last is something we did already, in Ukraine, waiting for her passport.

One small glitch: how she behaved if she could not get her way. If we said she could wear ripped jeans to a friend's, but not out to dinner or church, she became distressed—not willing to accept alternatives, instead quite rooted to the spot.

Early on, it was like trying to negotiate with a toddler. It also appeared that the issue was *not* her not receiving something, *but it was as if to her, the no was a form of rejection*—added to who knew how many rejections in the past—and she associated it with my love for her, as if "no" meant "I don't love you." However, she craved affection and warm hugs and was delighted when she "played" at a neighbor's house with a girl who was much younger than her.

Shopping and buying her own things delighted her or buying gifts for others—she was proud when she worked hard and was rewarded with spending money. Having an incredible sense of style, she dressed fashionably—with bright, patterned scarves and cute hair ribbons. When Anna met my friends, she was very complimentary and would often say, "You are beautiful!"

Quite obviously embracing her life in the United States, she dove into new activities and family traditions and taught us the things she knew about Ukrainian traditions. Very bright, learning English quickly—did I say she was perfect?—she looked up with me other Ukrainian traditions to incorporate where we could. In addition, observations from school noted healthy relationships with many of her classmates and sports teammates. She was a good friend, thoughtful, generous, and compassionate.

But there was no getting around the underlying tensions. Sometimes she got overwhelmed by how to deal with a world *where she had to understand different kinds of limits.*

For example, it's common for children from orphanages to become a bit brainwashed by the fantasy world of life in America, where "you will get everything you want." Although we went out of our way to address our daughter's material wants and give her a safe, loving home, with lots of exciting activities, we noticed that she reacted petulantly to normal parental boundaries, such as, as mentioned, her inability to accept "no" from us. Or, to take a good example, she liked the local hip hop class, but wanted to be doing hip hop on a stage in New York.

It wasn't that she wanted a ton of stuff. It was the inappropriate "stuff," like the dangerous phone apps and usage that later became the main source of risk and tension, we had to say no to. In most cases, I did not use the word no but instead explained when she could have something or do something. I learned this technique from Joani Geltman, MSW, a child-development and parenting expert, the author of *A Survival Guide to Parenting Teens: Talking to Your Kids about Sexting, Drinking, Drugs, and Other Things That Freak You Out.*

What was amazing was that despite the neglect and lack of stimulation in her first ten years, while still in Ukraine, she showed cognitive strengths, able to make great strides in the classroom and in her language development. She seemed on track to succeed academically and socially.

After the initial transition, Anna began her life in America, being funny, engaging, extremely social, sweet, and empathetic. We had a solid bond, and she would come to me with most of her feelings, but not all.

Beginning in middle school, however, all was not well. And this is why I write this book. *I have my hypothesis of what the trigger was, and you will follow our search for it.* For some reason, no longer could she maintain friendships in the way she could in fourth and fifth grade.

Other than in one significant and two minor incidents—slamming a boy against a wall in religious education class and attacking my son at home out of the blue—no additional aggressive behavior presented itself until the summer before high school. And it was typically in "fight or flight" instances. She did indulge, eventually, in three other major physical assaults in addition to attacks on service professionals (police officers and hospital staff). Each instance was, in effect, an ill-advised, dangerous reaction to something she did not like that stirred in her a sense of aggrievement.

I only witnessed one major assault, and it was horrifying. The sad part was that I believed she never set out to hurt anyone. But built-up frustration boiled over, complicated by an inability to manage her emotions and her deep-rooted fear.

She began to walk out of our home at the blink of an eye, creating a day of chaos as I searched everywhere for her. "Do you know what could happen to you?" I scolded her. "You will be alone on the street, and someone will just take you!" She still insisted that I "just let her go," not chase her; she should be able to leave the house without telling me where she was going or when she would return. Later she said she was "addicted to running away."

Even though I didn't know about Borderline Personality Disorder (BPD) when these instances began to surface, in retrospect, I can see that this flight and aggression was consistent with the BPD characteristic of intense emotional dysregulation and attempts to cope with overwhelming feelings of anger, frustration, or perceived abandonment that characterize the illness. The problem with this was that once it started, I never quite knew when the aggression would occur, which created anxiety that it might happen at any time, in any circumstance. Disordered Attachment (the formal diagnosis known as Reactive Attachment Disorder, RAD)—due to early childhood trauma and lack of consistent nurturing caregiving during critical development periods—is common in children adopted from orphanages. I learned about it from a psychologist, who used specialized attachment-based and trauma-based therapy to address underlying issues.

The psychologist tried to help my daughter develop coping skills and work through lingering emotional challenges. And expressed amazement at Anna's progress, often commenting on the exceptionally close bond my daughter and I had. I regret not having continued to have Anna see this therapist when she enrolled in middle school—when all the fireworks began. But that's ahead.

For our part, a lot of this involved learning how to respond sensitively, providing consistency and creating a safe, structured environment.

In 2019, six years after we adopted Anna, she was diagnosed with suffering from Borderline Personality Disorder (BPD) and Post Traumatic Stress Disorder (PTSD). This was after a previous diagnosis of Major Depression Disorder. Also, Disordered Attachment. I say she "suffered" from these illnesses because the symptoms of trauma-based issues are *extremely severe*. Your life, if this happens to you, becomes centered around the ramifications; they are emotionally painful, complicated to understand, and can be difficult to treat. No longer do you grow up in a straight line of childhood to adult, for now your course is sidetracked, hijacked, sprinkled with confusion and pain that, until treated, may only grow.

A person with BPD is often unable to trust their own feelings. Imagine how that would affect you—if you couldn't rely on that closest of personal things, your own feelings; couldn't determine how you truly felt and had to admit this to others for their own safety. You feel as though you are worthless and bad, it makes you so uncomfortable that you try to fill the void with things like drugs, food, or sex. But nothing feels truly satisfying.

Many people with BPD lack a strong sense of self, resulting in a sense of emptiness. It feels hollow inside. "Nothing's there." As a result, you may frequently change jobs, friends, religion, values, goals, or even sexual identity. At the same time, your mind is engulfed with thoughts.

Your feelings can quickly swing from one extreme to the other: love to hate, like to dislike. Emotional pain breeds helplessness. And hopelessness.

It was hard to get a conversation going about BPD with many of the healthcare professionals and caregivers we saw, especially when my daughter moved into residential treatment. I was aware of the stigma attached to it, but I didn't see why some psychiatrists and medical professionals were reluctant to formally diagnose it, or even at least talk about it openly. In our case, she displayed almost every criterion except for fast or reckless driving (she was not old enough to drive) and possibly sex.

The fear of abandonment and eventually the fear of reunification with me was deep rooted and tangled.

But I soon learned that this unwillingness to follow through on a psychiatrist's and neuropsychologist's diagnosis of BPD was backed by a lot of well-documented valid and invalid reasons, such as that some health professionals believe it is too difficult to treat and that it could interfere with insurance coverage. I am glad that that outlook has started to change. Personally, I would like to help create awareness to debunk the myths, highlight the treatment, and participate in any lobbying that attempts at making it more understandable, renaming it "severe emotional dysregulation" or something similar. My understanding is "emotional dysregulation" is a subset of BPD. *Anything to remove the current stigma.*

It pains me to reflect that if we could have talked about BPD openly with Anna, especially when it was first brought up when she was sixteen, she might have begun to understand why she had such complex feelings and emotions, and it may have helped her realize that she was not alone in feeling the way she did.

If BPD is hard to treat, it's even more complicated, problematic—difficult—to try to explain, when compounded with other illnesses. On podcasts I've listened to, books I've read, I've felt uplifted by *success stories*: people who overcame most of the symptoms and went on to lead reasonably stable, happier lives. The most-cited *successful* therapeutic intervention is Dialectical Behavior Therapy (DBT)—developed by University of Washington professor of psychology Marsha Linehan—who actually had this illness herself. Laying claim to a long list of impressive titles at the University of Washington in Seattle—Emeritus Professor of Psychology, Adjunct Professor of Psychiatry and Behavioral Sciences, and Director of the Behavioral Research and Therapy Clinics"—she went on to quite a life, with a primary research focus in borderline personality disorder. Listen to her description of this illness:

> At 17 in 1961, Linehan detailed how when she came to the clinic, she attacked herself habitually, cut her arms legs and stomach, and burned her wrists with cigarettes. She was kept in a seclusion room in the clinic because of never-ending urge to cut herself and to die.
>
> Since borderline personality disorder was not discovered yet, she was diagnosed with schizophrenia and medicated heavily with Thorazine and Librium, as well as strapped

down for forced electroconvulsive therapy (ECT). Nothing worked.[1]

The roots of my daughter's trauma probably started when she was an infant.

In 2019 we consulted a well-known clinical neuropsychologist, Matthew Jeffries, PhD, to conduct a neuropsychological assessment.

Dr. Jeffries recommended that she move into a treatment residence temporarily as the best option. You will see how the convergence of many factors unfolded into pure mayhem.

So many people were fascinated by the challenge and wanted to "fix" Anna, but did they even understand her basic needs for success? Not always. This was completely evident when the eminent Dr. Jeffries offered the state mental-health-department team a meeting, but they never were able to coordinate with him—and never raised the topic!

I imagine now, knowing her, that being a strong-willed little girl, perhaps she reacted to impositions or mistreatment, even abuse if it happened, with defiance.

With so many new people asking her questions, it gave my daughter the perfect opportunity to "divide and conquer." Even sometimes "split." People with BPD use "splitting" as an unconscious coping mechanism: "seeing the 'good' side of a person or thing as the part they find acceptable and the 'bad' side of the person or thing as the part they find painful or unacceptable. And, it's much more than just seeing both a good and a bad side to everything. They actually 'split' a single entity into two opposing realities."[2]

"Splitting is based on alternating between extremes of idealization or devaluation, all or nothing, and good or bad. The main problem with

---

[1]   John M. Grohol, Psy.D., "Marsha Linehan Acknowledges Her Own Struggle with Borderline Personality Disorder," https://lifehelper.com/blog/marsha-linehan-acknowledges-her-own-struggle-with-borderline-personality-disorder/.

[2]   George Simon, PhD, Understanding "Splitting" as a Psychological Term (counsellingresource.com).

splitting is that the way a person sees the world is distorted and minimized to a 'You're either with me, or you're against me' mindset."[3]

In a popular self-help book, *I Hate You—Don't Leave Me: Understanding the Borderline Personality*, by Jerold J. Kreisman and Hal Straus, I was glad—and it helped—to learn that, in the Amazon display to the third edition, it says: "Both pharmacological and psychotherapeutic advancements point to real hope for success in the treatment and understanding of BPD." A reviewer notes. Let's take a brief look in this book:

> BPD behavior is all over the place, manifesting differently from patient to patient. If you or someone you know suffers from BPD, you'll find that some of the anecdotes are irrelevant, but others are so hauntingly similar to your own life that you'll swear you wrote them yourself.

> This book is also pleasantly up-to-date. I'm reading another book now that was published in 2003, and the major difference that I notice is that the prognosis for treating BPD is a lot more optimistic than it used to be. The 2003 book paints BPD as a very challenging disorder, resistant to treatment. This book is more optimistic and has data to back that optimism up.

In these large team meetings, with competing priorities, it took months to try to hash out point of views. To make matters worse, this bureaucratic nightmare played out during the almost-daily incidents we experienced in our home at the time.

Essentially, parsing out the behaviors to come to one or multiple diagnoses is not an exact science.

---

3   Nancy Green, Moving Forward column: The dangers of 'splitting' - Shelter Island Reporter (timesreview.com).

The other challenge was using the diagnoses to help our daughter with self-awareness. *Why did she feel the way she did in specific situations? She wanted to know as much as we did.*

As our family life changed dramatically, I felt like I saw things happening in slow motion and could not do anything about it. My husband and I and our daughter often used the analogy of a fork in the road, where one path was mostly productive despite some setbacks and the other was stuck, with no forward movement; even, things might start going backward. Many times, despite facing struggles, my daughter seemed able to get back on the right path. But then there were the other times . . . I made mistakes that I continue to learn from. For me to survive I had to give up things I cannot control.

I find comfort in writing. I like the silence; there is no one in front of me, encouraging me to let go—*"You did everything you could."* I know we did, but I miss my daughter.

My mind wanders to other mothers, fathers, spouses, and family members who are on similar paths. Feeling misunderstood, powerless or worn out.

In chat groups, on podcasts and in books there are hundreds and thousands of stories like this. People pleading for answers. Yet, they're finding answers and getting help from the experts and each other while realizing they're not alone.

Finally, mental illness is debilitating and grueling for the sufferers and those close to them, but there can be hope and healing. Now come with me into the story.

PART 1

2013

CHAPTER 1

Special

We only knew each other for a day or so, but how many good days do we really have, you know?
—Karl Kristian Flores, *The Goodbye Song*

When I was younger, I always thought I would adopt a child. I am not sure why, but it was on my mind. I didn't think too much about it after I got married because I felt so incredibly lucky and blessed to have had a son, Max, with my husband, Mark. Then, after a series of miscarriages, unsuccessful IVF, and failed egg donation, we realized we most likely could not have more children. At that point, the prospect of adoption reentered my thinking.

Prior to pursuing adoption, we bought, for summer weekends, vacations, and retirement, an old historic house on Cape Cod to fix up. The house and property have an amazing history, and the positive energy is palpable. It lacks the modern comforts of our main home, such as a spacious kitchen and insect-and-spider–free rooms. But like many who "cross over the bridge" to Cape Cod, I always feel a sense of peace and lightness when I'm there.

In the early years, when I drove straight down Route 134, a 5.3-mile highway, instead of taking another route, I would pass an adoption agency. I did this for years without thinking too much about it, but yet I often paused a bit when looking at the sign. At some point I started talking to my husband about it because I'd always wanted more children. One day, I decided to stop there to pick up some information. I ended up speaking to a woman who gave me some tips and a pamphlet, but the director was out. Later, the director called me for a lengthy conversation. Towards the end, she asked me if my family would be willing to host a young girl from Ukraine the month of August. I was so excited that I said yes before even discussing it with my husband and son. The host family she'd lined up in New York had fallen through, and the child had nowhere to go.

I explained to the director that I worked Tuesday through Thursday but would have someone at home to be with my twelve-year-old son, and the child could do activities with him. The rest of the week, I explained, we could do fun activities on Cape Cod. She thought that would work out but then also mentioned that they would like the child to spend a week with a family in another part of the Cape.

Hanging up the phone, I was a little astonished but very excited. I called my husband, and he was initially taken aback, but fine with the plan to be a host family. Later that day I talked to my son, who was excited about the idea.

The following Friday the director brought Natalia to our Cape Cod vacation home, having warned me in advance that she was very scared and was crying alligator tears. I said I was planning to take her to the beach right away, and I thought everything was going to be just fine.

Natalia was still upset when she got out of the car, so I walked up to her and gave her a quick hug. I showed her some beach toys and a ball to visually communicate our plan for the day. We went to the beach, and even though she was shy, she quickly warmed up to me. We played catch with a ball for a long time, swam, and built a sandcastle. By the time we left, she seemed very comfortable and was smiling a lot.

I was really excited for my son and husband to come that evening to meet Natalia. During the week, while I was at work, she spent time at our home doing craft projects and playing outside with my son. Every Thursday after work we headed to the Cape. We played soccer and games in the yard, went swimming, fished—catching sunfish—and had barbecues in the backyard. At home on the Cape, she rode a skateboard-like scooter, and my husband taught her to ride a bike. We grew close quickly, and she seemed very happy.

When I came home, I often spotted her shy but smiling face. There she was, sitting on the curb in front of the house, waiting for me to pull up. She couldn't wait to usher me into the house to show me the bracelets or other craft gifts she had made for me. Monday nights, she came to my hockey games where I play for an adult women's team. Cheering from the bleachers, she ran from end to end in the stands, waving at me. How little it takes for the heart to glow. I walked around with mine glowing.

In the third week, the agency asked if Natalia could spend the weekend elsewhere. The dad spoke Ukrainian; they thought it would be good for her to have that connection to her home country. I was reluctant but had agreed early on for her to go with them for a week. However, since they had just moved into a new house and were busy, we decided she would only spend the weekend. I was so excited to pick her up at the end of the visit.

At that point, my mom and stepdad were visiting us at the Cape. We all went to a fishing derby, and Max, my son, and Natalia participated in the fishing portion and in the eel-catching contest. To catch eels, they stood in a small pool filled with slippery eels. Each participant had to grab as many as possible and transfer them to another pool or bucket. Natalia ended up receiving a trophy.

Natalia left the week before Labor Day weekend. We all went to the airport and met the group of kids who had come with Natalia from Ukraine. We said our goodbyes and let Natalia know we would write right away. We mailed a letter a couple days later, telling her how much we loved having her.

On Sunday that same weekend, I received a phone call from the director, telling me Natalia was available for adoption, and we had three days to decide. I was shocked and explained that this was too short notice. It was a huge decision, and I was caught off guard that she was springing it on us like this. I'd been under the impression that Natalia still needed to be on the Ukrainian registry—typically for a year—and we had to be approved for a foreign adoption. "Another family is interested," the director added.

For some reason, I thought I wasn't getting the whole truth. "How can we make this decision in three days?" I asked. Sure, we had had the idea in the back of our heads. But now we had urgently to decide. It felt unfair. We would call her that week, I said, then added, thinking of Natalia's best interests, that we would not want to prevent anyone else from adopting her. How silly to be so diplomatic. But I reiterated that we needed time to talk together as a family. A few days later, I called back. Had Natalia gotten our letter? I asked.

"I have some news for you," the director said. "The other family is going to adopt Natalia."

"What???" I stammered. "I asked for more time!"

I couldn't believe my ears. Is this how it worked? My mom was still visiting, and a friend was sitting with her on our outdoor patio. I was so incredibly upset. When I got off the phone, my mom asked me what was wrong. I explained. Though sympathetic, she also said that it probably wasn't meant to be.

I didn't believe that at the time but later thought that God had a different plan for me, so I tried to accept it the best I could. Nevertheless, I called the other family's mom. I tried to express congratulations but then broke down, crying.

We agreed that I could be involved in Natalia's life a bit, like an aunt or family friend. I was excited about that, and we decided to talk again soon. As you can gather, I had already grown quite attached to Natalia, but it wasn't in my family's nature to make snap decisions. It felt very hard to just let go, pull the plug completely.

Later, however, the adoption agency director informed me that the family thought while Natalia was settling into her new home, it was not the right time for my family to engage with her. It might bring up afterthoughts and confusion. That made sense to me, but I wished it had been different.

Even though her new adopted family lived on the other side of the Cape, we never heard from Natalia nor her adopted family again. However, a year or so later, the adoption director asked if a boy named Andrei and his younger brother could spend a weekend at our house during the Christmas holidays. My son and I went shopping at the mall with them, then to TGI Fridays for dinner. We got each of them a gym bag, sneakers, and basketball clothes. They were so excited. The funniest part was when Andrei (the older brother) called me "mom." My son thought it was hysterical. I got a pang in my heart, taking it as endearing.

Years later I was thrilled to hear that a family from another part of the Cape (the same town Natalia lives in) adopted the two boys and their little brother. I received an unsigned email from Andrei out of the blue that read: "Hi can you please give me a call tomorrow or tonight my phone number is..."

I responded with a cautious "? Sorry, not sure who you are and what this is regarding."

He then wrote, "Kathy drops me off at your house one day."

Ah-ha. I knew exactly who it was. I wrote, "Ohhhhh . . . hi!!!! Yes, of course, I will call you tomorrow :)."

The next day we had a great conversation. He gave me updates on his life and said he'd seen Natalia out driving—that she seemed to be doing well. I was thrilled.

CHAPTER 2

Excited

We do not remember days, we remember moments.

—Cesare Pavese

After the holidays, the same agency sent me profiles of children up for adoption. I told the director we were not interested at this time. That spring, the agency director emailed me, attaching a picture of a young girl who had not one, not two, but three cute, colored barrettes holding back the front of her hair. Her top was purple, and she wore a jean skirt and thick white stockings. From her expression, she looked shy and very sweet.

For other reasons as well, I felt an immediate connection. I literally wanted to give her a hug through the computer. Writing back to the director, I requested additional information. She sent me what she had.

Before long, I began having the adoption conversation again with my husband. After weighing all the considerations, we agreed that we still had the youth and means to bring a second child into our family and give her love and opportunities she might not have in Ukraine. We updated all our paperwork and, without further ado, pursued the adoption of Anna. We didn't want to lose out this time.

Part of the process included payments to the agency, the foreign adoption liaison, and others. It was hinted to us that we should bring gifts, such as an unlocked iPhone, and cash for any "tips" that might be called for. We were entering a realm unlike anything I'd experienced before, and I was excited yet wary to begin the foreign journey.

Reflecting on the decision to adopt brings me back to a lively, very promising time. I believed this was God's plan, and I still believe it today.

CHAPTER 3

Adventurous

A child born to another woman calls me mom. The depth of the tragedy and the magnitude of the privilege are not lost on me.

—Jody Landers

I t would take three visits to Ukraine to complete Anna's adoption. In June of 2013 we flew to Kiev and met with government officials at the adoption office to fill out initial paperwork. Mark, Max, and I then traveled to the orphanage for the Big Event—to meet Anna.

Welcoming us into her office, the orphanage director had us sit down on a half-moon–shaped settee. In front of us was a table with cookies on it. When Anna came in, the director suggested she sit between Max and me. Everyone was smiling. Our foreign adoption liaison who was from Ukraine also joined us as a translator for the meeting. Neither the director nor Anna spoke English; since we did not speak Russian, most of the talking was between the three Ukrainians and translated to us. The liaison mainly facilitated the introduction. Even though Anna was only nine, the way it worked in Ukraine, she would make the final decision. *Did she want to be adopted by Mark and me? Did she want Max for a brother?* It was up to her.

The highlight of the day was watching Anna and Max play with a bunch of new puppies outside in the back of the building. I took a photo of my son and future daughter, standing together, each holding a puppy. They looked so natural together in this far-from-natural environment. Anna walked us through a tour of the orphanage. We had been told that the director ran a tight ship, and this was one of Ukraine's cleanest orphanages.

To me, it was what I expected for an institutional building: a yellow brick façade, a large foyer with freshly washed floors, long sterile hallways, with musty-smelling rooms; a well-appointed, cozy director's office; and comfortable, clean classrooms, especially in contrast to the children's rooms.

Because we would be in town for another day, we asked if we could come back to visit. They said yes, letting us know Anna liked McDonald's. So we picked up a Happy Meal on our way. *So far so good*, we thought. A tentative bond seemed to be being established.

The second day was a little different. Outside, all the kids mingled around us. But Anna, for some unexplained reason, kept her distance. I wondered about that, and Mark commented on it to me as well, but I did not think much about it. Later, inside, after she ate the burger, she kept asking other kids to ask my husband if she could use his iPhone, which contained his personal and work information. *Why?* he motioned to her. She showed him she wanted to play a game.

He would have preferred to say no but gave it to her. Like many children, she became transfixed, and we had a hard time getting her to part with it so we could all spend more time with her. When she did ultimately give it up, she became withdrawn, seemingly lacking much interest in continuing the visit.

One thing Anna's first psychologist explained was that many young adults and teens in the States become mildly addicted to electronics and social media, but foreign adoptees can become highly addicted. Could it be that they "attached" to it socially? *Did it set the stage to how Anna felt passionate about her cell phone?*

It was intriguing to discover that in Ukrainian orphanages, as in other orphanages around the world, not all children housed there are, in fact, orphans (perhaps most aren't). Many of them were placed in these institutions due to their parents' inability to provide for them. I didn't learn this until later, when Anna wanted to call her friends there on their cell phones. We did this successfully. Her face lit up with a contagious and genuine smile while talking to them and in particularly her friend Aleksandra.

Reflecting on many of the conversations Anna and I later had about her time in the orphanage, I find myself feeling how sad it is to think that a young child would have to live anywhere without parents and family to love, nurture, and guide them. I shudder at the thought she might have been mistreated.

Through limited information from the court papers, we knew that Anna's birth mom went to jail when she was four. It was her grandmother who brought her to the "baby orphanage"—at four and a half years old. She moved to an adolescent orphanage when she was six or seven.

Anna talked a lot about older boys in the orphanage having bullied her about her weight. She was not overweight, but must have consequently felt self-conscious, regardless. She said because there was limited food, she and other children developed schemes to steal food from the kitchen. Yet it was bland food, such as tasteless soup and bread. The most difficult stories she told were about her birth mom. Anna said she had only one picture of her, and someone had ripped it up and thrown it in the trash one day. She was very sad about this, and it came up often.

One Christmas, I asked Max if he could draw a picture of a pretty Eastern European woman for Anna as a gift. He was a talented portrait artist, so I thought if he drew this, it might help her understand that we knew how very difficult losing her mother was. He drew the picture and gave it to her in an elegant frame for Christmas.

The most devastating fact was Anna's recollection of her mother and grandmother coming to visit only once. But at that time her mother told her she would be back to get her. She never came.

I cannot imagine how hard that must have been—another factor, doubtless, in her shaky sense of self, as well as the sense of loss and emptiness she felt by being truly abandoned.

In the court papers we have, it states, *"While at the orphanage parents or relatives expressed no interest in the destiny of [Child], did not visit the orphanage, did not care about the child's upbringing, did not maintain close relations, did not contact the orphanage."*

We are not sure what version is accurate, but one is a close approximation of the other. And the fact of the matter was that Anna was abandoned by her birth mom. I didn't know how much we should tell Anna, so we consulted with Dr. Sophia, who recommended that even though the best approach was to be honest, we should not discuss anything of the information we had until Anna was at least eighteen. She gave us the same advice about visiting Ukraine with Anna. She also noted that when many adoptees met their birth parents, it only took a few minutes to satisfy their desire, and they were not interested in anything more.

On our second visit to Ukraine, a few weeks later, Mark and I went together. We decided that due to the post-court waiting process, I would go back alone the third time to bring Anna home.

Anna made her decision. We were to be her parents. She wanted to come back to the States with us.

On the third trip, as it turned out, the director allowed me to take her a day early, so when I arrived at the airport, arrangements had been made for her to be driven there to meet me. Meeting the van and the driver with Anna, I was so happy, thrilled to start the journey before us.

From the airport we went to a beautiful, new Ramada Inn hotel. Just prior to 2013, there was a big soccer tournament nearby so there had been large investments in the stadium, hotels, and trains.

After checking in, we toured the hotel—finding a beautiful swimming pool and a small café—the doubtless-unfamiliar-to-her trappings of semi-wealth. We laughed as we savored every sip of smoothies we ordered, and, when we finished them, headed back to the room to change into our bathing suits. We had a blast, although it was a little scary because Anna could not swim. I found a swim belt, which I put on her, and so was able to enjoy the pool. The water was freezing. Anna lasted much longer than I did.

I would have loved to know what Anna was thinking during these moments. I knew she went to Italy a couple of times in the summer. Was it to a beautiful white stucco home on the edge of a mountain like I pictured? Did the mom want to envelop her and hold her hand while she slept? Later Anna and I talked about Italy, but she had believed the family was going to adopt her, and that fell through. So it was disillusioning—again—for a child so young.

Back in the room, I showed her the new clothes and sandals I'd brought with me for her. The clothes she was wearing were dirty and smelled bad, so I tentatively asked her, using charade-like gestures, if we could throw them away—giving her the shiny new sandals and colorful new clothes to put on. She was nervous and indicated no, we could not put them in the trash. I then realized that she must have to bring everything back to the orphanage. That night, we ordered take-out pizza, one small pickle pizza, and one small chicken pizza. She selected the pickle pizza from the menu, and I just started cracking up. I never knew there was such a thing! Both she and I ate fast. She, on the other hand, did not like eating in front of people. Early on, I tried not to pay attention to how she ate or what she ate too much of, in order not to make her self-conscious. She liked and ate healthy food, some in abundance. Later, we often laughed about the pickle pizza, reminiscing about that joyful night.

Remember, she could not speak English and I didn't speak Russian. We communicated through facial expressions, body language, and eventually Google translator on my phone. This was a lifesaver. During the eleven days that Anna and I spent in Ukraine the most difficult part was not being able to explain the plan and next steps to her before we were able to fly out. That said, despite speaking different languages and facing some of the issues related to acclimating to one another, we had a lot of fun. I was with my daughter.

While there, we went to the tax office, had pictures made for Anna's passport, went to the passport office and the notary. Before we left, we ran into one snag. Anna had a sister, and the liaison told me that siblings typically cannot be separated. It was a concern. The liaison ended up working through it and let me know that Anna had a half-sister who lived with her father, so it was not a problem.

After a couple of days we took the express train to Kiev and arrived at midnight. I could not rent a single apartment for the whole time we were there, so we had to stay in multiple places. The first one was on Lesi Ukrainky Boulevard. The second was in the center of Kiev, with a balcony looking out to the city square—a beautiful spot. Since the most recent invasion of Ukraine, in 2022, it has been devastating, seeing the destruction of the city square in Kiev and all the other beautiful places we visited that have now been destroyed by bombs and fire.

Our daily routine in Kiev was that Anna and I would leave the apartment after breakfast and sightsee, go to the underground shopping mall, and go to the grocery store to pick up supplies for lunch and dinner. After lunch we would often venture out to get an ice cream cone. I wanted to err on the side of safety, so we did not go out after dark. As we were walking out of the market one morning, Anna spied a can of cat food on the shelf. She pointed at it, and I smiled; then she walked toward it, picked it up, and gestured for me to come look at it. At first, she seemed to like the picture, but then she gestured toward the cash registers.

I shook my head, indicating that we were on our way out, I wasn't purchasing anything else. Unable to speak Russian, I couldn't explain why we were not going to buy cat food, so I made a few eating gestures and tried to play charades to indicate it was cat food. I then gestured again toward the door, and she stood firm. She didn't give an inch.

I did it again, and she then ran by me out into the crowded city street. Looking back, I think I should have just bought the cat food? What harm would it have caused? Swiftly catching up with her, I tried to stand in front of her so she would not go into the road. Quickly opening the bag of groceries, I showed her we had luxurious supplies to cook today, again smiling. She grimaced, then pointed towards the bookstore, where we'd shopped the day before and stocked up on ten large Russian children's series books called *Winx*, based on a popular Italian TV show.

Before I could object that "We're not going to buy more books today," she walked in, so I followed behind. And she picked out a few more books. I felt generous putting two fingers up, but she ignored me and created a pile of books. Putting two fingers up again, I motioned toward the door. She then dropped the books and ran out and around the corner. I wondered whether this was the first time she'd experienced the freedom of walking out into Ukraine, into stores at will, splurging on purchases. Maybe she loved being in control of her decisions—her life—for a change. Maybe it was a test.

This time I caught her just before she crossed the street. We crossed together, and I took her hand gently and led her to a bench. We sat, but every couple of minutes she motioned as if to run. I again opened the bag and gestured toward the apartment, but she would not move. We sat for a long time. All the while, her newfound defiance was making me anxious. To help her understand why we couldn't buy any more books in Ukraine, but that we would buy more in America, I decided to call my adoption liaison. After I explained my dilemma, I passed Anna the phone. She had a brief conversation in Russian, talking fast and agitatedly. She then passed me back the phone, looking more satisfied. I took it, and the liaison told me that she just wanted to bring a few books home to America. Frustrated, I explained that we already had over ten large books and could fit only a couple more. This was the beginning of me having a hard time saying no, realizing I would need to figure out what role to play in these battles over control.

Back at the apartment, I cut veggies, motioning for Anna to join me, which she did. We made a stir-fry and ate. I set a deck of cards out to play.

I am not sure what game it was, but we were having fun until, picking up a card, I slightly scratched her by mistake. She grabbed her hand like it was on fire and pulled away from the table. *Who knew what memories of dread of hurt this called forth.* I went toward her, but she turned her back.

I got some ice out of the freezer and wrapped it in a paper towel. She took this and put it on her hand. She still would not speak to me for a little bit, but when she did, I gave her a hug, and all seemed fine. There is something about hugs that are soothing and enveloping, and we continued to show affection this way as we moved forward together.

So she has an issue with control, I told myself. *It's not a big deal.* The incidents with the cat food, books, and the scratch were minor, and right now they seem so petty compared to what parents go through every day, but with each instance it took a long time for Anna to settle back to a point where she was willing to engage with me. It also happened with electronics. In one apartment, we could not get the TV to work, so I let her use my iPad while I read a paperback book. A couple of hours later, I motioned to turn it off so we could get ready for bed. There was a brief no/yes exchange; then I asked her to put it on the coffee table. She did that but then went to the side of the couch and became withdrawn.

I learned to first give her a little time, but not too much, before I went over and stroked her arm or cheek to attempt to draw her back in. On this day, I went to the other couch, where I continued to read my book. After a little while, I went to the bathroom and brought my toothpaste and toothbrush out to show her what I was going to do. I invited her in, but she stayed on the side of the couch in a crouched, seated position. I did not want to leave her like that, so I went over and gently stroked her arm, walked away, and sat on the couch. It wasn't for another hour until she got up.

When she went into the bathroom, I went into the bedroom, turned on the light, and pulled down the bedding. I liked to hold her hand when we turned off the light. We held hands a lot for fun, and I sometimes gave her a nighttime "massage," which consisted of touching her lightly along the lower back. Also, I lightly touched her temples and the side of her face. This light touch and simple comfort would put her to sleep within about five to ten minutes. And she slept like an angel. I found this interesting because we have friends who've adopted children from Russia, and I put their daughter to bed once. It took a mere five minutes of reading a book and stroking her temples and face before she was sleeping soundly.

We had a few more issues around control and wanting things, but we kept busy and had fun. One day, we went to a city festival and a haunted house in the city center. Prior to this, I thought I was a haunted house fan, but it was not the case for this one, which was beyond scary. Upon entering, I walked into a narrower space. Suddenly, our legs were being grabbed from below. I was petrified and screamed. At one point, it was hard to shake loose the grip that was on my leg. After that I ran out, screaming and laughing, with Anna right behind me.

After about a week and a half, we received the call that the passport was ready. I was extremely relieved to get the phone call.

During the flight, the attendant became aware that Anna was coming to America for the first time. She asked me if I thought Anna would enjoy a visit to the cockpit after we landed. I said yes, although I was a little nervous because there was a lot of subtle defiance on the flight: refusing to buckle the seat belt, refusing to put her backpack under her seat, and getting extremely frustrated when she could not find a cartoon to watch. I understood all of this because although she had been on an airplane before for a summer trip to Italy, I realized this must be a scary, stressful trip for her, leaving Ukraine and *going to an unknown new world*. How many people would be so brave as a mere child? That said, this was the beginning of the lack of control I felt, and the control she wanted over her situation and me.

I always look back on the last part of the adoption journey in Ukraine as playing an intricate role in our initial bonding process. I tried to make our time in Kiev feel more like a relaxing vacation filled with walking, cooking, shopping, and playing games.

A lot of people ask me about the adoption process, and for us it was relatively smooth after a few initial bumps. Prior to going to the Cape Cod agency, we wanted to explore domestic adoption, so we pursued this through a local agency, but we were rejected due to the health issue my husband had eight years earlier. I also have a GI issue, but with the proper medication it has never prevented me from doing anything. To the best of my memory, I have gone ten years at a time without missing a day of work—with, maybe one exception. We were also in the process of gathering information on other adoption resources such as Catholic Charities Boston, but during this time I stopped by the Cape Cod agency.

Before the adoption, Mark, Max, and I met formally at the agency with the director. She explained that the best places to adopt from at the time were Ukraine and China, due to the lack of red tape. We were both open to a child from China. My sister and her husband lived in Shanghai for a long time as part of his job. We visited China as a family seven years before. We ended up sticking with Ukraine because of both his and my European heritage. We still had to complete lots of paperwork and have home visits from agency personnel to make sure our home was suitable and safe for a child. We also had to participate in several health care assessments along with the online study course on adoption, foreign adoption, and adopting an older child.

There was also the financial cost of the adoption.

CHAPTER 4

Joyful

"The biggest and grandest adventure in life is life itself."
—Debasish Mridha

Anna and I arrived in Boston on August 1, 2013. She had turned ten on June 30. Mark and Max picked us up from the airport. I didn't know it, but our house had been broken into while Mark was in Cape Cod with Max and my mom. Outside the car, Mark told me. He said the damage was confined to the basement only; the intruders ripped TVs off in the family room and gym. To avoid unnecessarily worrying the kids, instead of telling them, we mentioned vaguely that there was a problem with the electrical system, and we would be getting the TVs replaced. Unfortunately, I was uncomfortable going into the house. But I could not worry too much about it because we were busy supporting Anna in her transition.

The day we got home, we showed Anna her new room. She loved it. Imagine. She had shared a room with other girls in the orphanage. Now she had her own private space and was excited that I had had it painted purple, which she had requested while we were in Ukraine. She also had her own bathroom. She was neat and organized and took great care of her belongings.

The next day we left for Cape Cod to show her the ocean and get some fresh air. The small struggles continued. Each in their own way, ten-year-olds are different. I didn't think of it necessarily as a huge hurdle. It appeared to be primarily about general control. If she didn't like something I said, or more likely a face I made, she would retreat. The gumball incident below is accurate, and she did hide in the hot sun for a couple of hours. I am trying to figure out how to express that it was not always about material things. I often felt manipulated and at times bullied. I wanted her to love me, just as much as I loved her. I learned that a lot of it was due to her own fear, and she was unconsciously testing me. Anna saw many things that appealed to her, and while I did buy her a good number of them, there were limits. That, she didn't seem to understand. If Anna didn't like a decision I made or if I said no to something she wanted, she would often hide. Usually in the yard behind a tree.

On the way to the Cape, for example, she wanted a sleeve of six or eight humongous gumballs, each larger than a quarter. I may have made a mistake by taking them away from her and putting them back on the low shelf in front of us, because when I did this and gestured to the other types of gum, even bubble gum, it was too late. She had shut down and wouldn't even go inside the house. My initial reaction was because she came to the States with lots of cavities—eight, to be exact!—maybe if I searched for and showed her a photo of a mouthful of rotting teeth, she would understand I said no *because* I loved her.

But in such instances, giving her a hug, pointing to where I would be, seemed to lessen the time she sulked. I would also bring a toy, a ball, or our sweet dog over to where she was to help coax her back to the patio or inside the house.

Despite all this, we felt like she was acclimating well. We began to enjoy the beach, the ponds, and the ocean waves. Our son now had a sister, and the two of them were having fun together. We learned a lot about each other during these first few months—including the fact that even in the front seat, Anna struggled with car sickness and nausea because she'd only infrequently traveled in a car. I laughed when she would stick her head out of the window while I was driving. With the wind in her hair, her face lifted toward the sun, she closed her eyes and consumed the fresh air just like a cute dog.

I also noticed some disordered eating and sneaking of food, but this was normal, considering how she'd been deprived for so long and snuck food out of the orphanage kitchen. Overall, Anna loved to snack on apples and other healthy foods. She often ate pears off a tree at the Cape, something she had also done on the grounds of the orphanage.

Before the summer ended, the director at the local adoption agency invited Anna and me to lunch in Boston with some other recently adopted local Ukrainian children. While we were at the restaurant, I noticed Anna's attachment issues. They were very subtle, but I felt I could now see situations as they began happening. She would pay close attention when I engaged with people and had the same watchful eye when people responded to me or were conversing together in general. My instinct was to get closer to her at those times, making sure I was paying attention to her and helping her feel as comfortable as possible.

On the last day of August 2013, Anna had her first day at the local elementary school. Mark was excited to take her and sent me a picture of them both with big smiles on their faces. After the first day, Anna and I, along with our dog, walked the couple of blocks to her school. I was in my absolute glory, so happy this reality now actually existed.

The rest of 2013 was full of first-time events for Anna. She adapted well to school, and we introduced her to many family and community traditions that she enjoyed. She took swimming lessons and fell in love with being in the water. We also discussed Ukraine and made calls back to the orphanage so she could check in with the director and Anna's friends. Once winter arrived, Anna learned to ski, we saw a performance of the *Nutcracker*, and we went to Mark's cousin's house for her first Becker family Christmas. Everyone in the family remarked how charming she was.

That New Year's Eve started out festively as we all bundled up to go into Boston to see the ice sculptures and have dinner with close friends.

Anna, still ten, and her older brother, who was twelve, were running around, enjoying themselves. Everyone was joking, enthralled in a light-hearted good time.

But as soon as we met our friends at the restaurant, Anna's demeanor began to change. It started with pouting; then she lay down on the floor next to the table, refusing to move. *Was she more comfortable with just us? Did she look on this as an invasion of sorts?* We let her be because by that time I was learning that she might be trying to get a reaction, trying to get attention.

Because she was ten and not an infant or a toddler, it would have been too difficult to pick her up and put her in a chair. Also, like many children, she did not like being grabbed or touched, and her reaction to that certainly would have been worse than just leaving her where she was. In my experience, if I reacted, it seemed to not only be what she wanted, but also it escalated the situation, so I just let her know she could stay where she was until she was ready to rejoin us. A similar situation happened over the summer on Cape Cod, and I learned that as long as she was in a safe space, I should let her be. These situations were tricky. If it was just Anna and me, I could engage early with smiles, or light touches . . .with more people she may have been looking for my reaction and it was difficult for me to try to help her other than leaving her alone until she was ready to join the group. If she did open up to anyone or try to get sympathy from someone else, it was most often another mom.

Other than a few bumps in 2013, Mark and I felt the adoption process and the beginning of a formal education program *could not have gone better*. We were so proud of Anna for her upbeat attitude, her kindness, and all the effort she was putting into so many things. You may ask why we were so upbeat. But imagine all our daughter faced, leaving her birth country, friends, and confidants in the orphanage, arriving in a strange country—in one fell swoop turning her life upside down.

PART 2

2014

CHAPTER 5

Magical

Dare to live the life you have dreamed for yourself. Go forward and make your dreams come true.

—Ralph Waldo Emerson

This was an exciting and hopeful time, filled with adventure, learning, and opportunity. It was winter, 2014, and Anna was in fourth grade, making friends easily, sharing in the excitement of events, such as the first day of school, Halloween, football games, birthday parties, summer camps, sports, singing, and so much more. She was always up for anything, apparently needing this type of stimulation because our quiet home environment was not what she was used to, and she got bored by it. Another thing I noticed early on was her compassion for people with illnesses, disabilities, transitions, or anything else where a person could use the support of a friend or an act of kindness. Anna had a friend in middle school who transitioned from a female to a male, and she was extremely supportive during the process and throughout the school year. One day the friend's parents invited Anna and me over for dinner. The family could not have been nicer, and we had a wonderful evening full of delicious food and sharing stories. The mom even went out of her way to make Borscht, a traditional Ukrainian soup.

In a chapter titled "The Upsides of Having BPD," in *The Big Book on Borderline Personality Disorder*, the upsides occupy ten paragraphs. *And in at least five, I felt that Anna had those same positive aspects: Spontaneous and Fun, Nonjudgmental, Intuitive and Sensitive to Others, Artistic, Creative and Talented, Resilient and Strong.* Traits anyone would want to have.

A week later, at Mount Snow for the holiday weekend, Anna took a ski lesson, and by sundown she looked like a pro—or at least like she'd been skiing for years. On Valentine's Day she dressed in a red dress with polka dots at the top and taffeta on the bottom. Mark gave us each a bouquet of roses. It was a beautiful scene to witness.

That year passed like a whirlwind, with her learning to play hockey; time outdoors at playgrounds and parks; and heading back to the mountains during February school break for sledding, skiing, and a hayride. Anna often asked me if she could sing to me in Russian, which I loved. I also observed a subtle inclination towards detachment in larger groups. She loved when I took a photo of her, or her and a friend but was reluctant to have her picture taken as part of a group. In April we traveled to Florida to celebrate my mom's seventy-eighth birthday, staying at her house and spending a couple of nights at the Marco Marriott, where we enjoyed the pool and the beautiful view from the room. We reveled in a day of paddle boarding with my brother and his dog, and Anna spent a lot of time with Max on this trip; they had fun together.

In May I was invited to her school for a special Mother's Day breakfast for English as a Second Language (ESL) students. As usual, I could not believe my luck to have my daughter in my life. Anna made me a cut-out flower that read, "You are the best mom forever." In the center it read, "Happy Mother's Day—I love you."

Her friend Lina, originally from Syria, was also there with her mom, so it was great to meet her and exchange contact information. After this, we began to go on playdates with Lina, who often brought her younger brother along to the park or for a hike through the woods. As Anna had a nice group of friends from fourth grade, there was no shortage of birthday parties, school events, and sports.

Each year we took a family trip to see my dad in North Carolina for his birthday.

In May 2014, we went to my dad's to celebrate his eighty-fifth birthday. Anna and my dad, hit it off right away. She loved his dog, Truxa, and would roll around with him or lie with him on the floor, regardless of how much dog hair clung to her clothes. At Walmart we got some sparklers and fireworks, and Max taught Anna how to light the sparklers and properly hold them to prevent being burned.

At home, the weather that summer was stunning. Anna, Max, and I had come to enjoy an abundance of activities at Nauset Beach, searching for hermit crabs at Paine's Creek, ice cream from Kate's, and hot chocolate from the Hot Chocolate Sparrow.

On June 30, we celebrated Anna's birthday at a trampoline park in Hyde Park with a SpongeBob-themed party. She invited six of her friends. Mark and I were so happy to see her with this wonderful and accepting group of friends. Showered with gifts and love, Anna smiled and laughed all day. Two daughters of my friend from across the street presented Anna with a very large birthday card: "Happy Birthday, Anna, 11 YEARS OLD! With love, Julianne, and Katy."

These were happy, carefree times full of love and excitement. Anna was precocious in learning English, and we were now able to communicate and joke verbally. We had absorbed her into our family, and she was a central part of its rhythms and traditions.

Then something happened. It was alarming.

After her eleventh birthday, Anna started developing tics and very odd, uncontrollable movements—mostly in her arms, a bit in her legs and head. I reassured her that everything was going to get better, I would call the doctor right away, and she would help us. The doctor asked me, first thing, after examination, whether she'd had strep recently. I said no and provided the limited medical history that we had been given with her adoption papers. The doctor talked about a condition called Sydenham's chorea that causes the kinds of uncontrollable movements Anna was so bravely experiencing. She put her on a ten-day course of antibiotics as a precaution. My first thought was: *What is happening to her?* Watching the fear in her eyes during this time, I felt thrown off balance, it was so sudden. I slept in the bed with her and held her hand like I used to.

Sydenham's chorea usually occurs between the ages of five and fifteen. However, there is another illness that often follows an attack of untreated strep throat. It's called PANDAS, which stands for Pediatric Autoimmune Neuropsychiatric Disorders Associated with Streptococcal Infections, a serious condition that affects some children. It is believed to be an autoimmune response triggered by a streptococcal infection. I was stressed. It was the first alarming health concern I'd seen in Anna. *Did we have the right diagnosis? Was it serious? Were we treating it properly?* These thoughts were uppermost in my mind. I was very happy that she talked about it openly with me, but she was scheduled to be going to day camp (or overnight) in a few days. *Should we cancel?* The doctor said this condition could take a while—typically four to eight weeks—to resolve itself. That is what ended up happening, and after a full examination the doctor ruled out PANDAS. The tic disorder persisted a bit longer, and later she developed some issues with rapid blinking, but eventually all the other symptoms went away. While the tics were happening, I never reacted openly, but focused on reassuring Anna. I told her truthfully that other children would probably not notice anything—that she didn't need to be self-conscious. Try telling that to a young girl, however. She asked if I could talk to the camp nurse and her counselor, so we did this together. The good thing about camp was that it was close by, right down the street in Cape Cod, so even though I was working near Boston, I could be at her side in less than two hours if need be. Fortunately, Anna attended camp and had a great time.

In the fall of 2014, we plunged back into an exciting period filled with more activities and opportunities. Anna was thrilled about the first day of fifth grade. I loved the walk to school with Anna and Lily, our Fox terrier who accompanied us. These mornings made my heart full, and I still could not believe that I had such a sweet, amazing daughter! Anna was practicing singing often, and her favorite singer/songwriter was Adele.

To encourage her interest, I asked if she wanted to do the local open-mic night at our art center. Yes, she did. No hesitation. Because she was still learning English and the lyrics to many of Adele's songs, she ended up having the song play in the background with light volume. Her performance was so beautiful. She told me she felt funny things in her stomach, which I explained were "butterflies." She laughed at this, so I went on to tell her that the funny feeling was probably nerves, and having "butterflies" in the stomach, in English, describes the common feeling before going on stage. Later that year, her school had a talent show. This time, Anna performed the Adele song by memory, in another amazing, touching performance.

Also in 2014, Anna played town soccer and did well, loving every minute. She won a school contest and was selected to be part of a team cooking-challenge event. On Halloween, a close friend of mine came over with her daughter to go trick-or-treating. The girls had a blast. As I look back, these memories are particularly poignant because I lost this close friend five years later. This loss happened while a lot of other things were going on that I will describe in detail throughout this story.

I still struggle with losing my friend and have not been able to fully process it. Not only was she good to me, but also, she was a positive person in Anna's life, bringing joy and excitement by inviting us out on her boat, teaching her to waterski, and demonstrating open arms and loving friendship.

The year end was peaceful.

Our family felt intact and complete, with Anna living a vibrant, engaged life full of friends and fulfillment. We wanted to make up for the lost childhood in the orphanage by giving her a rich tapestry of activities. As an eleven-year-old in fifth grade, she was thriving, and I was ecstatic to watch her embrace each new opportunity that fell at her feet.

PART 3

2015

CHAPTER 6

Empathetic

"Pain of mind is worse than pain of body." So wrote Publius Syrus in the first century BC (Aphorism, 166).

In early January 2015, the year after the tic disorder had come—and gone—Anna was not out of the woods. She developed symptoms of obsessive-compulsive disorder. At first it was hard to recognize and believe that's what it was. Most everyone has a touch of it. But this was pronounced enough to pay attention to, and as with other disorders and illnesses, once you learn more about what it is and why it happens, the easier it is to understand and stay close to offer support. Anna talked to me often about what she was experiencing; for the most part, she just wanted me to listen, or she wanted to write down what she was doing and have me look at it. This was key for me to begin to understand how she was feeling. I told her it was a very common thing, which can happen to anyone, often linked to stress and anxiety. "Let's continue to talk about it and discuss it with Dr. Sophia," I suggested. Dr. Sophia, who I mentioned earlier, was the psychologist who, since Anna arrived from Ukraine, had been working with her regarding trauma-focused therapy and post-adoption adjustment.

Dr. Sophia taught Anna that sometimes there is a little blip in the brain. Through their work together, she was able to help her, with the result that most of her OCD symptoms went away within a couple of months. The psychologist also brought me in to make sure I understood so I could support Anna, using the same explanation and terminology.

In one of my folders, I found a piece of paper from a workbook of Anna's, titled *What dangers does OCD try to trick you about?* It's likely Anna filled this out during her time with Dr. Sophia. But it's possible it was later.

She answered that she feared she would "have to go back to Ukraine."

Other fears were typical of someone her age, such as that she would get fat or lose her "beautiful, smart, helpful, nice, caring" mom. Not to mention a fear of spiders. Who doesn't fear spiders?

Very moved, I guaranteed to her that we would never allow her to be sent back to Ukraine. Never. Not unless it was her wish. Otherwise, this would not happen. Never by constraint, never against her will. Also, I told her, "You will never lose me as your mom." During times like this, I'd remind her that God wanted her to be with us, she was meant to be in our family. I reassured her that if by continuing to eat healthily and stay active, she would stay in shape, feeling good.

Anna's fears about being sent back to Ukraine and about losing me were common to adopted children, especially if having been abandoned by their birth mothers. Fear of abandonment is also a core symptom in mental-health conditions like Reactive Attachment Disorder and Borderline Personality Disorder, both of which I will get into in more detail later in the story.

> Fear of abandonment is *primal* fear—not something we get rid of. It is essential and universal to all human beings, a driving force in our connections . . .
>
> The key is how to deal with this primal fear so that we can best access its healing properties . . .

People frequently complain that the fear of abandonment imprisons them behind a wall of insecurity and isolation. Many get caught up in patterns of constant re-abandonment (*abandoholism*) or avoid relationships altogether (*abandophobism*) to avoid any chance of getting hurt or are in a relationship but feel chronic heartache. They're shrouded in shame for feeling so needy.

There is a way out of these self-isolating patterns.[4]

At the time, abandonment was clearly a focus of her therapy, and talking about it was an effective way to deal with the emerging symptoms of OCD.

Her OCD symptoms peaked in January–February 2015. The key to unlearning them was an Exposure/Response Prevention model.

This model is the most common and effective way to treat OCD. It involves confronting the thoughts and situations that make you anxious or that trigger obsessive behavior, while making the conscious choice to *not* engage in the compulsive behavior. In other words, retraining your brain to react in a new way.

You learn to control the symptoms. Another helpful tactic, which provided me with continuity and input, came when Dr. Sophia invited me to the end of Anna's session and they both talked through what Anna had learned.

I had never known anyone I was close to who suffered from this disorder. Often, I had to balance helping her face and overcome fears with, on the other hand, accommodating her need to avoid them so that she could function. I noticed that being involved in Anna's treatment helped me be more understanding and empathetic.

---

4   Susan Anderson, Fear Of Abandonment: A Primal Dilemma Of Insecurity And 10 Ways To Turn It Around | by Susan Anderson | Abandonment Recovery | Medium, published in *Abandonment Recovery*.

One thing I didn't think of at the time was that there might be support groups in our area we could go to. When Anna felt understood and/or that other people were experiencing the same thing as she was, she often felt much better.

Even as Anna worked through her OCD with Dr. Sophia, our family continued to stay busy with work and school and many fun activities on the weekends and during school vacation. We went to Bretton Woods in February to ski and celebrate my fiftieth birthday. One dynamic I started to notice was that family birthdays, particularly mine, began to have a strange vibe, with an odd dynamic between Anna and me. She seemed to stay closer to Mark on these occasions and keep her distance from me. This continued to happen on my birthdays. Just a subtle detachment, and an insecure or envious aura.

I didn't know exactly what she was thinking, but I let things happen naturally and gave her the space she needed. Overall, attachment issues can look much different in how the child treats their mom versus their dad. This is because the symptoms are typically expressed outwardly with the mom.

The mom becomes the nurturing opponent. I had a window into this. And to me, it was transparent. I began to realize that it was difficult for others to see it because the behavior was often much different at home than out of the house; there, it was subtle. This is when I began to "see" the attachment disorder" and later—sometimes reluctantly and almost against my will—"see" other illnesses as they began to manifest outwardly.

In March, I started a new consulting contract with a close friend and business partner, which I was thrilled about. Anna played local basketball on the weekends, seeming to enjoy herself socially and physically. Mark and I could not get enough of watching this strong, passionate basketball player running up and down the court with ease. I was also coaching boys ice hockey. When the season ended in April, I took the kids and my nephew to Florida with my mom. On one of the first days in Florida, we all went to Busch Gardens, and the kids rode the roller coasters and other rides and had fun playing arcade-type games. Then we headed to Orlando—Anna's first trip to Disney World. The boys loved the hotel pool, so they stayed there with my mom, and I was planning to take Anna to the Magic Kingdom.

Unfortunately, I got a stomach bug or flu. Rare for me. The good news was, I was still able to take her to the Magic Kingdom, but my stomach couldn't handle the rides. I felt terrible about it, but she didn't mind me perched on a bench or the curb. She was a complete trooper, hopping on the rides alone, bounding back to me afterward, brimming with animation and excited from the thrill! It turned out to be a great day.

Anna was still seeing Dr. Sophia, and other than having periodic tics, she was doing great. I think all the activities and the opportunity to participate in so many sports gave her outlets for her energy, ways to connect with other people, and positive reinforcement.

At that point, May 2015, all looked bright. Anna was functioning at a high level. Her OCD symptoms were stabilized. She was safe, happy, engaged.

Anna ended fifth grade on a positive note. The summer was like previous years, balancing time at home and enjoying the sunshine and magic of Cape Cod. Anna participated in her first theater camp. I often look back at the video of her and other actors, holding mops, singing "It's a Hard Knock Life" from the musical *Annie*. Sporting a glowing tan, she wore a memorable shirt that boldly proclaimed: "Be YOU, it's always in style." We were lucky to have another mom and daughter next door. The mom is my "summer friend"; each June our friendship picks up where we left off the previous September. We spend time walking, chatting with the girls, and enjoying our Friday night cosmos. We lounged in golf carts under an open sky, enjoying an outdoor movie. The girls participated in the annual "Brew Run," a road race that unfailingly occurs on a scorching Saturday in August, with the temperature never seeming to dip below eighty degrees. Such a happy time! The summer was topped off like the cherry on an ice cream sundae, with a beautiful note from Anna to me:

> A day without Sun, is a day without you! You are really smart and pretty plus a good hockey player.

September 2015

That fall, Anna started sixth grade—middle school. If you have read carefully, you know that this is where the trouble began, stomping into our idyl.

Against our better judgment, we had enrolled Anna in the *large* public middle school because of her need for services, as had been recommended to us. The middle school in our town is big; it combines four elementary schools. But she was used to a small academic setting due to the smaller size of her elementary school.

All her friends from the prior year were dispersed across different teams and classes. It's well known that teenagers don't want to transfer out of their familiar class. We had no idea beforehand just how difficult this would be for her. She seemed like such a popular, can-do young girl. But that was in her nurturing elementary school, where she had a secure sense of identity. The move brought a gradual shift.

As she hurried down the long hallways of the middle school, racing against the clock to get to her classes she burst through the door and plopped down in her seat; some classes she did well in, receiving top grades; in others her tendency to be overly social or lack focus resulted in feedback from teachers, indicating room for improvement.

She was only twelve years old. Isn't this when preteen girls are going shopping at the mall, hanging out, or attending parties and sleepovers? There were other things that preteens were doing. And that was using chat groups and social media.

We held off getting Anna her own phone until she was thirteen and a half. But her iPod connected to the internet, and she was allowed to use an iPad at home for games and movies. She knew the restrictions around what she could access and what not. I reminded her often—if it is something you don't want me or Dad to see, don't post it, don't write it, don't access. This may sound harsh. But we had a few open issues about electronics, and we dreaded having to police something like this.

Now, in the big middle school, she gradually drifted apart from all her elementary-school BFFs (Best Friends Forever), or "besties," which significantly impacted her social life. You can see how this could happen when there was limited time to chitchat at the water cooler. But then came her participation in the fall theater production—in the chorus. It kept her engaged and occupied, *and off electronics.*

One day around Halloween, Mark dropped Anna and our dog, Lily, off at work with me for a couple of hours. I proudly introduced her to my colleagues. She was so sweet and confident. If she hadn't been tethered to the dog, I could have imagined her joining in as a capable assistant. Anna also completed the Monster Dash, a road race, that Sunday—just a week after participating in a strong-girl trail run at a local park. *I don't think she realized at the time just how big these accomplishments were.* On the plus side, this left her little time for excessive downtime indoors.

I felt that Anna and I still had a tight, supportive mother-daughter bond. We still clashed, on occasion, mainly on my need for her to express her feelings, but overall, we had a positive mother-daughter bond that she reinforced in sweet notes to me, such as this one during the week of Thanksgiving in November 2015, part of which I quote below:

11-23-15

Dear Mom,

. . . I am the luckiest kid in the world.
When I am sad you make me laugh
And you always make me feel alive.
When I see flowers, I think of you. When?
I hear songs I think of you. When I see
you I always smile. Thank you! . . .

Your daughter/
Buddy Anna

But one day when we called the orphanage, we realized that because she was focused on English, she had temporarily lost her Russian. And we could not have a conversation with the director, unlike before. I learned after this, though, that this phenomenon is not unusual.

> *"The minute you start learning another language, the two systems start to compete with each other," says Monika Schmid, a linguist at the University of Essex.*
>
> *Schmid is a leading researcher of language attrition, a growing field of research that looks at what makes us lose our mother tongue. In children, the phenomenon is somewhat easier to explain since their brains are generally more flexible and adaptable. Until the age of about 12, a person's language skills are relatively vulnerable to change. Studies on international adoptees have found that even nine-year-olds can almost completely forget their first language when they are removed from their country of birth.[5]*

At the end of 2015, I posted an ad online "Help my daughter 're-learn' Russian via Skype" with a freelance company, Upwork. A lovely Ukraine woman responded, and from December 2015 through the beginning of May 2019, Anna logged 226 hours with her: over 250 individual sessions!! Can you just see her working in government as an international interpreter?

She was so interested in these sessions and loved then so much that she would wake up early and start her session on most days at 6:30 a.m., due to the time difference in Eastern Europe. The woman's name was Helena, and they developed a fast bond. First, they worked on vocabulary and language skills, then talked about culture and traditions. Relearning her Russian language was a way to stay grounded in who she is, while building new layers

---

[5] Sophie Hardach, BBC Future, "Losing Your Language," https://languagehat.com/losing-your-language/.

of identity through all the experiences she was having. Although this was a deliberate step to honor her uniqueness, I did not know that it would have such a positive effect. It was fascinating to see Anna get her Russian language skills back. This also allowed her to sing in Russian, and that became another thing we did together. Hearing her captivating voice singing in Russian was like being whisked away to a cherished memory of mine at a holiday concert in Vienna.

PART 4

2016

CHAPTER 7

Understanding

Second half of sixth grade

We were all going in different directions, but at the end of each day, we relished coming home, having dinner, and enjoying the things that made us comfortable. Anna had joined the school theater and was in the play. She also played basketball in the town league. Max was busy with school and hockey, and Mark and I, besides work, were engaged in several nonprofit charities. Max had never played on a formal basketball team, and as I mentioned, we loved watching Anna's games. Mark and I went to one of his close friend's destination weddings in Miami. In mid-January, Anna presented me with a beautiful "Mother of the Year" certificate.

While I was away on business at the end of January, Anna sent me a long email about the school play—explaining how, now that it was done, she was feeling so sad. She had the best time ever, she said, and some of her friends screamed their heads off just for her when she came on to bow. Being in Florida, I had sent her a picture of the ocean and she replied to the effect, "I'm about to jump on a plane because it looked amazing." She said she was thinking about doing the next play, even though she initially thought the first one was boring. Her closing email said, "I miss you so much."

For February school vacation, my mom invited Anna, along with her stepcousins, to Florida. She flew as an unaccompanied minor, so I was only able to take her as far as the security gate. I was so proud of her in times like this because she was confident and independent, bursting with excitement.

As in previous winters, Anna played basketball, went to hockey games, free skated with friends, etc. Along with relearning Russian, we, in other ways, stayed connected to her Ukrainian roots. That Easter, for example, we learned how Ukrainian pysanky eggs are decorated, using a wax-resist method, resulting in unique Easter egg designs that are deeply symbolic and meaningful. We copied some of the designs from pictures of the pysanky eggs, and we also bought some at a Ukrainian fair.

After sixth grade the school guidance counselor recommended that Anna do a review course in English Language Arts (ELA) and Math Enrichment summer school. Mark and I were not sure. We ended up agreeing. But Anna was bored and unfocused. It did not turn out well. In a rebellious attitude, she dismissed the need for the summer program. In this period she seemed a typical soon-to-be-thirteen-year-old. At one point, she asked about working (or volunteering where she could earn special privileges), so we investigated the animal shelter and the library.

One librarian did say she could use help with a couple of art classes. I said that would be great. But for whatever reason, Anna skipped out. When I went to pick her up, the library staff was worried that I did not know she wasn't there.

After summer school, we filled weekends on the Cape beach or at Cape barbecues and dinners at local restaurants. In August, Anna and I went to the Marshfield Fair. I asked her to come along with some friends from hockey to see a musician and then walk around the fair and go on the rides. She ended up going on some rides with other *daring* people who were up for the rickety, spinning Ferris wheel, where the carriage spun around too. And then off we went to New Hampshire, stopping at a friend's lake house for a cruise around the lake in their boat and an overnight visit on the way to summer camp.

When I dropped her off, she asked me to talk to the counselor about the OCD that still plagued her from time to time. Accordingly, the counselor explained to Anna she could talk to her anytime and call home and check in with me if needed. Anna asked me to make sure the counselor knew she might need some support.

This helped a lot because she would often need to see them, and they could easily help her without involving me. Typically, the day after drop-off, I sent a care package. Some kids were at the camps for longer sessions, so packages arrived often.

Anna loved the packages and always sent a nice thank-you. Tacked on at the end of the note there would often be a few words about an ailment *". . . I am having so much fun. My head was hurt (ing) on Monday I went to the nurse it helped a little but still hurts . . ."*

I often reflected about how brave it was that she fearlessly plunged into so many unfamiliar things by herself, such as going to a new camp where she knew no one; flying to visit her stepcousins; trying out acting in theater. Anna was always up for these experiences.

This pattern continued as a preteen. She was always up for "getting out."

We loved the drive to the Cape. She cheered Mark on at a bike race in the White Mountains, chasing him up the hill and across the finish line. She loved social activities and joining her younger cousins for activities or dinner. I could see these things brought her a sense of freedom.

CHAPTER 8

Distressed

Nothing could be as hard as middle school.

—Zooey Deschanel

Seventh grade—September 2016

Now comes the trying part I've been warning about. Seventh grade. A pivotal moment. There was also puberty to contend with and, for Anna, an increase in interpersonal and peer conflicts.

I noticed a significant shift in Anna's demeanor early in September during an Adele concert we attended together, a birthday gift for her. Suppressing the urge to repeatedly ask her, "What's wrong?" as she kept her face turned away, I fought down the words "Why are you ignoring me?" Again, the tricky thing was I could not tell what she was thinking, and the whole teenager thing could have been the culprit. Obviously, being with your mom and dad at a concert when you're thirteen may not be thrilling, but it was something she'd begged to do. And she was excited up until we arrived and showed our own enthusiasm.

The behavior that we were starting to see could have been "splitting." It was complicated—similar to pushing people away due to fear of abandonment. It also was hard to comprehend that she was *not intentionally* doing things like this, but that they were a result of *the way her brain was programmed from much earlier in life.*

Her friend circle seemed to dwindle to maybe one or two, but she did not talk about these remaining few like she had with the friends from elementary school. What we didn't know yet was that *she had a whole gang of friends online.* Maybe some of the group she met at summer school, or they might have been students in her grade. I did recognize one name, Aida.

The next morning while slipping her iPod touch into her pocket, she acted and looked cagey. I told her: "Give it to me"—that she should go up and get ready for school.

Anna may have assumed I'd forgotten her password. I had not. I opened the chat and was struck with one of the most appalling—vulgar— conversations I have ever seen on a chat or anywhere else. I am not a prude. This was way beyond the pale. I closed the iPod down and put it down. When she returned, I told her she didn't need it at school that day, she could go up and exchange it for an MP3 player if she wanted to bring music. She looked at me like there might be a stand-off, but did as I said, but became *very quiet and avoided eye contact.*

I didn't say a word about it until she got home. I was calm and matter of fact, reminding her that I had repeatedly said I would look at her iPod if I suspected she was using it inappropriately.

"Who is in the group?" I asked. "And why are they talking like that?" She explained that she did not know all the kids, but a few went to her school. She said she didn't write anything; this was true; I hadn't seen her name on any message. I warned her to leave the chat immediately, not to return to this group or any group like it—that if she continued to use the iPod inappropriately, it would be gone for good. I stressed the importance of encouraging this group to disband.

This was the beginning of the battle that I could trace back to Ukraine: us vs. the iPod, iPad, iPhone, Snapchat, and other social media apps. It was a long and intense battle because the iPhone became her lifeline, her identity, her confidante, *and a secretive, dangerous tool.*

Later that fall she wrote some very scary things on paper about wanting my husband to die; specifically, "I hope he dies tomorrow at three. I prayed to the devils and demons. They are my god now." But, as it was hidden away in one of her notebooks, I saw it only the following spring.

Still after-the-fact, I later discovered that shortly after writing the above text in a notebook, she wrote that she only pretended to walk the dog, but stayed on the couch all day, watching TV. The next line said, "Then later my mom (step) got the truth out of me." Referring to me as her "step" mom was also disturbing and odd.

When I stumbled upon these notebooks, she was in the hospital in 2017. She had asked me to get some of her papers, on which she had jotted down phone numbers of friends. I didn't want to tell Mark about these notes because he'd always supported her in every way, and some of the confidences took me aback. I thought it would hurt him too much. And besides, did she really mean it? No, I didn't think so.

He loved watching her play sports, and they had many engaging conversations about history, education, careers, and college. They did not get into the heavier topics like we did, and I did not mind taking on some of the emotional burden to relieve him from this because I was with her so much. These notebook confidences did not seem to come from that sweet little girl we knew our daughter to be.

Later, I felt that not taking on some of the emotional burden I did, he did not understand the gravity of what I went through daily, what our daughter was illustrating. The turn she had taken.

I tried hard not to unload on him too much of the chaos that began to happen. I often felt like it was when you have an infant or toddler, and your partner comes home exhausted, and you are ready to hand them the child and have a minute to just relax and kick off your shoes.

Often, it was very hard for me to understand how Anna was feeling, and it was times like this, when I read her own words, I got a glimpse inside her head. I constantly reminded myself that due to her trauma and attachment issues, these words could mean anything, but it was still upsetting.

There is a lot written about splitting—how people with BPD can love you one minute, hate you the next. It is also related to black-and-white thinking. Splitting was beginning to be a huge problem for us, even at this time. It made sense that Anna, having lived for years in an unstable orphanage environment, had developed some unhealthy coping mechanisms.

CHAPTER 9

Concerned

Darkness will always be a servant of light.

—Matshona Dhliwayo

Anna's report card continued to be peppered with phrases like "she has been a bit too social," "her attention and effort could improve," "is inconsistent in performance"—mixed with "a pleasure to have in class," "shows recent improvement." Or "drew a banana on a sheet of paper when she should have been doing a class assignment." By this time this information was also regularly passed along to us at parent-teacher conferences. Neither we nor they could put our finger on the cause of the inconsistent behavior and effort.

But as I have mentioned repeatedly, she was a thirteen-year-old girl in a big middle school; it was hard to tell if these were typical developments of a teen girl grappling with the confusing environment or something more concerning.

We did not have to wait long to find an answer. A call from the guidance counselor asked us to come in for a meeting after Anna showed another student some cut marks on her wrists. The school recommended an outside psychiatric evaluation. She could come to school after that, but not before.

On October 24, Anna was admitted to St. Vincent Children's Hospital for cutting and received care within the inpatient mental-health unit. Anna was hurting, and, the cutting, it appeared, gave her relief from pain. Later, she also started cutting herself if she was not allowed to do something or got her phone taken away for lying or for getting in trouble at school. Any little upset, and she cut herself. I felt helpless because as I tried to keep the communication lines open, she was withdrawing; this was all new, and the thoughts in my head were flying around, trying to make sense of it. In pain? Ashamed? Probably, but the disordered attachment was also rearing its ugly head.

At the time we had no idea a whole new set of challenges was on the threshold: trying to navigate emergency rooms, intakes, hospital stays, discharges, medications, follow ups, safety planning.

On Tuesday, October 25, I went into the hospital to visit, and we watched a movie together on her bed. She did not want me to leave, and it was hard to go. The stay was supposed to be five days, but they agreed to discharge Anna a day early with an individualized coping and safety plan.

During a hospital stay it's common for a safety plan to be developed by the patient with the social worker or clinical psychologist's help. Its primary goal is to minimize the likelihood of return trips to the hospital. One component utilizes a number scale ranging from one to six (other versions may use a different metric), indicating a scale from feeling at one's best to feeling at one's worst. Alongside each number are the patient's personal responses to questions, such as how I feel, how I act, what I need. There is also a section that lists coping skills that could be used to help manage intense emotions.

Having completed the plan, Anna was discharged. We were relieved she was home. All the time she was at the hospital, I'd been uncomfortable and restless. It had not been a good experience for her. Unfortunately, this was the first of many hospital stays over the next few years.

For us, as parents, a new role awaited, involving navigating the mental-healthcare system.

The next day Anna and I went out to get some Halloween decorations. She loved Halloween and was thrilled to be decorating and making plans to go trick-or-treating with her new friend. I have so many stunning pictures of Anna. I clearly remember her smile that stretched from ear to ear while she was putting the fake cobweb on the green bush that flanked the front stairs.

Peacefully, the Thanksgiving holidays wrapped up, with Anna and me at my dad's in North Carolina. Meanwhile, Mark and Max celebrated the festivities with the Becker clan, and Max enthusiastically kicked off his high-school hockey season. Anna and I made a quick trip to my mom's in sunny Florida for the Christmas break.

PART 5

2017

CHAPTER 10

Blindsided

There is a crack in everything, that's how the light gets in.
—Leonard Cohen

N ow came 2017. It turned out to be one long rollercoaster ride; there were some thrills but mostly we experienced deep, dark plunges.

It wasn't apparent right away. Anna was smiling and hustling on the basketball court with her blue "Court Crushers" team shirt on. Heading straight to the garage to shoot pucks against the wall after finishing his homework, Max wasted no time between his high school hockey games. As parents, we cherished every minute in the stands cheering them on.

As we planned to kick off a system transformation project at work, the year started excitedly. I was eager and grateful to plan the kick-off. Mark and I snuck away to Cape Cod for an overnight to celebrate my birthday.

We settled into the historic mansion wing at Ocean Edge Resort in Brewster. The room boasted crisp white bedding and elegant drapery enveloped in rays of sunshine. *Heaven.*

Due to the mild winter I had the luxury, offered by the surprising weather, of spending the day strolling on the beach in Cape Cod. I was so happy to be on the Brewster flats, virtually alone, in the beautiful sunshine, smelling the unusually warm and salty sea air. The Brewster flats are muddy, marsh-filled tidal flats that expand to twelve thousand acres at low tide as the water recedes, then gets covered again at high tide. My happy place.

For Easter weekend, Max, Anna, and I flew to North Carolina, to my dad's—for the first time taking our dog Lily, who will become important in this story, though she was always important to me, my companion for over fourteen years, till February of 2024. Lily, a small dog, loved cuddling up on the couch with my dad, and my dad loved having the whole gang for company. I hadn't the least suspicion that he was about to have a major stroke.

Returning to Boston, intending to attend a hockey tournament in Vermont on the weekend, I invited Anna to join me, but she was looking forward to a sleepover on Saturday night, so she preferred to stay home. Late Saturday night the phone rang. It was Anna, reporting some friction with the other girls. I told her Dad could pick her up. But she declined.

The girls had been mean to her, she explained when I got back on Sunday. I envisioned how the drama played out. In moments like these, I always tried to validate her feelings; in fact, Anna was more sensitive in group situations than one-on-one.

Maybe this stemmed from the orphanage, where she had been bullied. At least now, she had a home, a family, her bedroom, where she felt safe. Digging deeper, I found that Anna often spoke about her appearance and was fixated on it at times. She worried whether people liked her and, more importantly, if they reached out to her, as much as she reached out to them; she would often use the phrase "did the work." But there was something in addition that was hard to pinpoint.

Had there been an incident in Ukraine that caused her guilt or shame? I asked myself, or was something happening now that she was being elusive about? This possible secret, she carried with her, often saying, "You don't know what I have seen." *What?* Try as I might, I couldn't extract it out of her. In all the therapy discussions, the pieces of information that surfaced were that she saw her birth mother strike someone—her father, her stepfather, or another man—over the head with a frying pan. Maybe he was hurt badly? Maybe this is why her mother went to jail when Anna was four? The other thing that seemed to haunt her was violence she'd witnessed in Italy when she went to the same host family two years in a row.

She told me and at least one clinician that the father yelled a lot and may have struck the mom. I said "What? Did he hurt you or the other children?" She didn't know. "Why did they send you back a second time?" She shrugged. She also remembered once being in a park alone, maybe age three or four. This haunted her. An additional mystery was, why did her grandmother bring her to the orphanage? Hadn't she lived with her at the time? That's what she told us. I increasingly learned that if she got the validation that I understood her disturbing experiences, she typically felt better, able to move on. Now came a critical event of the year, frightening beyond anything I'd imagined possible.

It was Tuesday, April 25, 2017, approximately 5:15 p.m. A call came in from our babysitter. I was just leaving an appointment. Anna, she recounted, had taken a lot of pills and did not feel well. At least, that's what Anna told her.

Oh, no, she didn't really take a bunch of pills, did she?? shot through my head, although undeniably it was the case. I called 911 in a panic. I was just down the street from the fire station, so I saw the fire truck pull out, lights ablaze. *It's a false alarm*, I kept telling myself. *Let it be a false alarm.* But no matter what I said in my head, *it was very real.* In less than five minutes, I got into the house to find Anna sitting on the couch—the paramedics clustered around her. My babysitter and son were in the room too, looking as if they had seen a ghost. *My daughter was only thirteen years old.*

Anna was pale, shaking with cold. In that moment it hit me. *She took a lot of pills. They need to get her to the hospital. Right away.* I raced to the hospital in my car, grateful that it was only a mile and a half away. At the hospital, Anna reported having taken twenty-six Midols, five Tylenols, and five Advils. This incident is a bit of a blur because I was so worried, scared, and shocked. It didn't register that there was a security officer sitting right outside the room, but this vision became much more familiar with additional ER visits. I know they pumped her stomach and, to absorb the toxins, gave her a charcoal substance. When they let me see her, she was vomiting up the charcoal.

She allowed me to comfort her and hold her hair back. She also let me clean her up around her face with a towel. I whispered, "Everything is going to be okay." The doctor predicted that because she came in so fast, she would probably not suffer any lasting damage, but that it would be a good idea to have her do an additional twenty-four-hour special treatment at a Boston pediatric hospital, Kennedy-Parker Pediatric, to help prevent any issues. After he said that, we wanted to get her there as soon as possible.

Anna was admitted to the Kennedy-Parker Pediatric Hospital on April 26, 2017, at 2:00 a.m. She slept most of the day. The next day I sat with her. If I spoke, she became angry, which didn't surprise me in that she no doubt felt terribly sick. The nurse told me Anna was medically cleared to leave. From research I did, this meant that acetaminophen that can indicate liver damage wasn't found in the enzymes.

She would be transferred *later that day* to the inpatient psychiatric ward at the same hospital, Kennedy-Parker. I often reflected back, thinking: *Would our local hospital have released her to go home with us? Could we have avoided the psychiatric ward?*

This was a turning point, as I see it. I wondered what role this longer-term inpatient stay would play on her confidence and self-perception.

Meanwhile, Anna asked me if I could bring her some comfortable clothes. Anna was discharged to the inpatient psychiatry ward while I was shopping. When I returned from walking/jogging about a mile away to Marshall's, I found her tucked up and back in a far corner of the hospital. I left the clothes as they were getting Anna settled. Procedurally, they needed to go through every item to ensure her safety. And they wanted to do that alone. I got the hint: time for me to leave. The formal intake would be on Monday.

Notably, the instructions on the Kennedy-Parker Inpatient Psychiatry Service website warned about how frightening it can be to a caregiver to find that your child needs to be psychiatrically hospitalized, and even the environment itself can make you feel unlistened to and overwhelmed, or even, with regards to the outside world, embarrassed. Suddenly I felt thrust into an unfamiliar sadness—unchartered waters. Never did I imagine I would get accustomed to spending my days as a visitor in a locked-down hospital psych ward.

I learned about what's allowed in, what a sensory room is (think large lava lamps, fiber optic lights, comfy chairs, stress balls, and more . . .), the structure of the team, where the common areas were, how the med distributions worked, how the food distribution worked, how the passes worked, what a step-down program is, what you can and cannot bring such as razors, nail clippers, etc. It's a world behind a curtain that you would know if you had a child, relative or friend with a mental health issue who needed a safe environment for their emotional state to be stabilized so they can hopefully progress to a "step-down" lower level of care, or to home.

Anna spent two long weeks in the inpatient psychiatric ward *THIS* time, with an additional two weeks at a step-down program. A whole month! There was an eerie, quiet feeling at home. I missed the bouncing sound of the basketball, missed cheering on the sidelines at her soccer games.

On Monday—as we sat together on her bed, backs against the wall, my hand gently stroking her thigh—she walked me through what happened. I felt it was too soon to ask Anna explicitly why she did it. But she gave some details: the pills made her feel very sick and dizzy, she said—like she was going to die. She knew *at that moment* that she did not want to die. It was all too real. She DEFINITELY wanted to live. Whether she knew it or not, it had been a cry for help.

Thankful she'd been able to get herself downstairs and alert our babysitter to what she'd done. She talked about going on an online chat group to get help after she took the pills. It scared me to even think about what might have happened.

While in the inpatient psychiatric ward, Anna earned good-behavior passes so she could leave the floor with us and go down to the cafeteria or ice cream shop in the lobby. We started talking about what had triggered her into taking the pills. The culprit was social media. She had been corresponding with a boy (she assumed he was a boy) on a couple of social-media accounts, she explained; then he blocked her. That action set her off. She was devastated.

"Why didn't you talk about it with me? I could have helped you figure out who this person was and why he would do such a thing. People disguise who they are on social media apps; they could be any age, and it's dangerous."

Surprised, she looked at me with squinted eyes, trying to process what I was saying.

"He was my age," she said slowly—still finding it hard to fathom why a grown man, or anyone, would trick her into thinking he was a boy her age and they were "dating" online. I knew that thirteen-year-olds meeting people on social media apps, using an iPod and Wi-Fi, can be a slippery and dangerous slope.

I also knew that underlying things were at work, and she was feeling down. Depressed. Significantly, it came out that she had just read *Thirteen Reasons Why*, which she'd received as a Christmas gift from a friend. I had had no idea it glorified teen suicide. I bet the friend didn't either. The silver lining was that she said the incident scared her so much she never wanted to do anything like it again. Her thoughts of suicide were gone.

To my knowledge, since the cutting, self-harm had not been something we'd had to worry about, at least in this way. Later incidents, however, such as eating inordinate amounts of hot sauce after her doctor instructed her to stop due to existing stomachaches and pain, appeared linked to self-sabotage.

I never completely understood what led up to the overdose unless it was purely an impulsive emotional reaction from getting "dumped" online. It was all the information I could get at the time. I know it's a common symptom of depression and trauma-based illness, but it blindsided us, and I still feel like there was more to it. I say this because, afterward, while still in the hospital, Anna became increasingly angry with us, especially Mark. This was one of those moments where we seemed to get further away from each other, and I was confused about why. *How did it come about? Was it just her age, or was it more deep-rooted?* I also realized that the book she'd read that centered on teen suicide was *a big miss on my part.* I still asked myself: Could it be related to reactive attachment? Was this the mood disorder or another illness beginning to present?

Meanwhile, I developed a nasty case of shingles. Wouldn't you know? While her behavior and feelings toward us in the hospital became more distant—at times demanding—I felt very stressed out, and stress causes a weakened immune system. Anyone who has had shingles understands immediately that it brings radiating pain from the inside out and can itch for days.

I felt lucky that I only had the radiating pain, that it was caught quickly, when at a routine appointment I mentioned a small rash. I immediately bought a shingles balm online and layered it like paste under my clothing. Things like this hardly fazed me anymore, perhaps a testament to the pragmatic nature instilled by my German heritage.

Whether it was at this stay or another, Anna was informed that it was part of her "rights" to have her schoolwork delivered from the public middle school in Madison. She was a smart girl who, when able, put great effort and pride in her work. She did not want to get behind while out of school. For me, it was confusing because she demanded the work, then I would receive calls from the education liaison at the hospital because Anna was acting out and not doing the work that was delivered. I wasn't sure what they wanted me to do from afar.

Initially, I had the role of schoolwork fetcher. This should have been a straightforward process. I understood it could take a couple of days: an email to the guidance counselor, her follow-through coordination with the teachers, and a package ready for pick-up. It rarely worked that way, and my first trip to the school was a waste of time because, although promised, there was no package at the office. Overall, I was getting little support from the public-school guidance office.

During the stay we took Anna out of the hospital to a family dinner, the movies, manicures, lunches. I followed the team's lead, and we gave all the support we could, but it also began a time where *if we refused to take her up on a particular suggestion she considered fun or worthwhile, she would typically refuse the pass.* If she refused it, it was useless to beg; she was a determined human being. She would only budge if I "bribed her" with something of material or personal value to her. Did the social worker realize that this would give Anna an opportunity to push me away, just to feel more in control? Of course, to have been yanked out of her home, with all personal authority pulled out from under her, was it any wonder she expressed her freedom any way she could—however inconsequential. And, ultimately, useless?

Released from Kennedy-Parker Pediatric Hospital Inpatient Psychiatric Unit she was again sent to St. Vincent Children's Hospital, but this time would be enrolled in the Community Based Acute Treatment (CBAT) program. But right away, *at the intake*, she described having experienced family tension at home. Taken aback, I had not been aware of any. Surely, I would have noticed. This exemplifies the splitting—playing one side against the other. I have to say, she was deft at it, able to manufacture stories, but then, how was I to know whether she really believed them, given the fragile state she was in?

Initially at St. Vincent Children's, she lobbied to have the planned two-week stay reduced, but at this point, we were going to follow the medical team's lead, despite my gut feeling that two weeks was too long. I wanted her to be at home; the hospital environment felt cold, sterile, and lonely by comparison.

The good news was that at the CBAT she was talking and sharing her feelings in group therapy and one-on-ones with the clinician. *Positive reports filled her chart; she was initially hailed as a leader to some of the other adolescents.*

On May 14, Anna and I went to a trampoline park nearby. She was all smiles in the pictures and the selfie we took. Having dinner with Mark and

Max in Harvard Square, we celebrated Mother's Day. We sat in a cozy booth, and it felt so good to be together like this, especially on that holiday.

Things didn't change until after the first week, when she began to get bored and frustrated. Understandably. The closer she got to being discharged, the more she acted act out, precipitating setbacks. It appeared that she feared succeeding and being discharged, but also wanted out. I thought of this as a form of self-sabotage, in fear of the next step, the unknown. There was a lot going on in her head, and I can only imagine how overwhelming it was for her after the traumatic incident.

CHAPTER 11

Determined

The kids who need the most love will ask for it in the most
unloving of ways.

—Unknown

May 2017

THE CBAT program offered Anna an opportunity to talk a lot about
tension at home—tension she perceived but that baffled us. During
the meeting, Mark and I sincerely sought ways to improve by asking
Anna how we could offer our support. She had no answer at all, unable to
provide one.

Interestingly, she had her earrings on. I noticed it right away. Why had
they allowed that? She had made a big point of how because of the strings,
she wasn't allowed to wear some of the clothing I'd bought her. I knew that
rule applied to earrings, and in the meeting, out of concern, I mentioned
them to the social worker—only to get a blank stare. Later they informed me
that Anna had cuts on her arms. "New ones?" I asked.

Yes, but they did not know the source; a full sweep of the room revealed nothing. I was confused: she had not been cutting recently.

"Maybe her earrings?" I asked. They said that Anna said no; they believed her. Later she told me how she fooled them into letting her keep the earrings on, then used them to scratch her arm.

"But I didn't think you were having urges to cut anymore," I said.

"I just did it," she answered—half gloating, nonchalantly, as if testing me—"because you mentioned the earrings at the meeting."

Apparently, it had been a whim, a bit of mischief—her way to express displeasure at my attempt to "control" her. It was the old saying: tell someone not to do a thing, and it's the best way to get them to do it, especially someone with a rebellious streak.

A light bulb went on. This was a lesson to me. Now I knew that if I was not being asked for my opinion, I did not need to interfere. For better or worse, this was a seminal moment for me. I could not compete with delusion, or outright dishonesty. I felt a new sense of sadness and doubt about Anna and me getting back the closeness that we shared over the past three and a half years.

I keep mentioning her need to control. She had it, I say, even in the orphanage. But let's approach it another way. Think about how her first experience, at five, was of being taken from her home with no say in the matter. Then in these hospitals she is again with no say in the matter. *She doesn't exist. Other people can think and make decisions, not her.* It would be a terrifying way to make you feel you were a cipher. But she wouldn't go down into nonentity without a fight. Think of that side of it. Of course, her spark of life, the life force, her divine spark, said: *I exist. I need to control something, even my ten feet square of earth.*

Before her discharge from the CBAT, I took her to school for a few hours. She'd been out almost a month. In a reentry meeting with the administration team, we discussed putting supports in place that, hopefully, would alleviate her sense of overwhelming pressure.

The school administrators' backs were pushed against their chairs during the meeting, they were not *leaning in* as they talked about how they could work with Anna and us to support her. It was all superficial, with a lot of smiling and head nodding. Personally, I felt like they would have liked us to go away, *disappear.* I decided to reach out to her teachers directly and had much better luck. One had the idea to meet as a team during parent conferences, instead of me having to work with each one separately on whatever academic and behavioral issues they were seeing.

Back at the hospital, Anna called me in the afternoon, laughing and joking with someone in the background; she said to me she thought she was crazy.

Going back to the local middle school felt different, she revealed but then clammed up. She did not want me to come back that day and did not want a pass on Saturday, as planned. Mmm…was she looking for my reaction? I asked her if it was because of soccer (she didn't have to go if she did not feel comfortable, I assured her), but she said no, *she just wanted to think through things.*

Fine, I said. But also said that when she was ready, I would like her to tell us a bit of what she was thinking. Very gently, I added, "I think you are shutting me out. Please don't." No, she insisted quickly, she just needed time.

One thing struck me. The other teens had issues too, she said, and it was nice that "They understand me." *Did she just want to spend time with the kids there?* I wondered for a minute after the call. Yes, apparently. Just after another hospital-planning meeting decided to discharge her the next day (a Friday), she said, after the psychiatrist left the room, out of the blue, "Nah, I like it here better than home, so I am going to stay the weekend."

Later many professionals explained that sometimes a hospital psychiatric setting begins to awaken potential problems, such as in meeting other adolescents who might glorify risky behavior, push back on the rules and authority, and discuss problems they experience with their parents.

I knew she had a lot of unresolved issues; it was just hard because she was not able to express herself like she had in the past. Before we hung up, she said sorry and told me to tell Dad sorry. I told her there was nothing to be sorry about.

Anna changed her mind about Saturday. Happy, I asked her to go to the Cape for the day, but she passed on that. Too bad. It's not a fancy place, but it radiated good energy.

On Saturday, I picked her up to attend her brother's baseball game with a friend. It turned out the friend could not go last minute, so I brought snacks, cards, and a comfy blanket to sit on. It was a beautiful, warm day. The air was fresh, and the grass smelled like, well, sweet grass. When we got there, she was relaxed, but then veered into asking if we could go to the Cape. I explained that after the game would be too late. It was an emotional weekend, with the shingles gnawing away at me. I tried not to even mention this to Anna because, unlike in the earlier years, gone was the compassionate, empathetic young girl. She was oblivious now to anyone else's ailments.

Right after that she got all quiet, not wanting to play cards, go on swings, etc. We took a walk, during which time she basically vented about everything: the staff yelled at her, which got her day off to a bad start, she said; her stomach hurt. I was concerned, but soon the ice cream man came, and she wanted a pre-packaged cone with vanilla ice cream and chocolate swirl. After she ate the ice cream, she was cold, she said. And now she gets cold all the time. I felt the current negativity stemmed from not being able to go to the Cape, but this might not be the case. I found myself in a constant tug-of-war within my own mind, trying to figure out what were symptoms from the illness, and what were not.

At this point I just said "Sorry you feel this way." I did some tougher talking about communication, but then asked if I could braid her hair. That did the trick. The tension lessened and I could breathe easier.

When we got home, she made brownies and muffins while I made soup. It was fun. She did say that it would be better if we talked through things instead of fighting. I hadn't thought we were fighting! But I'd been tougher—or just frank.

I said, "Yes, we can talk through things," but also explained that the constant complaining and lack of wanting to do anything, including talking, made it very hard to "talk through things. I can't read your mind."

The rest of the afternoon I kept telling her how much I loved her—with a big smile on my face, sincerity in my voice—and that seemed to help too. I missed those happy times together at home.

The plan was for Mark to do the discharge Tuesday afternoon if all went well back at the program the next day. Then she would go to school Wednesday.

Things went as planned, and after-school Wednesday I took Anna to her primary-care doctor for the post-hospitalization visit, another procedural thing planned during discharge. Like many doctors, this one was hugely compassionate. But I remember no particulars. After the appointment, Anna seemed more sensitive and withdrawn, as if regressing to when she first came to the States. It seemed like if she was getting her way, she was happy, but if anything she didn't relish was asked of her, she'd go down a black hole, mostly complaining about people or a new ailment.

The tricky thing here was that *she was thirteen, so this behavior was consistent with that of other thirteen-year-olds.* That said, her emotional stability continued to decline, to the point where later, looking back, it was clear that this had not been just typical teen behavior.

CHAPTER 12

Sorrow

If there ever comes a day when we can't be together, keep
me in your heart. I'll stay there forever.

—Winnie the Pooh

That Friday, Anna and I went to the Cape—hooray!

I noted—and brightened to—the contentment in her face as
I drove. Mark and Max and some of Max's friends came later. Anna and I
went for a walk at Paine's Creek, our family's favorite place to walk and
paddleboard. It was an unseasonably cool day, in the mid-50s. We did a mini
photo shoot, and I was able to capture stunning pictures of her barefoot,
flip flops in hand, with slightly tattered blue jeans, a blue and white striped
top. Later the kids swam indoors and went into the warm, frothy jacuzzi. We
were lucky to have access to a pool club in Brewster granting us refuge from
the cold as we retreated to the warm, welcoming oasis of the warm indoor
pool and the steamy, soothing hot tub.

But that bright note was short-lived. Nobody's fault. We no sooner got
back home Monday than my dad was unexpectedly admitted to a hospital in
North Carolina with congestive heart failure. I was blindsided.

But by Tuesday afternoon he was feeling better. I talked to him at the end of the day while at work as did my sister. Unfortunately, one day later a call came in from the doctor. *I should head down pronto.* My dad had had a stroke, right in the hospital. I dashed to my boss's office. He was an amazing guy and in his Irish brogue said *"Go, go!"*

My mom booked me a flight while I headed home to grab some things. I called an Uber and set out for the airport, my heart in my throat. Just before midnight I arrived at the hospital. My dad's new caretaker, Chuck, who had only been with my dad six days, was in the room. I sincerely regretted not getting Chuck into position sooner because the supplemental caretakers I initially hired were incompetent in this role. I knew my dad had had a stroke, but I was unprepared to learn he was still unconscious. Holding his hand, I said, "Dad, I am here. I love you, and you are going to be okay." Wishful thinking.

However, he squeezed my hand, and I started to cry. Just to be sure, I asked him to squeeze it again, and he did.

I spent that night sleeping in the chair next to his bed—hopeful that he was going to wake. The next day I made phone calls to my sister, my brother, and my mom (my parents were not together but still cordial). I told my dad when each one was on the phone, and then they talked to him. It was beautiful.

I was very close to my dad, and I am also very close to my mom who is a young eighty-seven-year-old. My mom is an industrious, fun-loving lady, who loves watching game shows and sports on TV. She drives "old people" to doctor's appointments and enjoys her daily nap. You can often find her enjoying a glass of cheap champagne on the "Lanai" around 4:00 p.m.!

Back to my dad... Around midday the doctors talked about hospice, so I decided we would get my dad back home and have hospice come in. Like many people, my dad did not like being in the hospital; I wanted him at home. Chuck was already in the process of getting his hospital bed into his bedroom. Amidst the myriad of circumstances unfolding at home, I had delayed hiring him, something I mentioned before that I wish were different.

His presence, however, proved to be a solace, with a comforting and spiritual essence for which I am forever indebted to him. I have the same sentiments towards several other caretakers who loved and attended to my dad.

A little while later a neurologist came by. I told her the plan. But she put her hand on my shoulder to say, "If it were my dad, I would have him go across the street to the beautiful hospice building. They will take very good care of him." I knew she was telling me this for a reason. So, reflecting a bit, I agreed.

They did take marvelous care of him, but the following day when the doctors did the rounds, I was under the impression from them that he still had a few days. I was happy about this because I was not ready to let him go. He was snoring loudly; I was banking on his waking. There was a chance of it, I still thought.

Because I slept in my clothes again, the second night in a row, Chuck was a little worried about me. "Go take a shower at your dad's," he suggested firmly. I nodded my head yes, went to the house, made a cup of tea, brought the tea into the bathroom, showered, and dried my hair.

My phone rang. It was the hospice facility. "I think you should come back; it may be today," the voice said. I grabbed the keys and my bag and ran out of the house. While driving, I got a call from Chuck. I was screaming, "Is my dad okay? Is he alive? Or is he dead?" Chuck said I should pull over, but I said I'd be there in a minute. He met me at the front so he could park the car. I ran into the room. The nurse said he was still breathing but about to pass.

I still am not sure if he was breathing, but I chose to trust her. He looked at peace. There were so many emotions, and I just wanted time to stop *because I did not want my dad gone.*

The nurse said I could stay for a few minutes, which I did. I held my dad's hand and kept telling him I loved him. Eventually Chuck, at my side, said it was probably time to let him go. Chuck is very religious and spiritual, which gave me great comfort. I walked out, overwhelmed with sadness and grief. I was also upset that had I known it was only going to be twenty-four hours, I would have had Dad taken to his beloved, quaint, cozy ranch-style home nestled amidst the rich pine, sturdy oak, and delicate pink-flowered dogwood trees. However, my worries were quickly eased upon returning to his home, as the hummingbird he talked about paid me a visit right outside the window, a familiar spot where we often sat.

So many of our friends and family have lost a parent. Of course, this is my personal encounter. I had witnessed, years before, the utter grief that people went through and made a promise to myself to—during his last years—talk to my dad as much as I could and visit him. We also played Yahtzee against each other on our respective iPads: 473 games! Playing from a distance was not as fun as face to face, but it was a great way to connect and enjoy the game with him. Our win ratio was about 50/50; he was good. This lasted until the game changed, and he could never figure out when it was his turn to roll. During our last visit we played on paper, triple Yahtzee. Not one game, but many. I think, or know, he was the Yahtzee champion at the end. After my dad passed, a friend told me I would see dimes. A common belief regarding finding dimes is that it means a loved one who has passed away is visiting you. Later that day I saw a dime on the floor of my car. Since he passed in 2017, I have seen hundreds of dimes in many random places. Sometimes I put them in my pocket, and sometimes I leave them resting. I love this special spiritual connection we have.

CHAPTER 13

Heartbroken

Love is proved the moment you let go of someone because
they need you to.

—*Catherine L. Alder*

June 2017

But the difficulties of that heart-rending year did not let up. We were
tested to the limit.

A couple of weeks later, my sister and I traveled to my dad's home in
Pinehurst to determine what to do with his furniture, his tools, books, and
his precious encyclopedias, and get the home ready for sale. The massive
encyclopedias were kept in a small two-shelf bookshelf with a round world
globe on top. One of his prize possessions. His caretaker, Chuck, agreed to
stay on to manage things until it sold. On the second or third day there, at
a pizza restaurant we stopped in on the way to a carpet store, as we were
enjoying the time together, although it was a sad time, my phone rang.

Mark was on the other end of the line. Anna had violently attacked
him while he was belted into the car and then run off. The attacks were in

two parts; at first, she pummeled his face and head, which he was covering with his arms and hands. The second attack surprised him; he thought she'd stopped, so he was in the process of unbuckling his seat belt. He had recently hurt his back, therefore was not so agile. Already shocked, caught off guard by the new round of punches, he put up a flat hand to protect himself at the same time she was lunging toward him. Her nose hit the hand and started bleeding.

Anna freaked out, fleeing from the car.

Mark got out, dazed under the impact of what had just happened. He had a bloody cheek, body aches, and the beginning of a black eye. Trying to find her but unable to, he went into the store and talked to the security guard, then called me.

In utter dismay but relieved that Mark was not hurt too badly, with my heart heavy and pounding—still numbed with grief over my father—I said to let them look for her and that he would probably need to call the police.

A little while later Mark called to inform me that Anna had made formal statements about him trying to kill her! Because of this, he'd been arrested.

I was horrified and shattered. I felt terrible for him. For both of them. He did not deserve this, and I knew that Anna must have been in an awful mind state. Still only thirteen years old.

Anyone with any awareness of Mark—even just a little bit—knows he's a gentle guy who has never hit or hurt anyone physically. A caring, loving person and father, he has spent his entire life and career helping people. I told him I would call his brother and get home as fast as I could.

Canceling the plan to take my dad's caretakers out to dinner to thank him for the beautiful care of my dad, I called the airline, which graciously rebooked my flight. We thankfully had the opportunity to reschedule the dinner in the future because these caretakers were like family, and I was feeling profound sorrow and some anger when I had to cancel. On the way to the airport, I called The East End Café, one of our family's favorite restaurants in my dad's town, to cancel the dinner reservation. We had celebrated my dad's eighty-fifth birthday there three years back, and then recently gone for Easter and an early eighty-eighth birthday. We always sat outside in the covered garden. The food never disappointed; I still remember the large, plentiful chunks of lobster in my dad's bisque and the massive piece of red velvet cake with cream frosting they served him. We all shared it, and Anna and I ate as much as we could. My dad, having diabetes, had to watch his sugar.

Mark's face was bloody and sore, and there was a black eye developing on one side, but he did not need additional medical treatment. He was in shock. He could not believe what was happening. I also called my longtime friend and babysitter of my kids, Maryann. She agreed to go to the hospital on the south shore where Anna was, close by to her home. I was extremely grateful, knowing it was asking a lot—a godsend; my friend knew Anna very, very well. Unfortunately, though, her visit allowed my daughter to split. As mentioned, splitting is a common tactic of young people with mental illness or mood disorders.

Anna spent a lot of time venting to my friend—many extremely scary things. For instance, she vowed not to come home until "Mark" was out of the house. Maryann described a wild, manic side of Anna to us, a side she had not seen before.

I then received a call from the state children and families department. We all agreed it would be best if Anna stayed overnight with Maryann. When I arrived to pick her up the next day, she was lying on the couch. Still not wanting to leave, she made a couple of rude comments about Mark. "We'll have this discussion at another time," I told her. Needless to say, Mark was not going anywhere.

When Anna came home, she would shut down if we tried to talk about the incident. The most difficult part was that our relationship was so strained. I didn't show how incredibly upset I was about what she had done, and when she had done it.

But we were to learn she could not control her anger and emotional and physical response. She was resisting therapy and despite the introduction to mindfulness activities such as craft kits for bracelet making, journals with fun stickers, music, exercising at the gym, card games, skill games like Jenga, adult coloring books with colored pencils, walking at the park, fidget spinners, a basketball hoop for her bedroom door, and noise-cancelling headphones, it was not enough to calm her mind. She needed specialized treatment.

During this period, going by her actions and demeanor, nothing had even happened.

It was as if the incident had been wiped from her memory. This went deep into me. She lied about what happened, then refused to talk about it. To her, it was like it didn't happen. Much later she admitted she did it and lied.

At this point we were watching, aghast and feeling helpless: a pattern was developing—involving being aggressive.

Even though she didn't outwardly show any further disdain for my husband, she wrote in a notebook I found later: "I don't like my dad. He's annoying. I am also pissed that the people didn't come in to check in with me."

I'm fully aware that invading someone's privacy is not acceptable, but as in the case of any violent crime or unsolved mystery, I felt similarly compelled to look for any information to gain insight into what was going on in her mind. She just could not or would not offer it on her own. Also, she was a minor, and I was her parent, so during these apparent breaches I did not feel like I was overstepping my boundaries at all; I did not trust that she was going to share her honest feelings.

She just wanted to move in with Maryann, she added. But this is information I found later.

I got more frustrated a couple of days later at work, when I received a call from the Victim Advocate. Horrified, I listened as she asked me if I felt safe in my home because of my husband.

I said "Sorry, you have this all wrong. My husband has not *and would not ever* hit or hurt anyone." I told her that my daughter was ill, and not telling the truth. The woman, though very nice, did not seem to believe me.

I am not sure how it was possible to move on after this incident.

Despite feeling like it was a joke that the state children and families department was coming into our home to conduct an assessment to see if we were competent parents, I had to suck it up because this was serious stuff.

This incident really crossed a line for us on so many levels. Not only did Anna attack Mark, but *she lied about what happened*. Maybe rage had been building up in her, or her illness was starting to present in more intense ways, but she had to know that she'd attacked him twice, and he never had and never would strike her.

On further reflection, I think her anger could have related to her fear of my being away, her uncertainty following the loss of a grandfather, seeing me distraught over losing my dad, just general internal pain due to her illness, or wanting to deflect the attention back to herself. But how long could we go on like this? Sure, I loved her, my husband loved her, her brother loved her. That made it more agonizing.

But our day-to-day life was getting entangled in manipulation and confusion. And even lying. Not to mention the pain of this illness, to all it touched.

CHAPTER 14

Tentative

We are not people who touch each other carelessly; every point of contact between us feels important, a rush of energy and relief.

—Veronica Roth, Allegiant

Camp was approaching, so I took Anna and her friends out for an early trampoline bouncy birthday party, and then we went to Friendly's. The six kids squeezed into a booth, and I sat in one by myself to let them have fun. I was fine with this, but overall, everything seemed somewhat bizarre. I wanted her to have a fun birthday party with friends, but I felt the odd detachment. I couldn't shake the longing for the closeness we once shared.

On June 28, I emailed her therapist that Anna seemed to be struggling. For weeks she had been distant, hardly acknowledging my presence. she was not talking or acknowledging me much. Her behavior at the pediatrician's office was the new norm. One minute she talked about not feeling well, being angry, but then, as soon as we left, acted fine. The biggest challenge for me was to stay empathetic, while having some boundaries—how did one do it? What was the trick? How to give her all the love I wanted to while not letting her walk all over me (which is how I felt).

Despite her coldness during the daytime, I continued to rub her back at night; I thought the touch was critical, and I would never say no if she asked for a back rub.

It's sad and ironic that lack of touch and nurturing in infancy can have critical negative effects on a child's physical, emotional, and social development. This includes attachment issues, emotional and behavioral issues, cognitive delays, a weakened immune system, and social difficulties.

Later I learned that even though she might not verbalize it, she was struggling emotionally, and although things appeared manipulative, *on her part it did not mean it was a conscious decision to act towards me this way.*

On July 23, 2017, I took her to a town about twenty minutes away to catch the bus to Camp Marymount in Maine. Shortly afterwards, I received a call from the director or assistant director, speaking about her homesickness. I had put information on depression in her medical paperwork but did not call ahead. I should have since I was not doing the drop-off. I think that—feeling overwhelmed, at my limit—I had needed her to go away so I could stop and breathe for a minute to try to process everything that had happened.

They did not want her to talk to me, which I understood and appreciated, but then they agreed to. What did she need? I asked her. "A fold-up mesh laundry basket," she told me. I said "Great! Anything else?" Yes, she wanted to come home. But I wouldn't entertain it. "Nothing is going on at home," I said, adding lightly, "Chin up"—my sister sometimes says that to me—and told her I loved her. The note she sent me a few days later, full of thanks for the four packages she'd received from family, which she shared with friends, totally omitted any complaints: she was happy about trying horseback riding, it was like night and day. Or evidence of "Chin up" pursued.

As I stood at the bus stop on pick-up day, I was filled with anticipation. I was hoping to see Anna fly off the bus with a big smile on her face. It was even better than that, she was fluttering about entangled in a group of girls, jumping up and down, saying their goodbyes, laughing and crying. Back from camp—she'd loved it.

Around this time, I returned to practicing yoga, finding my mat and turning the space I practiced on into my refuge. I often thought about my dad and the wonderful and funny memories we had. I also processed many of my worries. Yoga is intended to clear your mind, but practicing this way, at times, helped me feel more confident and in better touch with my feelings. Practicing yoga also made me feel more spiritual, and closer to God. I wanted to work on being the best person I could be, and such growth often feels like it goes along with life's ups and downs, and it takes time. But I trusted others to guide me, and many did. For this I am grateful.

Knowing the benefits of yoga, I asked Anna to join me one day. I selected a beginner's class, which turned out to be a little slow for her (and me). It was too bad because she got bored quickly despite telling me she loved the "Shavasana" and described sinking into a meditative state. The Shavasana is the final relaxation pose at the end of the practice. Regrettably, I was not able to persuade her to give it another try.

CHAPTER 15

Light

Rest and be thankful.

—William Wordsworth

Ahhh . . . August, I spent as much time as possible with my extended family (my sister, mom, and stepdad), intent on enjoying relaxing summer rituals. We were required to meet with DCF—short-lived, because it was obvious to them that Anna was suffering, despite having parents who loved and cared for her, a brother, a dog, and uncles, aunts, and cousins, all who loved her, going out of their way to include her and show how much they cared. They did follow up by email, making sure I was following up on all their requests. I confirmed that I was but was annoyed that I had to be accountable to them. We were doing everything we could. Mark and I had a lot of long talks about ways to help Anna and about the fact that she needed to eventually tell the truth about what happened the day she assaulted him. I also knew that these events and Anna's behavior in general were not lining up with just RAD (Reactive Attachment Disorder) and PTSD. Some other manifestation was at the root of her issues. Knowing what, I thought, would give us new tools, give us hope.

Contacting a smaller local Catholic school, we explained the situation and enrolled her. Very welcoming, they were willing to accept her into the grade. Later into the school year Anna and I started the Dialectical Behavior Therapy (DBT) program.

After an extremely difficult first three quarters of 2017—which included the overdose, my Dad's passing, and Anna's assault on Mark—things brightened. In September, Anna switched schools, *starting eighth grade at St. Katherine*, a preschool through eighth grade coed, Catholic school in our town.

What a happy development.

Most of September was full to the brim with relief and fun. Homelife was going well, and at work the large implementation-and-integration project boomed along. We spent days and many nights in the office, working tirelessly to launch the project on schedule. My memories from that time will always have a special place in my heart because of the amazing team of people; my boss and the rest of the team could not have been harder working and more passionate about success.

Because the project had a successful launch in early September, from the work perspective I could breathe a bit, joining in on a couple of very special celebrations that the CEO hosted for the project team. The project team celebrated with a beautiful dinner in the North End and an amazing Boston sporting event. I felt a weight had been lifted and looked forward to having more unpressured time in the evenings. As project leader, I had worked until about 11 p.m. a few nights a week all summer and in the final couple weeks until 1 a.m. or 2 a.m. The last day we stayed until we went live at 5 a.m. I returned at my usual 9 a.m. start time after showering at home. I did not want to miss out on the excitement.

One team member was from Russia, so another colleague, Anna, and I took her to Cape Cod for Labor Day weekend. It was beautiful. I thought Anna was a little quiet, but we all enjoyed the sunny beach, the delicious food, and sweets from the candy store.

CHAPTER 16

Tired

I am not afraid of storms for I am learning how to sail
my ship.

—Amy March

At camp over the summer, Anna met a girl who was having her bat
mitzvah in mid-September. Anna was invited, as was another camp
friend. The bat mitzvah was in New Jersey, but the guests were all meeting
early Saturday morning on the Upper East Side of New York, so we made the
plan to take Anna and her friend from Boston on the train to Manhattan on
a Friday afternoon. I picked up her friend at her home, about thirty minutes
away, then headed to the train station.

We arrived in New York Friday night. I was so happy to be there because
it brought back good memories from another work project, years before,
when I commuted back and forth to Manhattan each week. I'd enjoyed
every minute of the work, and I loved walking around the city and getting
last-minute show tickets.

One of my favorite things about arriving in New York is transitioning
from underground to above ground at Penn Station. The smell of fried

sausage, roasted peanuts, and the vapor-rich exhausts was inviting to me. We followed the wide, crowded sidewalk to Times Square to drop off our luggage at my favorite hotel and went out shopping. Ahh, the lights, the hustle and bustle, the city that never sleeps! I loved it. We ate late, then went back to the hotel. We were scheduled to meet the girls and the bus at 7:00 a.m. the next day. We woke up early and took a taxi to the meeting place. All the girls were dressed up, and it was very cute.

Since arriving in New York, the night before, neither girl was engaging with me very much. This seemed like typical teen behavior, but it was slightly uncomfortable, as I felt like I was nothing more than their foreign tour guide. On Saturday, I ended up walking around the city and having an early dinner because the girls were due back at 8:00 p.m. or so. While I was at dinner, Anna called to ask if they could stay over in New Jersey, at the home of one of the girls. I wasn't particularly thrilled, but I also did not want to say no and give them more reason to accuse me of being a boring mom. I said her Boston friend had to call her family for permission. They said yes, but then they both wanted me to still meet the bus uptown and bring them additional clothes. I tried to encourage them to wear what they had, not the dresses, but the clothes they packed for an outing in the afternoon, but they did not want to, so I walked the nine blocks back to the arranged spot and waited another thirty minutes outside because the bus was late. Immediately, they rifled through their bags and complained that I did not bring them everything they needed. At that point, I told them to have a great time and call me in the morning.

Some would say this is how all teens are, but it felt different, and I began to experience this type of behavior over and over. The next phase was where Anna would say, "all teenagers hate their mother" or "all teenagers hate their parents"; I disagreed and often gave her examples of neighbors and friends her age who had great relationships with their mothers. When I was a teen, I could never imagine hating my mother. To this day I am as close as ever with her, and there has always been love and respect (and a lot of fun) between us. In addition, I have another teenager, and we have always been very close.

From about age thirteen till eighteen, he wanted to spend less time with me and more with his friends, but he has never said anything remotely related to hating me.

Anna's behavior on the New York trip was also a form of splitting, where she was cold to me in front of her friends, and even though it may not have been conscious, it still didn't feel good. By the end of the trip, I was drained. We were in New York City at a beautiful hotel, and there was little sense of gratitude. On a brighter note, we met my brother-in-law on Sunday for lunch, so that ended up counteracting some of my feelings. By Sunday afternoon, I couldn't wait to get out of there.

Looking back on this trip, I feel as though perhaps I overreacted. These were two teenagers going away to New York together vs. me and Anna going alone. They seemed entitled, demanding, and ungrateful to me. It didn't feel right. But I realize now that I could have been feeling overly sensitive. I was physically and mentally exhausted and wished we had planned the trip differently. This was one of my favorite places in the world, and despite being independent, and loving being alone, I wanted to share this experience with Anna.

Things improved with Anna settled into her new school, busy with activities that fall; the season continued with fun charity events, road races, Halloween, and a beautiful Ukrainian festival Anna and I attended. I was also playing hockey and coaching boy's youth hockey, but because it was high school age, the season only ran through Thanksgiving. This was good; I felt the need for more balance and more time at home. This was another activity that I was so happy I could do because I loved it and could use my mentoring skills. The players treated me with the utmost respect, and the other coaches helped me run practices when I needed them.

The new school—the way classes were structured, not to mention all the activities—was having a positive effect on Anna, and Mark and I loved watching her play town basketball, looking so professional in the expansive, bright high school gym. We went to several events and fundraisers, volunteered in the kitchen, and kicked off the holiday season watching her participate in a holiday pageant. The pageant was more like a play, and Anna enjoyed wearing a different costume for each act and being giddy behind the curtain as she waited to go on. A compelling little actress, she was a hit in her part.

PART 6

2018

CHAPTER 17

Mindful

Meditation is a vital way to purify and quiet the mind, thus rejuvenating the body.

—Deepak Chopra

The highlight of the New Year was the Dialectical Behavior Therapy (DBT) course. I had gotten Anna and myself on the waiting list in 2017, but that got diverted to a hospital stay, as you remember. We were lucky to get her back on the list. And in February, with luck, she got enrolled.

Here, I had a preteen daughter, and I just made the statement that the highlight of the year was a behavior course. It hits me what I've just said. But for me it was true. For Anna, perhaps not.

For one and a half hours each week, we attended the DBT mindfulness class. It was an amazing opportunity to spend time together, meet other teens and parents, and get this specialized treatment. I loved it. Anna tolerated it.

I will admit, the concepts weren't easy. It took a lot of attention and participation. The DBT Skills training is made up of four modules: core mindfulness, distress tolerance, emotion regulation, and interpersonal effectiveness.

They are designed to specifically assist individuals in better managing behaviors, emotions, and thoughts.

We each had a large binder of handouts that contained our homework between sessions. The handouts came from the book *DBT Skills Manual for Adolescents* by Jill Rathaus and Alec L. Miller, Foreword by Marsha M. Linehan.

Helpfully, meditation and meditative activities began each class, that is, we closed our eyes, taking a minute to breathe and settle in.

At the beginning and end of the meditation, the instructor struck a small, beautiful, gold gong. It helped us transition into a state of calm, focused awareness—Anna as well—using mindful breathing. I noticed that she seemed able to let go of distractions, as I was. In my case, I then turned my attention to my inner self. That was the goal. Anna sat quietly, seemingly at peace. The instructor led us in a short meditation, typically giving us something to hold, feel, smell, and get acquainted with in some way. To close it out, striking the gong to gently awaken us, she signified the end of our collective contemplative experience.

Anna enjoyed the guided meditation. And she was particularly interested in aromatherapy scents, so I made sure to pick up small containers or rollerballs of fragrant scents I thought she would like. Citrus and eucalyptus were two of our favorites.

Ohm… we introduced Anna to meditation, and we did the DBT mindfulness course. I also bought books and fun journals for her, but they were usually short lived. I had mindfulness cards and asked her to use them with me as a game. But once her trauma started to present, during ninth grade, her only go-to coping mechanisms were music, gum, and shooting baskets. She was too down to do a lot of the fun things we used to do. Her trauma may have been so deep, and she had difficulty opening up to these modalities.

Later Anna's DBT counselor told me Anna was just going through the motions, not really internalizing the concepts and how they could help her feel better. Was she too young? Too distracted? Unable to retain?

Tired of me? I don't know. I thought the same thing at times, but because it was something Anna and I did together and she was participating in each session, I still feel confident that a lot of positives came from our attending the course. In one respect, the proof is in the pudding; during the six months of the course our family life and Anna's life at school and with friends was the calmest and brightest since fifth grade.

I did notice that her attachment issues were prevalent during some of the mindfulness exercises, where we reviewed and tested our knowledge about a specific concept. For instance, on a sheet titled "Pleasant Activities List," she was to circle things she would like to do, so she circled or checked more than half of the forty-four activities listed. A similar sheet, "Parent-Teen Pleasant Activities List," had instructions to check off the activities you would enjoy doing with your parent. It was a homework exercise, and when I noticed that she wasn't completing the sheet after we opened our binders, she said there was nothing she wanted to check off.

The exercise turned into an opportunity for Anna to create distance from me: pretending, in her list, she had *no interest in doing anything with me*. These years later, I can see it as funny because obviously not true.

Such subtle jabs happened often. I ignored them, aware of the underlying reasons, not taking them too personally. For sure, there were many activities that she liked to do with me; on the other hand, I knew she loved her independence and didn't always want to do things with her parents.

This kind of subtle jab got a little harder later and very difficult as she got older because they felt planned and manipulative.

For me, if not so much Anna, DBT was a godsend.

It supported our relationship, but also, I looked at it as an opportunity to learn and reflect on my own behavior, responses, tone, and PATIENCE. I knew I needed to work on sticking up for myself better and learn how to listen more, as well as not be impulsive in my reactions. I felt the practice of mindfulness, as taught in the course, did wonders for me. I am a much better listener. I try to communicate clearly about things I may not like. And I tend to stay quieter if I do not expect my words to be productive.

During the six months we attended the course I was proud of Anna for attending without any fuss, even to a degree participating in class. She was less interested in doing the homework together, but I would set out a snack and offer a cup of tea to make it more enticing.

Would that it had been a life changer for Anna, but she seemed impervious to the practice of mindfulness, unable to learn the techniques of stillness and calm or meditation. Again, perhaps she was too young. But we tried to introduce these practices again as she grew older and struck a brick wall. They did not penetrate.

Emotional control was outside her grasp, as is usual with this illness. She could not help herself.

Around this time, I was focused on our spending more quality time together, and we were having fun. While riding in the car one day, we heard an ad for an open-casting call—to be held at a Boston hotel. Why not go? We decided to, and it was like something you would see on TV, with teens all dressed up, waiting for their audition. Anna looked adorable and read the lines perfectly.

After the audition they told everyone in the ballroom they might receive a call that night. In between the audition and the call, I did some research online and realized it was a bit of a scam. If you got selected, you needed to join the program, etc.

I should have known, but I think we might have done it anyway. Anna loves singing, dancing, and acting in theater and was so happy to be part of this process. When we received the call later that night, I explained to her what it entailed and how it might be a bit of a scam. The next step was to go to New York for the class; we realized it was not going to work at the time. I asked her if it would be okay if we looked for a local theater program that she could join, and she was thrilled.

We laughed a lot about the experience with the audition and have great memories from it. I was proud of Anna for being flexible and open-minded to an alternative option. I also captured a picture of her from that day that we ultimately sent in for the playbill of her performance. She looked like a star.

Things were going well. Something was working. I continued to use information from books and articles to develop my own skills. Although simple, I found the following advice helpful:

- **Set firm boundaries.** Examples include:
  - "Yes, but this is the last time I will say this today: I love you."
  - "Please respect my right to form my own opinions about others."
- **Use "yes/and" statements.** Examples include:
  - "Yes, I am setting a boundary . . . *and* I still love you."
  - "Yes, you are having a really hard time right now . . . *and* I still need you to help out around the house."

The advice above comes from a great article from The Wellness Society: "How to Deal with Splitting Behavior."[6]

As mentioned above, when children do not receive consistent and responsive care, they may develop insecure attachment styles, leading to difficulties in forming healthy relationships later.

With my son on the high-school hockey team that winter, Anna didn't always want to attend. She wanted to start a job to make money for the holidays. One day I asked the coach if there was an opportunity for Anna to do the timekeeping. He said absolutely. New to it, she picked it up very quickly. Her handwriting was super neat, and she was able to multitask with the clock, logging penalties and goals. She loved it and later in the season started working for a Club league. These games were even harder, but she kept up very well. We were proud of her initiative and commitment, and she was proud of herself. She got paid by the club, and the high-school coach gave her a very generous gift that covered lots of her holiday shopping.

Midway through eighth grade, things seemed to be going well for Anna. In February, attending her school's award ceremony, we proudly watched her receive the St. Francis Award for "consistently exemplifying the life of St. Francis by demonstrating faith, love, gentleness, kindness, forgiveness,

---

6   https://thewellnesssociety.org/how-to-deal-with-splitting-behavior/

respect and fairness towards others in daily life at St. Katherine." Wow. We were impressed. She had a group of friends and kept busy with a variety of activities, for example, hip hop dance class, church choir, singing lessons and piano lessons after school.

It wasn't long before along came a minor setback: she got caught vaping at school. With other girls, of course. This was the school's first incident of students vaping. It was so disappointing because of how welcoming the administration and faculty were to Anna. The good news was that she finished the year with great grades and a very well-orchestrated and special graduation mass and ceremony.

My birthday was great. Despite the same light tension and withdrawal on Anna's part, we had a family dinner at a favorite restaurant and then all went to the local high-school hockey game.

The year continued to be full—more settled. Anna enjoyed being with me. She relied on me for advice. And I loved spending time together. During the winter a friend in town took Anna to a boxing class with her son. She loved it, and her friend appreciated having someone to go with. One night they went to a live boxing match in a town close by.

Keeping kids safe on the internet and more specifically social media is one daunting task. I was lucky to attend an event on internet safety for kids—this one hosted by Katie Greer who is an internet safety expert for kids. The information presented helped me set up Anna's internet access in a way I believed created a safer space for her including accountability to follow the agreement we discussed about practicing online safety. She didn't like it, but I did.

In June, Anna and I visited my friend Erica and her daughter at her cottage in Connecticut.

We all went out on her boat so we could teach Anna to waterski. Erica and her daughter were experts; they belonged to a club and participated in performances where they would ski in large, two-level pyramids, ski backwards, and once Erica sent me a picture with her waterskiing with a coffee and cell phone in her hand.

The cell phone may not have been real, but I think the picture was legit! She was a true type A personality, always reminding me of Annette Bening in the movie *American Beauty*. A wild but endearing real estate agent.

Anna took to waterskiing. This was no easy feat. Usually when learning, you pull too hard on the rope, taking a nosedive before getting above a crouch. Anna may have done this once, but the second time I kept shouting, "don't pull, don't pull!" and she was lifted to standing—sailing around the water on two skis. I can still remember the happiness exuding from her body.

Thinking about this beautiful day breaks my heart. Erica took her own life in April of 2022—I have only processed it a little bit at a time. It hurts too much.

CHAPTER 18

Positive

Keep your face always toward the sunshine—and shadows
will fall behind you.

—Walt Whitman

The summer of 2018, we had just "graduated" from our DBT course,
and I was feeling very optimistic. Anna was very excited to be enrolled
at an all-girls Catholic high school not far from our home. We continued
spending weekends on the Cape, celebrated Father's Day, and the kids'
birthdays, and spent a lot of time swimming and walking with the dog.

In mid-July, Anna attended a basketball camp. One day I received a call
that she was threatening to beat someone up. They thought it would be a
good idea if I retrieved her, so I did.

Around this time, Anna was also acting very strange with me. One
day I asked her to leave her phone in the car. I saw her most recent texts,
in which she was conversing with someone named Dave. The gist was that
he was telling her she couldn't post certain things on social media, and he
claimed she didn't say that she loved him before she went to bed. She wrote
back to say she loved how overprotective he was with her. She agreed to not

post whatever he was asking her to not post. They were also talking about getting engaged. A lot of the conversation was in slang. I wasn't thrilled to be looking at her phone, but I was glad I had because it was distressing. No, let me tell you what I really thought when my heart slowed down enough for my head to get in a reaction. I was ready to jump through the phone and strangle this creep. It was "baby" this and "baby" that and I was sick over it. To make matters worse, she was falling for his ridiculous exhortations and apologizing for posting pictures. I am certain that she never met this guy.

Nervous about escalating the situation, I did not want to directly confront her. Next thing I knew, she might run off and elope. This was not easy.

Tossing around in my head what I wanted to say, how to say it diplomatically, I took no action until the next day. Then I sat her down and went back to our conversation a little over a year ago, after the overdose, reminding her who this guy might be: a creepy man in disguise. I also took her phone away for lying to me about the way she was using it.

She was upset, of course. But in this situation, she wasn't a typical teen—lashing out and yelling or otherwise expressing feelings about how unfair this was, indignant that I was snooping and ruining their life. Instead, *she'd just hold her feelings in, ignore me, and complain to others.* Eventually she would just walk out of the house if I even tried to have a simple conversation about something. This was unsettling, and I wish there was a way I could have told her it would be better to shout her feelings out if she was mad. Explaining that it sometimes feels good to "get things off your chest." For me, the silence was unsettling. Anyway, she was heading to surf camp on Cape Cod, over the weekend—excited.

"Enjoy miles of unspoiled coastline while learning to surf or continuing to develop your skills under safe, professional instruction at sites along the Cape Cod National Seashore," the website announces. "No previous surfing experience is necessary—most of our campers are new to surfing!" Camp was only a week long. She'd looked forward to learning how to surf for years. When I picked her up the following Friday, she was sun-kissed, glowing, and exhausted. She loved it and was looking forward to surfing in the future.

At the end of August, for Ukrainian Independence Day, we attended a celebration at a church near Boston. We ate the traditional food and bought a Ukrainian cookbook; not only that, but she talked to some of the other attendees in Russian. Like so many other fun events, we have beautiful pictures from the day. We both look happy and content.

Looking back, I again try to decipher the up-and-down cycle of behavior. Was there more chaos and uncertainty in the summer—perhaps because of the lack of structure? Or it could have been that Anna could have used more of a break and more downtime after the long school year. Also, though, she spent more time on social media in the summer, and I knew nothing good would come of this, especially because of her unclear or always fluctuating self-image. I believe she turned to social media to get the attention she often craved, even without these issues. Anyway, there was a social-media epidemic for young girls and teens across the country. It was her lifeline.

CHAPTER 19

Over the Moon

Failure is not falling down but refusing to get up.

—Chinese proverb

September 2018

At the start of ninth grade, Anna was happy, and I was thrilled. She had not made her volleyball team, but I encouraged her to ask the athletic director and soccer coach if she could have a late tryout; the coach willingly accommodated. Now on the team, Anna did very well in her classes and on the soccer field all that fall. After the Thanksgiving holidays she made the JV basketball team—*a huge accomplishment for a freshman who'd started playing basketball only a few years back.*

Prior to tryouts, Anna and I looked up tips on how to have the best chance to make the team. The tryouts ran multiple days, so she had fun telling me how she worked hard, how she asked questions . . . but not too many; always kept moving. When I picked her up after each try-out day, she would tell me how well the plan worked. We both grinned and nodded our heads implying our shared feeling of getting away with something.

Both Mark and I always went out of our way if she wanted to do something fun. One Friday night in the fall, she asked us if she could go to a football game at a high school in the next town. I dropped her off, and my husband was going to pick her up. He got there a little early, so he decided to go into the stands to watch the rest of the game. But he couldn't find her. He texted her but received no reply. When the game was over, she texted him to pick her up at the front of the school.

Eventually, it came out that she didn't even attend the game, but instead just hung out with friends on the other side of the school. We told her if she hadn't lied about it, it would be one thing, but because she lied (multiple times), in future games we would need to be there too.

The next game we went to was also in another town. We said she could go, but we would be there. Through social media I found out she was drinking under the bleachers.

I told her I was going to ask her a question, and she should take her time before answering because I wanted the truth. This was a tip that I received from a therapist or book previously. It allows a child to think about their response without just blurting out a lie because they are nervous of the consequences. She ended up admitting to drinking. Even though this might be considered typical teen behavior, the way I looked at it, Anna was only fifteen; she already suffered from emotional issues and was on medication for anxiety and depression. The medication did not mix with alcohol. It was written right there on the pill container.

We began the dreaded punishment of taking her phone and other social media applications away. One piece of advice we received later related to her cell phone was to remove her phone or apps for twenty-four-hour periods since, according to researchers, punishment only appears to work in the short run. In the long run, however, it could make your child resent you. An article written by Olga Khazan, a staff writer at the *Atlantic*, points to theories of Alan Kazdin, the director of the Yale Parenting Center; that "punishment might make [a parent] feel better, but it won't change the kid's behavior."[7]

Kazdin isn't alone in this theory, writes mindfulness mentor Hunter Clarke-Fields. Many researchers agree, she tells us, that . . . punishment . . . can:

- cause resentment
- cause psychological damage
- encourage self-centered behavior
- encourage dishonesty
- prevent [kids] from developing their inner moral compass[8]

Quite a list of undesirable traits.

---

[7] Olga Khazan, "No Spanking, No Time-Out, No Problems," The Alan Kazdin Method for Making Your Children Behave, The Atlantic.

[8] Hunter Clarke-Fields, "A parenting expert shares the common mistake that psychologically damages kids—and what to do instead," https://www.cnbc.com/2019/12/11/the-common-yet-parenting-mistake-that-psychologically-damages-kids-according-to-expert.html.

CHAPTER 20

Understanding

You are not your illness. You have an individual story to tell.
You have a name, a history, a personality. Staying yourself is
part of the battle.

—Julian Seifter

At this point, Anna was continuing to act oddly aloof and sneaky; it was baffling and disturbing. We celebrated Thanksgiving at home. Both Anna and I helped prepare the meal with my brother-in-law in the kitchen. She laughed while peeling a large bag of potatoes.

In mid-December, I traveled again, to New York and New Jersey with a former colleague to meet with a new work prospect. The reason I bring up traveling is because reflecting back, it seems as though I only had to go away for things not to go so well. It was tricky to get to this fact because Anna, contradictorily, on the surface, expressed joy at going over to friends' houses and being with our babysitter. Reflecting, I have a sense that in her mind she wanted to be independent and not have me hovering around, but if I was gone, it was a destabilizing unknown, which made her anxious or scared. A big push and pull for her emotionally. I believe she was not trying to sabotage my day. At this point, she had a very good relationship with three or four friends from school. To them, she was perfectly "normal," someone they liked to hang out with. Her school was small and tight knit, and she was a bigger fish in a smaller pond, unlike the year before.

She maintained these friendships, and I believe her friends enjoyed her sense of adventure, her talent in school activities like the Christmas pageant and the musical recital. What was different was she wasn't interested in having friends over to watch a movie or "hang out"; she appeared more interested in social media and developing an online following. I am sure this is more of the norm today than it used to be, but to me, this seemed to happen quickly and exploded during what seemed like a manic-type episode a couple months later.

Then came another day I will never forget. On December 22, 2018, my husband and I planned to attend a local holiday party. I was ready to go, but he hadn't yet returned from what I thought was going to be a quick trip to Home Depot. When I called, he was running late because at Home Depot he'd had a hard time reading the small print on the packages; then after making his purchases there, he'd gone to a small gourmet-type market down the road and was there now. I said, "You should come right home." When he walked in, I could right away tell there was something wrong.

I asked what it was and when he didn't answer I led him over to a small loveseat in our kitchen. Pointing to our daughter, he astounded me and sent chills down my spine, asking "What's her name?" At that second, I grabbed the phone and called 911. He'd had a stroke.

It was not a ministroke, I could tell. I left right after the ambulance and told the kids I'd call them as soon as I could.

The good news was he recovered his memory and speech within a couple of hours. The bad news was the doctors wanted to get to the root cause, so they began conducting scans and tests and checked him in.

I called to let the kids know he was fine but needed to stay for observation. I also began phoning the family to change the plans for the annual Becker Family Christmas Party we were hosting the next day.

Once Mark got settled in a room, and a couple of family members left, I headed home. The next day, I split my time between the hospital and home. I had done the back and forth to the hospital trips before when my husband fought and beat stage four throat cancer at only forty-two years old, with my son five.

On Christmas Day, I had the kids open their gifts, and we brought Mark's to his room. Anna gave me the prettiest little jewelry box with "MOM" engraved on it. I see it every morning while getting ready for the day. Max took Anna in his car because I planned on staying late. Mark still needed an MRI and needed to be seen by a specialist, which was going to take time. After Max and Anna went home, I took a walk in Boston to get a latte and a few newspapers. This was Mark's typical ask when he was sick or in the hospital.

The city was desolate—the air chilly and fresh. It was good to be outside. I walked around for a while before going to Starbucks, which was open, then back to the hospital. I am not sure why I stayed as long as I did, but I remember calling Anna at 7:30 p.m. to let her know I was on my way. She told me she had a bad stomachache; I assured her I would be home very soon.

At home, I sat in my car in the driveway a few minutes to breathe. When I went in, I went right up to my daughter's room—finding her rolling around on her bed, almost in tears. She said her stomach hurt more than it ever had before. I told her she should just relax, and we could put a warm compress on it, but like other times, she said this pain was something different than ever before.

I tried to convince her she was going to feel better soon, but she kept saying *she had to go to the hospital*. I asked if she'd eaten a lot; to my best recollection, she said yes. I was sure it was all stress related and felt bad that I had not come home earlier. Because she'd had lots of somatic-type stomachaches before, I did not think she needed to go to the ER.

But she was acting like she was dying, and it crossed my mind: *What if something was seriously wrong? You never know. This time might be the one time it's different*. Well, I should have listened to my gut because after we waited an hour, a doctor examined my daughter while asking her a few questions. Looking annoyed, she left and after a few minutes came back with an enema. Did she want to use it there or at home? There, Anna said. Ugh.

The doctor then told me if she did not have a fever and wasn't vomiting, it would not constitute a trip to the ER. I felt scolded, but being at the end of my rope, I didn't let it get to me. In fact, she was basically giving me permission to trust my gut a bit—underscoring that it had guided me correctly.

We went into a large one-person public bathroom in the ER so I could help administer the enema. As, obviously, she was sitting on the toilet, I took a seat on the floor a few feet away. I told her I would find some music to play to muffle the sounds. We started laughing, and even though she was slightly embarrassed, she got through it, and we left.

Both kids were stressed.

I later learned that this was most likely somatic: "Somatic symptom disorder is diagnosed when a person has a significant focus on physical symptoms . . . to a level that results in major distress and/or problems functioning. The individual has excessive thoughts, feelings and behaviors relating to the physical symptoms."[9] It is fascinating to learn about this complex relationship between the mind and body. I know today there are therapists just focusing on somatization. I recently met a friend's daughter who is a somatic therapist. She said the therapy she practices is called somatic experiencing therapy. I just looked it up and found this very clear definition written by Theodorea Blanchfield, AMFT on Verywellmind.com:

> Somatic experiencing therapy is a type of alternative
> therapy geared towards helping people find healing from

---

[9] Philip R. Muskin, M.D., M.A., "What is Somatic Symptom Disorder?" https://www.psychiatry.org/patients-families/somatic-symptom-disorder/what-is-somatic-symptom-disorder#:~:text=Somatic%20symptom%20disorder%20is%20diagnosed,relating%20to%20the%20physical%20symptoms.

trauma. Created by Peter Kevine, PhD., this therapy works on the principle that trauma gets trapped in the body, leading to some of the symptoms people with PTSD or people who have experienced trauma might experience. Through this method, practitioners work on releasing this stress from the body.

I believe Anna's issue no doubt was precipitated by Mark's being in the hospital and the fact that on top of her being anxious about that, I was out all day. Especially at Christmastime. I say this tentatively, but who am I kidding? I see a direct correlation. I'd be foolish not to. But it's important to bear in mind that, to her, it felt real. She could have been feeling the pains, even if psychosomatically.

PART 7

2019

CHAPTER 21

Supportive

Sometimes it's hard to tell what derails a train and with life,
it is the same.

—Sima B. Moussavian, *As the moon began to rust*

To say that things went downhill in 2019 would be a massive understatement. I wonder where words like "making headway" and "breakthrough" went. Certainly, I had no need to call on them in this period. As the year began, I watched, horrified—or maybe I should say helpless— as Anna's emotional state changed before my eyes, and my heart was splintering, and my mind was spinning like a top.

My bundle of energy and confidence was now unmotivated, becoming increasingly allergic to rules, boundaries, and/or authority figures—no matter what type.

Less interested in spending time with me apparently, she no longer asked for or welcomed her nightly "massage." Looking back, I think this was detrimental; when I rubbed her back or stroked the side of her face or head, it typically comforted her. I have to believe falling asleep this way had some benefits too.

As far as her being angry with me, I almost never knew why. But at least part of it must have been a ramification of her just not feeling well. If you don't feel well, being kind is often secondary.

If having negative feelings, she didn't yell or argue. Rather, a tension seemed to hang in the air as she withdrew and mostly ignored me. Prior to this, she used to cut herself if in such a state. Insofar as I knew, she didn't yet drink alcohol, except in the instance cited earlier, or use non-medically prescribed drugs. This unfortunately all changed sooner rather than later.

Only a few times do I recall raising my voice to her during these ten years, once when she was punching the walls in her room and once when I gave her a very direct lecture about having gone halfway around the world for her, and how she said yes to us; that she wanted to become part of our family.

I was driving home the point that the difficulties we were encountering were not just affecting her, but that they impacted the people around her *because we all cared about her.* I needed her to know we were working on her issues *as a family*, and we expected her to share how she was feeling, or communicate when she wanted space, or if she wanted to talk about something.

This conversation about going halfway around the world for her took place early in the year, and she didn't walk out. She cried and then after a little while came over to say sorry. She did apologize a few times to me about the way she'd been treating me, and whenever she did, I always told her I understood—that I appreciated all the nice things she did for me (which were a lot). Also, I empathized with how hard it can be to be a teenager. Neither Mark nor I ever expected apologies, but we looked for accountability or acknowledgement that her emotional responses and behavioral choices were not good and that being violent would have terrible consequences. From this point forward, she had no acknowledgement of any of her unwise behavior and no accountability—on the contrary, to her thinking, whatever she did to someone "was their fault"; that this was the way she thought only became more apparent.

I was walking on eggshells because if I said anything she didn't like, she wouldn't talk back, but would instead walk right out the door.

CHAPTER 22

Unavailable

You may be out of my sight, but you're all I see.

—Ahmad Shawqi

Anna mostly wanted to talk to me now when she was feeling sad or having a difficult interaction with someone. This was fine, but when I was traveling for work, I wasn't always available right away. I was never gone for more than two to three days, but many times I'd receive a call just as I was leaving to go or getting on a train or plane. During the first week of February, I received a text while I was away in a meeting. It said she knew I might be in a meeting, but she was very upset. She typically would not call or text me when I was at work, so I was slightly alarmed, thinking whatever was going on might be a little more serious this time.

My response: *Please call Dad—I love you!! It's going to be okay. Call Jane if you want to chat with someone—I will send you her number. Did you take your medicine? Please call Dad right away. He understands.*

I was worried and knew I only had a minute to text before rushing back into the meeting, so I tried to give her options:

Response: *Yes, I took my medicine, I don't want to call him.*

Me: *Please, he loves you and cares deeply. I am worried.*
He will call you.
Response: *I'm fine, I'm just listening to music I don't want*
to call anyone.
Me: *You just told me you could not stop crying*
Response: *I am not going to do anything.*
Me: *I know that. You may just need to talk to someone.*

I think it is somewhat normal for teens to cry out to their mom and not want to talk to their dad. When they do get your time and attention, they often feel better.

Unfortunately, or perhaps in explanation, the same day we received a note from the school, requesting that Anna see a professional due to the list of reasons below:

- Intensified feelings of depression
- Feeling empty and not wanting to feel anymore
- Having made previous suicide attempts and engaged in self-harm activity
- Having issues with food restriction, binging, and purging

The school had determined that she needed therapeutic intervention to feel safe. They asked that she stay home until she was cleared to return. I emailed her therapist that day and worked with her on a short-term plan, which included seeing her that evening and then the next if needed. I was happy when Anna reported to me that she was already feeling better after seeing her therapist, and her therapist thought their spending time together the next day, doing something fun, would be a good idea.

The next day Anna continued to feel better, and she did not think she needed a second therapy appointment. After I canceled the appointment, Anna said she was not feeling well again. We decided to do one of our favorite things, which was to cozy up on the couch and watch *Gossip Girls*. We typically did this after dinner, sharing a bowl of popcorn or another snack. I also turned her on to tea, so were warm and cozy under a blanket, cups in hand, with a hand or limb touching.

She told me she did not want to do her timekeeping job on Saturday. It was not like her to not fulfill her commitments. At any rate, I had to tell her that it was too late to cancel so she would have to give it a go, and I would stay with her in case she could not do it. She ended up doing the timekeeping, but I could tell that she was off.

The following week she was starting to struggle with basketball. Her ultimate passion. This was alarming. Specifically, she got frustrated if she did not get much playing time in the game. I tried to impress upon her that being on the team is not only a huge accomplishment, but that it allows you to practice with the team and establish a foundation and friendships for the next few years. We were thrilled that she crawled over the finish line after a season of hard work and perseverance. She was proud of herself too because she had fun with the other players and was able to join in the end-of-season activities.

One of the hardest things to think about these days is that this ended up being her last formal basketball team. When she was out on the court, she never missed a beat, hustling from one end to another. She learned how to block shots and grab rebounds in no time. She was passionate about basketball, practiced outside at our hoop often, and loved the team spirit. Sports, singing, dancing, and other activities not only filled most of her free time, but gave her a huge sense of pride.

CHAPTER 23

Still

We are not our trauma. We are not our brain chemistry.
That's part of who we are, but we're so much more than that.
—Sam J. Miller

Despite taking Anna to multiple healthcare-related appointments each week, one area I had a hard time figuring out my role in when it came to her was medication. It wasn't an area I had expertise in, nor an area that I thought I should. I could track, call in, and pick up, but Anna wanted to be in control of her meds, and she had a very fixed approach. From the perspective that only she knows how she feels, it's understandable. But there were other aspects, such as how her mood and energy were—how they fluctuated.

At this time, she was very independent and responsible with her medication; she appreciated the control she had. We kept it in a kitchen cabinet, and she would take it on her own each day.

Later, she became more focused, borderline obsessed, looked up medications, and often made recommendations to her healthcare providers. As many of us know it can be tricky trying to find the right med for an individual and it often takes some trial and error. This can be very disheartening for an adolescent, especially where they expect to feel better soon after swallowing it. Any recommendation from her psychiatrist, where she did not like the sounds of the listed side effects, she would refuse.

I was able to have a good understanding of why a particular medication was prescribed. I had a basic sense of how Anna's moods and behaviors responded during different periods of time. The reason this was important was I was asked *a lot*. Later, especially when she was not living at home and refused to see her long-standing psychiatrist, things became more difficult.

CHAPTER 24

Discerning

Do not withhold good from those to whom it is due, when
it is in your power to act.

—Proverbs 3:27

On my birthday that year our son had his final high-school hockey game,
so we all went to cheer on the team. It was an unforgettably fun day.
As we attended an end-of-the-year celebration at one of the player's homes,
I was presented with a cool "hockey mom" birthday cake—bright blue, with
a picture of a mom with a hockey helmet on her head, equipment and sticks
in her hand—it was hysterical! The party filled us with laughs, good food,
and appreciation to the coaches and players for their hard work and tenacity.
Anna enjoyed herself, playing air hockey with one of my friend's daughters.
My friend remarked how beautiful and sweet she was, and I agreed. It was
touching to see her laughing during the air hockey competition.

Afterwards, Mark and I had a quick dinner out because I was taking
Anna on a ski trip the next morning for school vacation. We thought skiing,
fresh air, and getting away might help her feel better. I invited a friend and
her daughter to join us for a couple of days, so we were looking forward to

that. My friend asked if we had room for one more, and I said "Yes! The more the merrier." On the ride up to New Hampshire we sang songs. Anna sang to me, which was great. When we arrived, the condo was musty and dank, so we set up our things and tried to make it cozy. It was late, so we went to bed shortly after we got there. I didn't like the fact that the bedrooms were not next to each other, and looking back, it would have been better if Anna and I had stayed in the same room. The next day, she was crying a bit. This was new and it made the already gloomy condo seem sterile.

She had a couple specific social-media apps turned off on her phone because she had solicited drugs the week before. I asked her if that was why she was upset. But she didn't know and couldn't quite put a finger on why she was sad. I told her if things went well on the trip—and she didn't run off or do anything unsafe—she could have one of the apps back before we went home. She complained about wanting the other one, but I said that one was not coming back anytime soon.

Reflecting on this, it seems silly that I wouldn't just let her use them while we were away, trying to get her head in a better space. Things like this could be added to the *what-if's* list, but from what I knew about kids—and I read a lot about adolescents with various illnesses and boundaries—they need to feel safe, and to feel safe, they needed some guardrails to keep things in check.

"I feel empty," Anna told me the next day. Reaching out to her therapist, I jotted some notes down on a piece of paper. We discussed a plan for her meds and appointments. My friend and the two girls joined us the next afternoon. That night for dinner we went to a pub. They had a fun trivia game, so we all played while we ate. But Anna was not up for skiing the following day, so we switched plans, to go tubing instead. But as we were leaving to set out, I could tell that Anna was not feeling well. During the tubing, the bright sun bothered her eyes, and I could clearly see she was not her adventurous self. When I look at pictures, I can see a dramatic difference in her eyes and face.

Later that day, the girls went out for a ride. It was good for her to get out with them. When they returned, she asked if I could talk to her in the bedroom; she said the girls were excluding her and she wanted me to ask them to leave. Not knowing the backstory, I was empathetic but said they were staying so she should try her best to have a fun night. Reflecting now on this time, when Anna seemed to really be struggling with mood swings and feeling sad and empty, makes me think it was then that the BPD (borderline personality disorder) began to present.

CHAPTER 25

Concerned

Just because no one else can heal or do your inner work for
you doesn't mean you can, should, or need to do it alone.

—Lisa Olivera

As things got more chaotic, I just tried to keep my head above water, not
having time to do the reading or research I would have liked to. Not
that it would necessarily have helped. I would always like to go back to the
information explaining how much of this is out of the sufferer's control.

Back then, based on Anna's sensitivity, her unstable emotions, and her
physical aggression, I thought that there had to be more than disordered
attachment, depression, and PTSD that was causing her internal pain. I didn't
fully understand the basic differences between RAD and BPD. Through
reading lots of individual descriptions I learned that RAD can improve over
time. It starts in childhood. It shows in a push and pull I'll mention later, but
mostly the pull: withdrawing, not attaching, avoiding comfort from others,
and a lack of trust.

BPD usually starts later: in late adolescence or early adulthood. It
apparently lasts longer and is more pronounced, entailing intense emotional

dysregulation, mood swings, anger, relationship issues, a fluctuating self-image, and fear of abandonment, among other disturbances. Every person's expression of it is different, based on their individual circumstances, genetics, and co-existing conditions.

CHAPTER 26

Uneasy

The best way out is always through.

—Robert Frost

In February and early March, Anna texted an old friend to see if she could get her some pot. The friend was not eager to do this. But they reconnected well, to the point where Anna became infatuated.

Also, through text she began complaining about life, then stated that if she killed someone, she would not care. Where was this coming from?

With her permission, we still monitored her social media to watch out for things like this that needed addressing. Sometimes, however, I wondered if this made things worse.

If I did see anything harmful or otherwise disturbing and tried to discuss it, she got angry. In the case where she was soliciting marijuana, I told her—matter-of-factly—that she was going to lose her phone for twenty-four hours.

At the time of this exchange, Anna and I were upstairs, and I asked her to sit down in a TV room near her bedroom. I explained that it is not okay to ask for drugs, and what's more, it is illegal. "Give me your phone," I told her;

she said no quietly. I started to ask again but decided not to rock the boat right now.

She was still visibly upset and angry. I told her we would pick up the conversation later when Mark came home. I gently proposed it might be a good idea to stay home from school the next day and have a mental-health break or consider going to get help. The note from the school lingered in my thoughts urging me to pre-empt an emergency intervention. She went to her room and closed the door.

When Mark arrived, I told him she was in her room. I had talked to him earlier about the phone situation and the subsequent outburst, and he said he was prepared to go talk to her.

I said to be gentle *and* cautious. He walked upstairs and a minute later I heard her rebuff his overtures; also, he took her phone.

At some point he told her if she was not willing to talk, we would get help for her. As he walked out she slammed the door, then started yelling about not having her phone and how she could not talk to her friend. Since she was escalating, I went back upstairs and spent a little more time trying to encourage her to let us take her to the hospital so she could talk to someone, but she was completely out of sorts, appearing manic with awkward movements, mumbling mixed with shouting out; she would not agree. I pleaded with her that it would be better if she went with me and Mark to the hospital than for me to call and get help. I said, matter-of-factly, it was *time* to get help.

My heart was hurting. My anxiety was increasing. And things were getting tense. We were worried about her safety and ours. Eventually I called our local police on the non-emergency line to ask them if they could come convince her to go the hospital with us versus calling an ambulance. There were several reasons why we thought this was better. If we brought her, we could choose which hospital ER to go to, and even though her last experience at Kennedy-Parker Pediatric Hospital had led to two weeks in the psychiatric ward, her records were there, and we chose it this time because it is one of the best hospitals in the world. If you go by ambulance, you typically cannot choose where you go. There was a good chance the EMTs would take her a mile and a half down the road to the closest hospital. This is convenient for emergencies, but not to have an adolescent psychological evaluation.

After the fact, I struggled with the decision to call the police. On the other hand, it was all so tricky, with razor-thin margins for error. I was worried about things escalating. *But what if we had instead worked through it or given her time to cool off and gotten her buy-in ourselves?* Safety was the one thing I promised myself not to jeopardize, so although it wasn't easy, I still believe taking these actions was the right thing to do.

When the police arrived, seeing the car through the window, Anna flipped out. She could not believe we had called them.

They came in, and Mark explained what was going on, giving them a little history. They asked to speak to her. Mark and I went into the kitchen. They did convince her to go with us to talk to someone. At that point, she was shouting that we took the only person she cares about away from her. What she meant was that we took her phone.

We decided it was best if Mark dropped us off at the ER. As soon as they called her in, the splitting began, and she ignored me.

My heart was breaking for her. I could clearly see she was in distress, and it was very difficult for others to understand what she was going through. After the evaluation, the hospital psychiatrist told me that due to her current heightened state of anger, with some signs of mania, they did not think it safe for her to go home without first attending the Kennedy-Parker Community Based Acute Treatment (CBAT) Program, which specializes in intensive, short-term residential care for children and adolescents dealing with behavioral health challenges.

As in her earlier CBAT stay at St. Vincent's after taking the pills, it would be a step-down residency and treatment program before being discharged to our home.

CHAPTER 27

Relieved

What mental health needs is more sunlight, more candor,
and more unashamed conversation.

—Glenn Close

This was Anna's third inpatient stay. The first was a brief admittance to St. Vincent Children's in 2016 for cutting; the second a four-week stay after the overdose, beginning Tuesday, April 25, 2017; it included two weeks as an inpatient at Kennedy-Parker psychiatric unit and a two-week step-down residency at St. Vincent Children's Community Based Acute Treatment (CBAT). We knew by now that whenever she left an ER to be transported to another facility, we had twenty-four hours to get there and do the formal intake. Because I began to dread these, mainly due to the emotional gap that seemed to be at its widest between me and Anna during these times, I often gave myself a couple of hours at home before I left to go. When I went to the Community Based Acute Treatment Center for the intake, I learned that Dr. O'Shea, our daughter's psychiatrist, was the resident psychiatrist there. We were thrilled with this news because it typically took a long time for healthcare professionals to get to know Anna and to understand how she was feeling.

After a couple of days, Mark and I went in for a meeting with the team. Anna refused the family meeting, so Mark and I met with Dr. O'Shea. He explained that along with her attachment issues, major depression, and anxiety disorders (PTSD), she met, he believed, the diagnostic criteria for borderline personality disorder. I had read about BPD, and this confirmed what I'd been thinking. Unfortunately, the current medical information at the time said this illness should not be diagnosed before the age of eighteen, in much the same way that Reactive Attachment Disorder should be diagnosed by age five.

As part of Anna's treatment work, she began creating a safety plan with the hospital social worker. I talked about Anna's first plan way back in 2017. It listed coping skills she could utilize. The list she created during this stay included wonderful activities such as music, stress balls, scented products, gum, herbal tea; also, play games, cook, take a bath, sing, create in arts and craft, to name a few. In the section *Feeling Safe to Unsafe*—on a scale of one to six—she did a remarkable job in expressing these feelings, these true emotions, onto paper.

Down the side of the page was a line to list Friends/Family. Anna put down Aida and Elaine B., her then-therapist. She did not include any of us under "family."

As in the past, looking at this plan, anyone would think it had the proper criteria for success. Unfortunately, it wasn't that simple. Anna *wanted* to be able to do these things, yet her mind had a different agenda. As her emotional state escalated on the scale, her emotions overwhelmed her. It was impossible for her to slow down, breathe, and engage in activities intended to calm her mind and body. Because she had been through this sort of thing time and again, she didn't believe in these plans; she would tear them up as soon as she was alone.

Throughout the stay Anna continued to refuse to participate in family meetings. This was discouraging. At that time, Mark and I were due to go on a bike trip for our twentieth wedding anniversary. We went back and forth with the hospital team, and they all agreed we should go on the six-day trip. Before we left, Anna earned a "pass" for a visit outside grounds. She agreed to go for a walk with me and get some lunch. The walk was mostly quiet.

She did not want me to ask her any questions, so I didn't. At lunch, we got falafels and salad. A gentleman behind the counter joked about us being sisters. This was a bright spot because I saw Anna smile. She loved it when people commented about us looking alike. We talked briefly about her friend she recently reconnected with—Aida. She said she was the only one who understood who she really is. Anna also said that *she was not going to be the person we want her to be.*

"What do you mean?" I asked. "I don't understand. We want you to be yourself, if that means being respectful to people and follow the law." I could not get more information out of her about what she meant. She reiterated the same message to Mark. We wondered what was behind this eager need to convey her point.

We coordinated a plan for Maryann, the same family friend and babysitter who went to the hospital after Mark was assaulted, to discharge Anna when appropriate; the plan was for her to be discharged a day or so before we returned. Our friend agreed to do this—a godsend because it was asking a lot. So we set up a meeting to go to the CBAT and prepare the paperwork. My husband and I were torn about leaving; we thought it might cause increased feelings of abandonment, but in the grand scheme of things it was six or seven days, out of some very long years. At the same time, Anna was very close to this family friend.

CHAPTER 28

Rested

When you recover or discover something that nourishes your soul and brings joy, care enough about yourself to make room for it in your life.

—Jean Shinoda Bolen

We left on the bike trip March 23, and every minute was amazing. We rode through Majorca and Menorca, Spain, ate delicious local cuisine, and socialized with the other twenty-four people on the trip. Getting away from all the chaos gave us a breathing space. We called every couple of days, but Anna did not call us back.

On March 28, two days before we came home, Anna was discharged from the CBAT and went home with our babysitter. The discharge diagnosis was Major Depressive Disorder (in other words, depression), which affects 21 million Americans, and PTSD.

After our conversation with Anna's psychiatrist, we were surprised that the discharge diagnosis did not include BPD. That said, many experts are cautious about diagnosing BPD in adolescents because their personalities are still developing. So to ensure that the diagnosis is accurate, it's important to have a thorough evaluation. She did receive the formal BPD diagnosis several months later, in July, as the result of a full neuropsychic evaluation. She was sixteen years old. According to the National Library of Medicine on the NIH website, a diagnosis as early as sixteen requires that the patient have difficulties that are "pervasive, persistent, and unlikely to be limited to a particular developmental stage or an episode of an Axis I disorder" and that symptoms "have been present for at least one year."[10] The Diagnostic and Statistical Manual of Disorders, Fifth Edition. "DSM-5 also indicates that the pattern of behavior begins in adolescence or early adulthood, if not earlier.[11]

When we returned from the trip, Anna again proclaimed to us that "I am not going to be who you want me to be but am going to be who I want to be."

Fine, I think it's what most all parents want for their kids—for them to blossom, be fulfilled, discover their calling. Just don't, as I told her before, be disrespectful or disobey the law. Barring that, we were on the same page.

Though there was a great deal of tension in the house, we had the utmost interest in supporting her. I suggested trying meditation or yoga again or going together to get massages. But no, she said, she had a list of coping skills from the hospital and would use those. I was thrilled to see several additions on the list: positive affirmations, scented products, and strength training. Also: singing, word search, music, and pet the dog. This was the same sheet where she listed her therapist and her friend that she was infatuated with under "Friends/Family."

Yes, the infatuation continued. So we arranged a trip to the mall, during which they could shop while I did some work elsewhere. The trip to the mall seemed to release whatever Anna was holding on to.

---

[10] Marie-Pier Larrivée, "Borderline Personality in Adolescents: The He-Who-Must-Not-Be-Named of Psychiatry," *Dialogues in Clinical Neuroscience* June 2013 15(2): 171–179, doi: 10.31887/DCNS.2013.15.2/mplarrivee.

[11] R.S. Biskin, "The Lifetime Course of Borderline Personality Disorder," *Canadian Journal of Psychiatry* (2015), Jul;60(7):303--8, https://doi.org/10.1177/070674371506000702.

Shortly after that, the friendship started to go south, and Anna took it hard. I can guess she again felt abandoned by someone she cared about. She continued to act out in school and was starting to show additional symptoms of BPD, including feelings of emptiness, anger, paranoia, difficulty in relationships, marijuana use, and more.

Reflecting, I see, apparently, that more BPD symptoms were emerging here, starting with self-destructive behavior (looking for drugs) and then the explosive anger and being consumed by rage. Anna was completely obsessive in her infatuation, maybe needing the friend to make her feel whole. I understood that it was common for someone with BPD to become infatuated. It was just unfortunate that we could not talk things through like we had done so much when she was younger. The ups and downs of this relationship seemed to be causing her a lot of angst.

I thought more about the discussion with Dr. O'Shea and BPD and knew I had to learn more. On March 30, I jumped onto Amazon and bought three books.

- *Stop Walking on Eggshells: Taking Your Life Back When Someone You Care About Has Borderline Personality Disorder* – Paul Mason MS and Randi Kreger
- *I Hate You—Don't Leave Me: Understanding the Borderline Personality* – Jerold J. Kreisman, Hal Straus, and Jerold Jay Kreisman
- *Get Me Out of Here: My Recovery from Borderline Personality Disorder* – Rachel Reiland

I like them because they offer such different perspectives, all relevant to our situation. Randi Kreger passionately supports individuals and families affected by Borderline Personality Disorder, and over the years this book has been a valuable resource to me. She gets it and is compassionate towards both—the person with a BPD diagnosis and the people trying to support them. It particularly helped me understand Anna when she was having trouble understanding what was happening to her. I learned that it is okay to call the police if you find yourself in a scary situation, which prevented me from continuing to dwell on those decisions. Most importantly, the parenting techniques that related to feelings of guilt, setting limits, offering choices, and having expectations were invaluable. After each section of the book, she offers "key takeaways"; this has allowed me to use it as a reference without being overwhelmed by the vast content. Unfortunately, it was hard to use this or any book during this period I am writing about. For me, my life was like a turbulent, long-haul flight, and I did not take the time I should have to slow down and read, or just regroup. Looking back, I find that much of this information would have armed me with additional knowledge to bring to the table when meeting with the state agencies, the hospital, or the schools.

CHAPTER 29

Present

Rarely, if ever, are any of us healed in isolation. Healing is
an act of communion.

—Bell Hooks, author and activist

In April 2019, I continued to get calls from the guidance counselor about Anna disregarding the safety plan she'd developed with the counselor and the school nurse; also walking out of classes. Despite causing safety concerns, she kept being supported by the guidance counselor and the administration. One evening, hearing her crying in her room, I went up and asked if I could talk to her. She said she didn't feel like doing any work. I told her that "I know it's difficult, but if you commit to it and put your mind to it, the weight in your head may be lifted."

A few minutes later, seeming much better, she came down to where I was. "Is there any fish left over from dinner?" she asked. I heated up the leftovers for her. We also talked about veganism, in which she had expressed an interest. I asked her if we could put it on hold for a bit, until she was feeling a little better and we could stabilize her medications. She eventually agreed, but I think to her, it still fell into the category of me telling her what she could and couldn't do.

That morning, April 2, Anna was bright, like her old self. I felt relieved. Was her internal pain lessening? She got herself ready for school handily. I was proud of her. Around 1:30 p.m., I received a note that Anna yelled, "I hate my life right now!" at school.

I picked Anna up and made the mistake of asking her what happened. "I can't remember," she said. Was she telling the truth? Possibly. It was hard for me to tell. Many times when the situation was more chaotic and things may have been fuzzy in her head, I believed her. On this day I felt like she should remember shouting that dramatic sentence as she was walking out; she'd certainly made clear she felt it inside; it wasn't like she wasn't sharing her pain with actions or words around this time.

Then I prompted her: "'I hate myself!' you said."

Hearing me repeat it, she still said she could not remember. She started pushing and punching and kicking the back of the seat, obviously distraught. Pulling over, I asked her to take some time to breathe—we could talk about it another time.

When we got home, I suggested playing basketball. This often gave her time alone to regroup, possibly to process what happened. She played basketball for ten to fifteen minutes. Later, we ended up talking a bit and then agreed it would be a good idea to write the math teacher and Ms. Mathers, the guidance counselor, to apologize. After Anna sent the emails, she seemed better. She also wanted to take Lily out for a quick walk. I asked if she wanted me to go with her, but no, she said—she loved to walk to clear her head. She came home, ready to do her math, did that, then went down to the basement to sing.

All these things, she enjoyed and was doing less and less. But it was obvious that she did not feel well.

A little while later, we went to her therapy appointment. I was in the waiting room. She came out crying and requested I go in because her therapist wanted to talk to me. The therapist recounted that Anna told her the "food thing" was out of control, and she wanted to go back on appetite suppressants (not sure if she was on these in the hospital). But she'd just told Elaine B. it was hard to resist binging at the CBAT, where there were lots of snacks and meals (temptation everywhere). I listened in surprise. This was news to me, but I believed it.

Anna came back in, and Elaine B. explained that any meds related to food, such as appetite suppressants, should be discussed with her psychiatrist, Dr. O'Shea.

Anna was frustrated, then quiet, on the way home. I asked her to clarify "the food issues," reminding her that she'd told me the bulimia started again *today*, but, to the contrary, she'd told Elaine B *it had been a huge problem for some time*. I stopped talking, as I sensed an argument brewing. She changed the subject to planning her birthday party.

Below is some advice from The Bulimia Project, "How to Help a Child or Teenager with Bulimia." How to talk with your bulimic child:

> Be honest. Tell your child you'd like to discuss bulimia. Don't tiptoe around the topic or open with a discussion of weight or appearance.

> Focus on yourself. Sentences that start with "You" can seem aggressive. Look for ways to put your observations first. For example, don't say, "You always throw up, and it's a sign of bulimia." Instead, try, "I've noticed that you visit the bathroom during family dinners, and I am worried about bulimia."

> Stay calm. Your child may deny what you've seen or get upset. Denial is part of the disease. Don't react with anger.[12]

---

[12]   The Bulimia Project, "How to Help a Child or Teenager with Bulimia," https://bulimia.com/bulimia-affect-relationships/teen-child/.

It was scary enough, knowing Anna was suffering from trauma-related illnesses, now having binging and purging episodes; bulimia was heart wrenching. The best thing we did was talk openly about it and with the doctor.

Repeated eat/binge cycles "can cause potentially dangerous chemical imbalances in the body, as well as physical damage."[13]

I was able to share such information with her about the internal effects. This is what ultimately helped her stop. A miracle really. This was not an easy feat.

Around this time, Anna's therapist, Elaine B., didn't think that once-a-week therapy was sufficient. More specialized help was called for. Elaine B. was excellent, and Anna liked seeing her, but coincidentally, we had just started the DBT class, and one of the requirements was that Anna see a DBT therapist weekly. To participate in the program, she would need to stop seeing Elaine B. and start meeting with the DBT therapist, a support instructor. The problem was that personally, initially, I did not think this therapist was experienced enough, and then more so during the time she treated Anna. The DBT therapist, Joan S., brought me in after Anna's first session. But not again.

After that, she never brought me or my husband in at any time, unlike so many of Anna's providers, she rarely reached out to us to discuss any tips or approaches for working on family relations, and she did not discuss BPD at all. The lead instructor of the DBT course was amazing; so was the other support instructor. Anna was, at the same time, seeing Dr. O'Shea for psychiatry/medication management, which was helping a lot.

Unfortunately, April 5, I received a long email from the guidance counselor, letting me know they could not locate Anna, she had skipped class. I know Anna trusted me to listen without judgment at this time and to give her the best advice I could from a mom's perspective. I would approach this recent event gently in an attempt to understand the root cause.

---

[13]   Ibid.

I was also armed with more education and resources about mental illness so I could validate her concerns and prevent her from feeling judged. She described many ailments to me: her head was itchy, her stomach hurt, her throat was dry. There was always something bothering her physically, and I initially questioned whether she was making the issues up, but when I learned that this "somatization" is real, as previously mentioned, and is the expression of psychological or emotional factors that pop up as physical (somatic) symptoms, I was able to validate her concerns and support her much better.

One day I grabbed a yellow legal pad and suggested that we start jotting down any health concerns she was experiencing so she could track them. We called it "the list." We couldn't run to the doctor for every minor issue, but I assured Anna we would go if anything was serious.

What began as something practical turned into a playful exchange. Whenever she mentioned anything bothering her, I'd jokingly say, "Let's put it on the list!" We would laugh together as we added items. When Anna eventually took the list to the doctor, she found many items had resolved on their own. If they hadn't, her doctor listened attentively and provide sound advice.

Going way back to when she took the pills in April of 2017, Anna began to have issues with her stomach; she "ruined her stomach," she believed. Maybe she heard the nurses, doctors, social worker talking about the treatment—to prevent that from happening—she needed; maybe another resident had a similar experience or knew of someone who did. This started a never-ending merry go-round of stomachaches and pains, doctors' visits, GI specialist visits, scans, IBS diets, recommended MiraLAX use, and the need for enemas.

It may not have been the trigger that started the somatic episodes involving her stomach, but it at least likely contributed.

I read another study from 2020 in scientific reports titled, "The relationship between abdominal pain and emotional wellbeing in children and adolescents in the Raine Study," with a conclusion: "Abdominal pain in children and adolescents associates with depression, anxiety, being bullied, unhappiness and reduced overall health-rating during adolescence." These were all health issues that Anna was dealing with.

Another new thing around that time was that whenever we rode anywhere, Anna would put sunglasses on, pulling her hood up over her head. I appreciate a little communication at the beginning of a ride. Anything, even, "Mom, do you mind if I crawl into my hood; it makes me feel so cozy and warm."

"Of course not," I'd say. That is, if she'd made this remark. I believe she put on the hood to curl up and hide—listen to music and "chill out"—and in no way because she thought I did not like it, or that she specifically did not want to engage with me.

I later learned that like weighted blankets, weighted hoodies are available for purchase; some have additional features, such as attached fidget poppers, tactile bubble textured sleeves, breathing loops to practice slow and deep breathing, chewable toggles, motivational quotes, calming colors, and more. They sound cool and are all over the web and Amazon.

Around this time, I began purchasing audible books. Listening to a historical-fiction novel or any type of novel allowed me to escape to another world. Or if it was a nonfiction or business book, listening on audio was efficient because I rarely took the time to sit down and read at home.

If we were in the car and she wanted to sing to the radio, or sing to me, we would always do that, but if she wanted to listen to her own music with headphones, in the back, I would say "good night" with a big smile, and she would smile back and put on her headphones. This is something we used to do in the "good ole days."

On Saturday April 6, Anna went to the gym in Boston with Mark. Their discussion on food and eating went well, he thought. But later Anna told me it made her angry. This is a good example of how things often happened. Since Anna had difficulty expressing herself, she couldn't always communicate her feelings in a way that we fully understood. So, discussions like this would come up later, and she would say they made her mad. It's difficult for a teenager to be consistent when describing their feelings about situations, and this made it challenging to know if a conversation was helping her or causing frustration. It led to a lot of confusion.

That Sunday, I was playing in a hockey championship game out in Boxborough. Anna came along, and her mood seemed brighter, as I saw her cheering—watching us play. After the game we celebrated in the parking lot. Now she acted very differently, not wanting to join us or have any snacks. We left shortly after, and she was quiet en route home.

On Monday her mood was up and down, but we had a nice talk about the upcoming talent show at school. Anna said she'd had a pretty good day but binged at school. She was a bit all over the place during our talk in the dining room. She said that day was the first time over the past few months she'd thrown up, and she felt sick. She said she ate a lot, felt like crap, and wanted to go to the gym. I dropped her off at the gym and I took the dog for a walk.

The next day I excused her from school after lunch to go to Dr. O' Shea. I also formally asked the school district for an expedited assessment so we could try to enroll her in a therapeutic school in the fall. *The expedited aspect of the assessment was ultimately denied, so that didn't happen for a couple of months.*

There were a lot of appointments in April I was running around, trying to figure out how to help Anna on top of working and doing a lot of pickups, and driving to appointments.

I received information from the school counselor that Anna made a lot of statements about her well-being. *She was not well.* She expressed a lot of the issues to me: irritation, sleeplessness, food restriction, forgetfulness, lack of concentration, vomiting, and one heartbreaking statement, "I don't like myself."

The items above are clearly related to BPD and depression. I am still disappointed that I was not able to get Anna the proper help and treatment. I felt things were daunting and happening quickly.

CHAPTER 30

Scrambling

Feelings come and go like clouds in a windy sky. Conscious breathing is my anchor.

—Thich Nhat Hanh

After each hospital discharge, Anna needed a follow-up with her primary-care doctor (PCP). Her PCP was excellent: she always took time to listen to any concerns and never appeared to rush Anna, nor did she mind me being in the room, and then for the exam portion I would leave so they could have private time. It was hard to not chime in when I heard things I questioned, which happened a lot, but I had to remind myself that this was how Anna felt, or how she remembered things, so I follow the doctor's lead.

At that appointment, the doctor gave her strict orders to avoid hot sauce or spicy food. This "boundary" was helpful because when she complained about stomachaches in the future (after eating hot, spicy foods), I was able to share the doctor's advice with the staff at her group home.

As the food issue persisted, I was busy, calling all around to try to find a suitable program for eating disorders. I was focused on disordered eating because it was causing Anna a lot of stress. None of this was completely foreign to me: in high school, for a brief period, I severely cut back on my eating, and then at the end of college I indulged in a few binge episodes that got out of control. After college and after a couple weeks of celebrating having my own place with my best friend, whom I grew up with—eating late at night and toasting with beer—we joined a gym together. We both worked hard to get back in shape, and I started distance running, which was a huge turning point for me. After that, I spent the next twenty years running road races and marathons. I feel lucky, looking back, that these issues did not resurface.

I picked up hockey again when Max was in kindergarten. Another mom said, "Come play hockey with us on Sunday night." I said, "I haven't played since eighth grade!" and she replied "It's like riding a bike." It *was* like riding a bike . . . pure joy. I played that Sunday night over fifteen years ago and have never stopped.

Due to Anna's hospitalizations, I needed to talk to a liaison from our insurance company. At the beginning the conversations seemed helpful, but after I investigated the suggestions for programs or next steps, I never found any of them to be suitable or viable. Pretty soon, I stopped asking for recommendations and just tried to do my best to update her so she could make the appropriate assessment for insurance coverage.

I continued working to identify the right supports and programs, in addition to the nutrition programs and programs that would be helpful in the summer. The following Monday I found a local eating-disorder program and scheduled an initial phone intake.

On Thursday, I asked Anna how her day had been. She texted me, describing having fought back the urge to binge; she was cured, she wrote. Not true. *Not at this time.* But she would one day be—she would then stop "cold turkey." She often told me that if something means enough to her, she can control herself and stop. In this case, I believed her, and it proved correct. She stopped.

4/19/19

Another area I needed to stay on top of was Anna's medications. A frequent question from healthcare professionals at intakes was whether I saw any changes when she took certain meds, so I was careful to take notes at appointments and when Anna and I had our chats in the dining room. I encouraged her to keep her own record of how medications made her feel, but she didn't like to write things down. Looking back, I could easily have done this for her. She enjoyed dictating her thoughts and having others write for her.

I had to keep a lot of people updated because there was a growing cast involved in Anna's well-being, and it was difficult to keep everyone on the same page. Overall, it was a good team, but things did not seem to be improving in a way that made me or my family feel safer at home. Reflecting back, I wish I'd pulled myself out of this management role and focused more on identifying the themes and patterns I was seeing—in order to learn more about strategies to help Anna.

In regard to the medications, the most positive aspect of this is that one medication, Lamotrigine, seemed to help a lot for her mood stabilization. Lamotrigine is often used in cases of bipolar disorder.

On the other hand, she wanted to be in control of what she was taking. For instance, she passed on medications with side effects of drowsiness or potential weight gain. I understood these concerns but sat frozen hoping she would listen to the potential benefits before shutting down the conversation. The multiple doctors who recommended these medications explained that they only recommend drugs whose benefits they believed outweighed the negative side effects.

She was typically on only one additional medication in addition to the Lamotrigine, but the more she got involved in trying to find a "silver bullet" to make her feel better, the more the water got murky.

April continued to be filled with phone calls and appointment scheduling. I was able to secure the neuropsychological intake for Wednesday, April 17th. The actual testing was scheduled for May.

The rest of April was a little better. Anna was communicating with me. She would let me know when she felt better in specific areas (usually somatic); her vision was improving; her focus was not; the dry mouth was still there; she was better physically—no vomiting, digestion a little better, and anger and irritation increasing. The Friday before Easter, she went to a friend's house but was feeling sad on Saturday. She said she did her best not to purge. "What about doing the deep breathing exercises that the nurse taught you?" She agreed and we practiced them a few minutes.

She woke up on Easter Sunday, feeling better. We went to church, and she did some reading afterwards. My son and I went to do some planting at my dad's grave, which was one of the highlights of my day. We had Easter dinner. And Anna was excited about watching a show together.

4/22/19—Monday

The Easter break began, and Anna told me the night before that she was not able to control the urges; now, each time she ate, she felt like she needed to purge. She had difficulty telling me this, which I understood, and I validated that it is very difficult for anyone to talk about things like that. She had not told her psychiatrist.

In addition to seeking support for the disordered eating and from the Department of Mental Health child, youth, and family services program, we hired an education consultant for help in assessing any next steps related to Anna's education. Based on her recommendation and the recommendation from the neuropsychic report, we were confident that she needed a therapeutic environment for school—the sort that helps trauma-afflicted adolescents or adolescents struggling with mental illness by helping them build their internal skill sets, encouraging learning and growth, and teaching them to create healthy relationships.

Things had stabilized a bit, and I told the education consultant that Anna was now on Lexapro, in addition to the Lamotrigine. Later the same day, Anna threw up after lunch, she told me. She said she did not tell her therapist but was fine. The next day I received a call from the nurse. Anna was throwing up in the bathroom. After school Anna and I had a long talk, in which I explained that she needed help.

The next day, Thursday, coming home tired and discouraged that a lot of things had gone wrong, Anna said she worked hard to make it through the day. We met Kirsten and Adrianna from the Department of Mental Health after school. The goals were to prevent multiple hospitalizations, provide mentors for youth to practice social skills, identify family partners (families that had gone or were going through similar challenges), and give in-home support. After the meeting, Anna told me she had thrown up before we met them.

Anna's guidance counselor requested a meeting on May 1, due to the bathroom incident a week earlier. When vomiting at the time, Anna had refused to give her name or come out of the stall. Prior to the meeting, I told Anna if she needed to take a break, I would be happy to pull her out. Ideas *like this often came from my therapist to help her not feel like everyone was ganging up on her.*

That Friday, in early May, I came across a very disturbing Snapchat correspondence Anna had been having with a young man or teenager (it was hard to tell which) from a town close by. They were basically threatening to beat each other up. At one point, Anna said she would get her brother to beat him up. She posted a picture of a huge bodyguard-looking man (not her brother).

This was particularly scary, as it brought our son, Max, in.

When Mark and I talked to Anna about it, it angered her, and she swung and hit Mark in the chest/shoulder.

A couple of minutes later, she tried to chase him up the stairs, but he told her to back off and go downstairs.

I spent time calming her down because her anger was not assuaged. Eventually she mellowed, and we spent Saturday and Sunday together. On Saturday, she shared with me that she was very upset about what the purging was doing to her body—the physical side effects. She was going to stop, to heal, she said. That day, we went on a charity walk, then to the grocery store to shop for a healthy lunch and other items she liked. We discussed the purging together while looking through a book titled *Intuitive Eating,* by Evelyn Tribole, MS., R.D. It was 300-plus-page paperback, so we just reviewed a section on "Coping with your emotions without using food." There was a corresponding workbook, but she decided she did not want to use it. We exercised together on Sunday, and she said that helped. The vomiting stopped.

That weekend, there was tension about her phone, as she insisted on going on Snapchat—once again battling over a social-media app. I tried to be mindful of Dr. O'Shea's advice that *we should eliminate the boundaries for now and not take away apps/electronics as punishment.* I am not sure what I did at the time; I hope I just gave her access because these restrictions were not helping her ability to regulate her emotions.

I look back on this period as being marked by volatile swings—ups and downs where Anna would struggle (with purging, anger, sadness) but have periods of relative calm and a resolve to be done with the bulimic patterns.

The next week, on 5/4/19, we received a note from Nancy, Anna's guidance counselor, informing us that Anna left a class and did not return.

The gist of which was: "Please speak with Anna and let me know what happened. Thank you."

When I spoke to Anna by phone, she admitted that she had no explanation and knew what she was doing was very wrong. But did not seem remorseful. I wonder if stopping the purging meant she had to find another outlet for her trauma. Maybe she just needed to flee, like she did at home.

That weekend I was playing in the same out-of-town National Hockey Tournament that I did the year prior. For my own sanity, I went on the trip. Maryann, my friend and babysitter, picked Anna up from school and was going to stay at the house until Mark came home. She gave Anna a stern warning, that if her misbehavior at school didn't stop, maybe she would have to be sent away.

That night between 11:00 p.m. and midnight, Mark heard the garage door open, so he checked in on Anna and realized she was gone. Then he found her computer, left in the garage when she crept out. Looking at her browsing and chat history, he found the name of a girl, Ava.

Since Anna had a good friend Ava, he assumed it was her. He called Ava's dad, who let Mark know that Anna was not there. He then went on to find additional information about a different Ava.

The police ended up finding Anna at Ava's home, hiding in a closet (planning on showing up at the large local high school on Monday morning); she did not want to go back to her current private school, Aquinas, any longer, but to transfer to the 1,100-person public school).

Anna had told Ava to tell her mom we kicked her out of our house; that she had no place to stay. I had gotten used to this lying. I called it that, but to Anna I think it was just strategy: seeing a problem and finding the most "logical" solution. She did not appear to consider it lying if it was tactical.

At this point, I regretted my decision to go away. On the other hand, did Anna do this because Maryann scared her? Later she said as much. Did she believe she could hide out for the weekend and just walk into classes on Monday morning at the town's high school, where she wasn't enrolled?

The police brought her home. I was on the phone with Mark at the time, in the bathroom of the house the team was sharing. But Anna told the police she did not feel safe, being home, because she did not know what she was going to do to Mark, that she might hurt him. My heart was petrified for Mark and at the thought of her not able to control her impulses to such a degree; sad, too, knowing all he wanted to do was take her in and have her get a good night's sleep.

I felt terrible for Anna because I knew she was desperate. Anna wanted out of her school and believed that there was no way to change paths. Angry, she directed at us her rage for the situation she was in.

What else could they do? They ended up transporting her to Kennedy-Parker Pediatric Hospital for an evaluation. Mark followed in the car and returned home early in the a.m. of May 5. Anna was admitted to the inpatient psychiatric ward. I went to the hospital to do the intake on Monday, May 6.

The whole time this incident was playing out, I spent most of the night talking to Mark. This again made it practically a cinch to conclude that although she appeared very excited to have Maryann coming over Anna characteristically acted out when I was away. So maybe the deeper cause this time was that she felt let down when Maryann burst her bubble with the "straight talk."

CHAPTER 31

Calm

And sometimes I have kept my feelings to myself because I could find no language to describe them in.

—Jane Austen

Kennedy-Parker Pediatric Inpatient Psychiatric 5/6/19–6/21/19

The spring of 2019 took its toll. I could only describe it as a cross between the movies *Girl, Interrupted* and *Silver Linings Playbook*.

First off, even though the two movie settings were quite different, I was personally familiar with both: a hospital psych ward and a loving home.

To me, going to psych wards was like going to wakes to express sympathy for someone's passing. Initially I was reluctant. However, once there, I found myself at ease, thankful that I came. In the psych ward in *Girl, Interrupted*, despite the rules and structure, it's almost as if "anything goes." Outbursts, defiance, rule breaking seemed almost part of the "norm."

In *Silver Linings Playbook*, on the other hand, drastic mood swings are not the norm and are therefore much more noticeable—in the middle of a living room, for instance. And are sadder when being played out in this everyday environment, especially if the person is really trying and wants to get better and lead a "normal" life.

Girl, Interrupted is a story of a young woman, Lisa (played convincingly by Angelina Jolie), the tough, rebellious one (sociopath) in the psych ward of what they called back then a mental institution. She has been there a long time, knows the ropes, and causes a fair amount of chaos. The lead character, Susanna (Winona Ryder), has a BPD diagnosis and is struggling with her mental health issues, trying to fathom what her diagnosis means. A sensitive young woman, she is smart and challenges the treatment at the hospital. The movie brings you inside the psych ward, where you can see these two characters' relationship, and the influence the more rebellious one has on the others, along with the complex range of mental illnesses they have. I could relate both characters to what I can only imagine Anna may have been experiencing. Some days she was collecting cell phone numbers from her "friends"; other times she was demanding to see the hospital human rights advocate so she could be emancipated from us. One day she was friendly with the social worker; another day she was screaming about him. I knew a lot (or was it the bare minimum?) from meetings with social workers and the resident psychiatrist, but so much more happened within the unit behind locked doors. At times she could be the rebel, demanding meds, and at times she could be more sensitive, openly wondering what was wrong with her and why she felt empty. Most interesting, as in the movie, she was exposed to a range of illnesses the other patients had. She learned that some were in for eating disorders, and this made her think about her own disordered-eating issues. She was also exposed to patients who were not as high functioning as she was and often exclaimed there was nothing wrong with her and that being there embarrassed her. I worked with her on this feeling, always trying to impress on her that there was nothing to be embarrassed about, everyone has something. Of course, though this might build self-esteem and inner strength, I had no control over others' reactions—and how they might turn their biases against her. Did they?

In *Silver Linings Playbook*, the main character, played by Bradley Cooper, was released from a mental-health hospital with a bipolar diagnosis. Now living at home with his parents, he has the delusional notion of getting back together with his wife. This movie reminded me of Anna at home after a hospital stay, much more sensitive and fragile, trying to build back friendships and participate in more "normal" things like basketball camp. She was trying, but at times delusional about what that really meant. And unfortunately, like "Pat" in the movie, Anna depended on medications for her mood swings and to try to control outbursts. If she did not take them—especially later in the group-home setting—it would result in quite the commotion; the household would be thrown into disarray.

In June 2019, therefore, Anna mostly still lived at home. How things would change. How I wish we could have kept to this protocol. But you will see why that was not to be.

During the time Anna was at Kennedy-Parker Pediatric psych ward, she requested a lot of things through the social worker—not wanting to engage with us at the time; I didn't realize but now do that she probably made the many requests to have contact with me or see me, without being vulnerable and asking. I started to push back, though—a bit of an understatement—through the social worker.

On one call I was raising my voice to the social worker; the requests were unreasonable, I told him. I was holding the back of my neck, while my volume escalated, at that point I realized I was screaming into the phone. I let him know that under no circumstances was I going to bring new clothing or anything else nonessential.

At the same time as the clothing and make-up requests came in Anna was requesting meetings with the human rights advocates, seeking her "emancipation" from us. She wanted to break ties. Wasn't there a better place for her? She imagined it so. "Emancipation," in this terminology, is when an adolescent wants to cut parental ties. She wasn't bluffing—in her mind she thought there was something better out there . . . an apartment or home that she could live in and come *and go as she pleased.* She *did not want any authority over her* and did not want to be watched anymore.

Anna would not participate in family meetings at the hospital, but she did want to meet one day to read us a letter—the gist of which was *that we never listened to her: that she was not mentally ill, she should have a say in her future, and she wanted to go to the local high school in Madison.* It would make her happy, she said, explaining why.

To no avail, we tried to remind her that she chose Aquinas, we had not prevented her from attending the public high school, but we understood she felt Aquinas was no longer a fit. Instead of a private school, she apparently wanted to enter the large-scale public school, just as she had in middle school—but there, she had felt lost, without her old friends.

Agitated, she told the social worker she did not want to talk anymore and wanted to leave the room.

We were already including an education consultant in our meetings with the team at the hospital and looking for support for a *residential therapeutic placement* where Anna could live in a safe environment, receiving treatment. At the time we did not know how this would impact her education.

The hospital team was having none of it, however, as much as we tried to break rank on this. She would be safe at home, they insisted. Reflecting, I wish they'd helped me understand *why* home would be better, versus just saying they thought we would *all be safe* together there. However, they were not in our shoes. We did not think the latter was true.

Did I truly think Anna was going to hurt us in our sleep? No, but we had no peace of mind and were always on high alert now when she was in the house, her moods could change so unpredictably. The hospital was on the receiving end of the stomach complaints and many more somatic issues that arose. They kept tabs on them and shared details with us. Towards the middle to end of the six weeks' stay, there were far less somatic complaints.

I am not sure if this was because Anna felt heard—her issues addressed—or if it was something else. Did she realize yet that the only place they were offering her to go was home, so she was resigning herself to that, instead of fighting for "a better place"?

We believed they were trying to push her home because they felt that was the best for her and that, in their opinion, she did not require the level of care she was receiving in the locked-down psychiatric ward. We understood this. The problem was we did not feel like we could parent her at home safely, especially now that she was so angry with us. She appeared to have developed some kind of psychosis or delusion in which she imagined a life without us that would be better but had nowhere to go and was not able to care for herself and keep herself safe. How that would influence her actions, what actions it might drive her to—what was going on inside her head, even—no one had any way of knowing. Our sweet little girl was growing up with unpredictable inclinations that even she could not control. Such is mental illness. During this time, I chose not to move forward with an application for in-home family services, not knowing it was a prerequisite to a longer-term residential treatment program.

While completing the reapplication paperwork, I simultaneously enrolled Anna at the large local high school, a required step in the application. In parallel, I corresponded extensively via email with the team chair of the special education program at the high school she had just transferred to.

We would finally meet in early June; they would approve or reject the request for an IEP (Individual Education Program). Even if they approved, this would scratch the surface of Anna's needs.

Our education consultant compiled a comprehensive package, highlighting *why a therapeutic school placement was necessary—that Anna would not thrive in school otherwise*. It was essential. To no avail.

The IEP was granted, while the request for therapeutic placement was denied. The school's special education committee assured us they had the right tools and support to educate Anna *at the large high school*. What folly that led to.

Disheartened, we left the meeting. This decision to deny the forty-five-day assessment at a therapeutic school turned out to be a major misstep on the high school's part.

Back at the hospital the social worker continued to push for Anna to come live at home. We brought up the need, in that case, for a documented safety-and-coping plan. Not because we needed a piece of paper in our hands and not because we had success with such plans before. Rather, because we felt strongly that Anna needed to go through the exercise of documenting and discussing her feelings.

In the past this tool was a prerequisite for discharge for all her hospital stays. So why was it not required now? Why wasn't the team working with Anna to assess her readiness to come home? *She was so angry at us.* If she refused to go through an exercise to discuss coping skills and the support she thought would be helpful and accessible if she was feeling sad, angry, or dangerous, wasn't that a red flag, dangerous in itself? It didn't feel like we were setting her up for success; it felt quite the opposite.

Because Anna was resisting this exercise and we were asking for it, they asked *us* to create the plan—what did we expect at home?

Looking back, what a misguided request it was for us to put our own expectations and boundaries on paper, no matter how straightforward and reasonable they seemed to us at the time.

The day we gave it to them, they sprung it immediately on Anna, in a poor attempt to let her establish some buy-in. Why on earth would they think for a minute this would be okay? They were the experts here. But we knew better. Predictably, she reacted badly, which was a huge setback for all of us. Mostly our family.

The plan blindsided her; the execution was ridiculous. Anna did the same thing with it as with all the other plans: she ripped it up and threw it in the trash the same day we arrived home. I know now that many of these stipulations caused her regress. It was the black-and-white thing.

The social worker explained that it had already been over four weeks; they did not want to keep her as an in-patient much longer. We agreed but asked how they could send her home when she had a vendetta against us, to slightly overstate.

At some point, Anna was informed that foster care, which she had been interested in (anything out of hospital and not with us), takes months to put into place. And someone told her that maybe the next step was a residential program. But that, she knew, would curtail her freedom. So it was clearly not an option to her.

Anna called me to say she had thought things over and wanted to tell me that if she came home, she had demands: for one thing, to be put in a "better school. And if we "sent her to a boarding school" (her words), she would either not go or flunk out. This referred to our discussions about an institute in Connecticut where Anna's admission was denied at the eleventh hour due to concerns about potential aggressive behavior and the risk of her leaving the campus without authorization. "You never listen," she went on, and "You do not do anything to make me happy."

"I've been listening, loud and clear," I said. I also asked her why she thought coming home was an option right now.

"Well, if I can't go to foster care," she said, "then I'm not going to boarding school."

"We should have this conversation with Dad and the team," I said. Talking about my own daughter with "a team" by this point seemed normal, so far from the way things started, when we used to decide everything together. But the needle had moved.

She hung up after saying her piece. As usual, I felt extremely agitated during and after the call.

Basically, the Department of Mental Health denied our request to place her in residential therapeutic treatment—that is, temporary live-in therapy—because the hospital team believed that with some short-term work, Anna could safely live with us. Unfortunately, we had seen nothing positive from Anna towards us or at Kennedy-Parker Pediatric Hospital that would make us believe she would not run away or be violent. Ben Hernandes, her assigned social worker at the hospital, stated in the meeting that he had seen glimpses of Anna wanting to go home, but when pressed he really couldn't add more. She was still oppositional and angry, saying our visits triggered her anger. So she didn't want us to visit.

I called Anna on Sunday, and she said hello pleasantly but then did not want to talk. She said she had been feeling weak for the past forty-eight hours; she felt nobody cared.

On Monday, Mark asked Ben again to make a recommendation to the Department of Mental Health that *she needed to be in a safe, residential therapeutic treatment program that had an education tie-in for the fall. Unfortunately, they were still not going along with our view.*

In-home family therapy had to precede a residential treatment program, they said. This is where we began to think about how the transition to home would look and what interim services to put in place.

The goal would be for her to understand that making visible progress was the path to coming home. Kennedy-Parker Pediatric Hospital stated that the reactive attachment disorder was very present, which we understood, but seemed to be dismissing everything else, including her school behavior, her unstable relationships, her feelings of emptiness, her fear, her anger, and her oppositional and dangerous behavior at home. I believed additional DBT treatment at Kennedy-Parker Pediatric Hospital would be beneficial, but I was not able to bring it up to Anna without her getting extremely frustrated with me.

Anna was discharged to us on June 21, 2019. The day before, Anna and I went for a walk on the hospital grounds. The hard shell present over the past month was starting to soften. We talked about some fun things we could do and how we could celebrate her birthday. While sitting on a bench, she confessed to me she was still purging and was adamant that I talk to the social worker about it. I called Ben later that day and told him. He said that Anna was being observed from outside the bathroom and they did not feel as though she was purging.

This was so interesting to me because Anna had just spent weeks expressing her hatred for us, requesting emancipation, and in the first heart-to-heart conversation we had, she was asking me to tell the social worker what was happening, but when I did, it turned out perhaps she was not telling the truth and wanted either my attention or the staff's. In other words, she was being manipulative, not open hearted.

As I reflect, this may have been another attempt for closeness with me, or even a test of my support. Would I take her side? She also might have been telling the truth. Things like this were very hard to figure out.

Also prior to discharge, we worked with the team and ultimately decided a step down to a day program (about twenty-five minutes south of where we lived) would be better than an in-patient facility.

On the second morning of the step down at the day program, the clinician there asked me to come in for additional paperwork. They reported that Anna's behavior the first day was a little out of control and when they tried to redirect her, they had minimal success.

Once out of the meeting, I saw an unanswered call to me from my sister. She was at the hospital with my mom. My stepdad, she told me, had unexpectedly passed away that morning from an aortic aneurysm. Later I found out he literally died in her arms, coughing up blood in the sink. It was horrifying. My stepdad was one of the nicest, gentlest, most humorous people I knew. While I was in the car, I called his daughter-in-law. She was in shock and busy calling people. I sat in the car and cried for a while before going home. I was overwhelmed with sadness, but I was also overwhelmed by everything that was consuming me at home.

Later that week I left for Florida to attend the services, with plans to return to celebrate Anna's birthday. We intended to take her out to eat and to the movies with some of her friends. Unfortunately, my flight was late, so Mark took her out, and the next night we went to a hibachi restaurant she chose.

A few days later we did the discharge from the day program, a day early due to the Fourth of July holiday. We hoped the fresh air and sunshine would be helpful. The report from the partial-program director was that Anna did not engage in the therapy per the expectation—that she used foul language and was disrespectful.

I only remember that the weather at the Cape was a little cloudy but warm. We spent time at the beach and got big, soft-serve ice creams before leaving. Because summer school started on Monday and Anna had an appointment that evening with Dr. O'Shea, we only stayed until Sunday.

The process of navigating my way through the school district's policies and procedures to develop an IEP was slow, but if I hadn't stayed on top of everything, there would have been even longer lags. The plan was for Anna to attend summer school so she could get caught up from missing most of the last semester. She would take traditional summer school English, plus math. Mark and I were working closely with the education consultant to advocate for her to attend a *therapeutic school instead of the public high school.*

In late June we hired an education attorney. Turns out we were a tad too optimistic about the school system "doing the right thing." We hear stories every day—financial politics messing with educational and mental health needs. I was on a constant treadmill of pushing, prodding, emailing, and calling, advocating for placement in the proper therapeutic school for Anna. But was met with extensive delays, broken promises, and a tunnel with no light at the end.

One night right before summer school, Anna became upset in the parked car, trying to kick me from the back seat. Not having started summer school yet made her frustrated, as did being offered only two courses. I reassured her that we would figure out what it would take to get her into tenth grade. She felt somewhat better after that.

On the first or second day at summer school, Anna got alcohol from another student. It appeared that she went to the other student's house to get it. She drank some there and took the rest in a water bottle to the library and possibly home. She was sixteen years old.

The following Thursday, I again stopped at CVS. Anna told me she was not going in but walking home. I said, "Not today. You are coming home with me."

She said, "No, I am not. I am walking home."

She jumped out and walked away from the car, not towards the store, adamant, "I will walk home!!!!!"

"I will call the police," I threatened, meaning it. I called my husband instead because, upon reflection, I should not have mentioned the police to her; that could escalate the situation. Trying to give her some freedom, my husband and I agreed I would follow the path home. Unfortunately, she was not on the one-mile route I traced; I could not find her. She called a little while later and asked if I "called the cops." I did not answer.

"I need to go to my friend's until late tonight because I do not feel safe, coming home," she said.

"Why not?" I asked, but when she did not explain, I told her that plan was not okay. She hung up. At about 8:30 p.m., one of her (at times troubled) friends texted me she was there, safe, and that her mom said it was okay. I thanked her, asking for the mom's number. I also said Anna had school tomorrow, so be sure she got home soon. By 9:45 p.m. she was not home. I called the mom. Introducing myself as Anna's mom, I said she had to come home. But the mom knew nothing about the situation. She'd just arrived home and did not know Anna was there. I brought her up to speed. And Anna came home as if nothing had happened.

I just repeated that it was not okay, what she did. My nonchalant demeanor was deliberate, I wanted to avoid the scenario of Mark and me being engaged in a late-night search party. Mark also told me he found a picture posted to her Snapchat. It revealed a significant amount of skin and flaunted minimal clothing. He intended to have a conversation with her about the potential risks associated with dressing this way and posting such photos, at her age.

It took until July to get things in place for the in-home program facilitated by Metro Community Services. This Department of Mental

Health program was necessary to participate in, as a prerequisite, to any residentially based treatment. The state team was optimistic. Unfortunately, despite the excellent structure, it was not well managed, so it turned out to be an unusually chaotic, stressful time for Anna and our family.

CHAPTER 32

Misled

The light shines in the darkness, and the darkness has not overcome it.

—John 1:5

On Friday, July 12, we began the in-home family-therapy program. I asked Anna to walk home from school because I would be on a call until 12:30 p.m., and the therapeutic mentor was coming at 1:00 p.m. At 12:45 p.m., with Lily on a leash, I walked to the end of the street to meet her, but she walked right past me. I told her lunch was on the counter. She wasn't hungry. I stayed with Lily at the bottom of the street for a few minutes. When I returned, the sandwich was gone.

When the state services program director and mentor arrived, I found Anna's mentor was an amazing young woman who exuded positive-energy warmth.

At the end of Anna's session, we all came together to fill out a safety plan. Did I want to say, "Been there, done that"? Yes. Did I? No. I inserted goals of not hurting herself or others. We had already had three minor incidents since her last hospitalization.

From that day forward, the program director only ever focused on the topic of reactive attachment. If her expression could talk, it would be saying "You're the mom—and you need to do something about this. It's not *her* fault." I continuously expressed back to her, the family clinician, and the rest of the (DMH) team that the breadth of issues went way beyond attachment. It was for naught. Their convictions were firmly established long before the meeting took place. In my head I was picturing myself standing on hot coals at a tribal council on the show *Survivor*. I certainly was not aligned with them. After the program director and mentor left, I went out to sit on the patio. I asked Anna if she wanted to sit out with me. She started to cry a little and talked about Ukraine; she'd had a dream where she was sent back. "Sent back to Ukraine?" I told her to sit next to me, hugged her, and asked her to tell me more, to which she responded that *she felt like her brain/head was different than in the years before; she couldn't control herself now, wanting to do risky things like run away.* She also mumbled something about having suicidal thoughts.

I asked her how I could help because this was the first time she'd opened to me recently. She said she knew how lucky she was and how she had a great family and a great life. We then talked about going to Cape Cod on Saturday, and she asked if we could paddleboard; "of course," I said.

A couple minutes later she went upstairs, then came back down. She asked me if she could go get face wipes at CVS in the square, about a mile away. I was a little concerned about letting her go alone after her dream and our conversation with the counselor, so I suggested we go together. But she said, "Mom, I would really like to take a walk and clear my head, and I would love to go to CVS." I relented.

After she left, I called Metro Community Services, the family-therapy-program liaison, to let them know about her suicidal thoughts because I had not heard anything like that since her overdose in 2017.

I said we had a long conversation, and she seemed brighter and kinder. The liaison said she'd be more concerned if Anna weren't saying anything, and we agreed we thought the visit with the therapeutic mentor made her feel better overall.

Looking back on this, I feel like I was fooled again. It was just another time I let down my guard.

A little after 5:00 p.m. the local police called—my daughter was in the hospital, brought in by ambulance after being found extremely intoxicated lying on a bench at the square in town.

But how could that be? I didn't think we had alcohol in the house at that time. But up in her room, I found a bottle of bourbon that had been a holiday gift—one third empty. A lot of alcohol. *A lot* of *strong* alcohol. I then remembered walking Lily right before the in-home family services program director and mentor came earlier that day. I'd told her there was lunch for her on the counter. Later I realized she'd used that time to take the bottle out of the cabinet and bring it up to her room. I am not sure how I had not noticed the alcohol on her breath, especially whiskey, because I have a keen sense of smell. I can only chalk it up to her covering it up in some way.

She had many strategies because she had to survive under very difficult circumstances; we'd seen other tricks and schemes play out in the past that were astonishing. We joked—and sometimes were more serious—saying, "*Anna, you should be a Ukrainian spy.*" She liked this idea and for a short period thought maybe she would go into forensics.

I jumped into my car. At the hospital, I met the EMT, and he told me how he found her. He looked disgusted. I tried to explain it was complicated. Her blood alcohol level was .191 (twice the legal limit). The nurse and doctor reckoned it would probably take eight to ten hours to come back down to a normal level and she would have to stay there until all the alcohol was out of her system.

They said I should go home and come back and meet with the crisis counselors later that night or in the morning. In her room in the ER, Anna was crying, telling me she wanted to be like her birth mom, so she drank the alcohol.

It was a very sad situation—with her begging me not to take her to the hospital. I told her she would have to stay a little while where she was, then come home. Because the staff had to administer charcoal to absorb the toxins, she was still throwing up. I went home around 7:00 p.m.

Mark went back around 9:00 p.m.; then I took a turn from 11:00 p.m. to 12:30 a.m., in case the crisis team came. All this while, she was begging me to take her home, vowing never to drink like that again. I told her everything was going to be okay. The crisis team was delayed, so I went home again. At 3:45 a.m., I got a call to meet with the crisis-team social worker. When I got there, he had been talking to Anna for a few minutes. I briefly went through her background and hospitalizations. He explained that he had seen this a lot, and despite her illness/diagnosis, she knew right from wrong. He told me she needed to go home and get her act together. He added that she was being manipulative and that we were spoiling her. He was very cut and dried about the situation and let Anna and me know that her behavior was inexcusable, and no, she was not being admitted.

He told her she needed to get herself to school, focus on school, and get herself home afterwards. OR, if the behavior continued, she would be sent to juvenile detention. "Do you know what this means?" he asked her. She did but she said no, so he explained.

Before we left, Anna was holding my hand and saying sorry. This did not happen often; I felt it was genuine. This mood lasted a few more minutes, but by the time she was discharged and we were walking to the car, her attitude had already started to shift. It was like an electric light switch.

The sad, apologetic demeanor was gone; she began to ignore me.

Despite feeling like he did not know anything about her trauma—and was dead wrong in thinking it was correctable by "bouncing back"—and that she wasn't spoiled (but was intentionally manipulative and could stop that mindset)—I was glad the crisis-team social worker was discharging her. She was discharged at 5:15 a.m. I was hoping we could use this as a major learning experience and work through it as a family. Her attitude took a 180-degree turn. She was angry because some of her clothes had been ripped.

The next day she was frustrated and complained about not feeling well.

Anna's moody, ignoring behavior continued until Sunday evening, although Mark spent time with her, with better results than I was having. I told Anna that one of her consequences was that she would walk a couple miles to summer school that week. She tried to protest to Mark, but I stayed firm. She was kinder after that.

I was surprised that the social worker was so tough on Anna, calling her manipulative and spoiled, and threatening juvenile detention. So many times, I would have liked to be tougher like he was, but how difficult and confusing it was to understand why Anna acted as she did and what effect my reaction might have on the situation. Not in this case, but many other times, I wanted to scream my head off and get things off my chest. I never did. I always held my tongue. Would it have helped to fire back? Or just broken our bond?

It would have been a relief to at least be able to ask, "What the heck is happening? Why are you angry at me? What have I done??" That, I did do sometimes but, as I've mentioned, she was mum.

July 15, 2019

I sent the second formal request for a forty-five-day extended evaluation placement in a therapeutic environment for Anna to the district lead for special education in our town. This was after the initial request was denied in June.

CHAPTER 33

Split

Show respect to all people but grovel to none.

—Tecumseh

End of July 2019

As I look back, it's clear the summer we spent working with the DMH/Metro Community Services in-home family services team was a disaster. Things escalated, with poor choices on Anna's part, such as drinking a lethal amount of alcohol (and walking out of the house when she didn't like something I said (I did not say much these days), wanting to control the in-home family therapy, and playing caregivers off against my husband and me. Unfortunately, Alex, her appointed clinician for in-home family therapy became very chummy with Anna, participating in bizarre "pre-meetings" at Anna's request. Before the family session, they would talk outside or in another room. That would have been okay if effective. However, predictably, it just resulted in a tremendous amount of "us against them" mentality. This is what the blunt social worker brought into the hospital had meant by "being manipulative."

The following Monday I decided to visit the local police station. On the one hand, I wanted to make sure they were not going to charge Anna for public intoxication, but on the other hand, I did not want them to allow her to run amuck, claiming that *we* were the problem.

"Your daughter has an alcohol problem . . ."

I said noooooo, that my daughter drank too much alcohol that one time but was struggling with trauma and illness, and it was a very serious situation. I left the station, feeling like the sergeant had a good understanding of the situation and how their support could be helpful in any type of emergency situation that might arise. He provided me with additional resources that worked with our local high school and with the court system. Two of these women proved to be invaluable to me, offering support and guidance whenever I needed it.

The following week we had a second meeting with the Department of Mental Health. After about ten minutes into the session with Alex, the assigned in-home family therapy clinician, Kevin, the assigned case worker, and me, Anna left the meeting. Soon the others left the house. A few minutes later Anna was about to go out with a backpack, I asked where she was going. "A friend's," she said. I said, "Okay, I'll just grab my keys. She wasn't listening. As she went out the door, I grabbed the backpack arm. During a struggle, Anna punched me a few times in the shoulder and chest and then bit my hand.

I released the backpack, and she flew down the steps and driveway, continuing down the street. I spent the afternoon driving around town and calling or texting her friends. I ultimately found out she was across town at a friend's house. It was the same friend whose mom made us the Borscht at dinner a couple of months back.

If I had it to do over again, I would have done things differently. *No way would I have gotten the police or the hospital involved.* Because things happened so fast and it was just seven days after she drank the alcohol, I was nervous. She also had the backpack, which, as it turned out, did not include any alcohol, only clothing and makeup. When I spoke to her friend's mom, I told her I told Anna she could go anywhere, provided she just told me where. Anna did not want to come home, but I told her I was coming to get her and that because I'd called the police, I was going to meet them there.

The parents of her friend were very kind, and I think they would have let Anna stay to allow her to cool off. That way, I could have come over to have a conversation with her about leaving the house without communicating her plans. I could have also explained that my stepdad's funeral was the next morning, so maybe she could stay with them, and we could pick her up in the afternoon.

Unfortunately, it was me this time that may have called an ambulance unnecessarily.

I also asked that we go to Kennedy-Parker Pediatric Hospital (because that is where her records were) instead of a hospital closer to where we lived. Another mistake.

By the time I arrived at Kennedy-Parker, she had already talked about how I wouldn't let her go out, and how there were problems at home . . . the resident psychiatrist consequently advised me I should play more board games with her and such. I let her know that I absolutely loved board games, but my daughter was at a very fragile place emotionally and not up for playing games these days, especially with me. The psychiatrist did say she would do us a courtesy by keeping Anna overnight so we could go to the services for my stepdad. She also asked me, *in a highly patronizing tone,* if I needed my hand looked at where Anna bit me. I wanted to say, "Are you kidding me?" but I just shook my head.

Another thing I would have done differently: I always went right into the hospital room to see her. But not this time. I couldn't bear to walk in while Anna was charming the nurses or the official sitting, as required, just inside or just outside the ER room.

I say "charmed" because perhaps I have not stressed enough that if she had not been ill, with quick-changing moods, she could indeed charm people. She had a quick smile and appeared to be taking the person into her confidence while also appearing innocent and vulnerable. These qualities often took me in as well. They were a part of her. If only she had had stable, manageable moods, she could have been, often, "the belle of the ball."

I knew she would be acting like she had done nothing wrong—telling them I was the problem. This was part of the illness and kept rearing its head.

Mark came a little while later. I was beyond frustrated that we were there because of Anna's reckless behavior, with so many trying to help and support her. It was also upsetting that I could not be with my mom. I could not wait to get out of there, and I was not looking forward to going back.

After the funeral I did not go back. Mark did the discharge, and I spent the afternoon with my mom and other family members.

The following Monday, I took Anna to her psychiatry appointment. After Dr. O'Shea met with her, he called me into his office so the three of us could talk. He told her that assault was very dangerous—not to mention illegal—which she knew. He underscored that he wanted her to go on another mood-stabilization/impulsivity depressor, but she refused. He then presented information about filing for a CRA (Child Requiring Assistance) and insisted that Mark and I apply. He explained the process to Anna. Not wanting to add on working with the court system, in addition to the healthcare system, we had been holding off on this, despite the recommendation from the advocate within the police department and another therapist.

After the session Anna was giddy. In retrospect, it was probably nervous energy. It was like nothing happened at all, but as with other things, I found out later that she was furious. It would be a few more weeks before I did apply, but when I did, I was ready. My personal therapist highly recommended the book *Addicted to Anger*. I already had a bunch of other books and resources that Anna was not interested in, so I did not buy it.

I went to the court, where I filled out the paperwork and left it—pending the assignment of a Child Requiring Assistance (CRA) lawyer for her. This was one of the reasons we'd been hesitant over the past year. Our sixteen-year-old daughter was going to have legal representation? It seemed unconventional and awkward, but that was the procedure. When the lawyer was assigned, I arranged to take her to a local Starbucks and have them talk. This CRA lawyer was retired from general practice, with some experience with Department of Mental Health, but not a lot of experience with trauma-related illnesses, such as reactive attachment disorder; he allowed Anna to talk when we went to the next meeting, a pre-hearing: a meeting where the probation officer got back papers from the lawyer to refile, getting more specific about the terms. When she listed the terms, the one thing that was missing was abusing alcohol and drugs. I wanted that in the terms because I felt as though that put her, and us, at risk. Anna was stating that she wasn't going to stop doing anything that made her feel better; the probation officer asked her if she was, in fact, doing any drugs, and she told her yes—she was smoking pot and not going to stop. She also voluntarily told her that she was shoplifting and didn't care.

My mom was in town for a few more days, and originally, we had planned to go on a fishing trip with her and my stepdad. She loved fishing but initially was not up for it. I begged her to go to the Cape with us for just a few days so we could go fishing and spend some time there, and I was so happy when she agreed. The night before, a few friends and I took her out to dinner. One of my best friends came down to the Cape, and the three of us went fishing the next day. We caught five huge striped bass. It was a blast and felt like a way to breathe after all the stress from the funeral and dealing with Anna. After fishing, we went to meet friends out at the beach bar at Ocean Edge. It felt so good to be away and to be with my mom and close friends.

The following week brought more episodes with Anna. On July 28, between 12:30 a.m. and 5:00 a.m., Anna left home (we think around 4:50 a.m.). She left a note, saying, "I'll be at school." She went to school but did not come home afterwards. One friend said she asked how to get to Boston, which made us especially nervous. We ultimately took out a missing persons report but later found her across town.

On Monday the twenty-ninth, Anna skipped her school counseling session, was not where she was supposed to be at pick-up, and again did not come home. At family therapy that week, she confessed she was addicted to running away, she liked risky behavior and wanted to be "out there." The meeting overall went well. Anna's active participation, even a few words, proved invaluable. The next day, we had a follow-up at the Metro Community Services office, the lead agency for the program we were in. The follow-up was for the incident on Monday. Five minutes after we returned home, she walked out again.

The police brought her home and threatened her with the Department of Children and Families (DCF), scaring her. That night, she cried because she thought she had almost been taken away. *She was not well.*

Anna was all over the place: one minute behaving as if she didn't care about any consequences and the next being upset about not being able to be home, go to school, be supported—exhibiting rapid swings from defiance to engagement. In this whiplash situation, things moved too fast to fully research them, prepare, resolve.

Telling this story, I have tried to restrict the content to my relationship and daily interactions with Anna, and how we have tended to her trauma providing love, support, guidance, resources, and opportunity, all of which Anna deserves. The parts that are left out include all the other daily, weekly, and monthly commitments in our life such as work, family, dog walks, bills, getting food on the table, health, volunteer and charity commitments, medical appointments, and so much more. Things all parents and families must juggle every day. We were at a breaking point, and nothing seemed to be changing. We would absolutely go to the end of the earth for Anna, but would that even be enough?

In early August, we enrolled Anna in basketball camp. But by Friday, she called and said she was going to fight someone, so come pick her up. This was a shame because she loved basketball and usually by the end of the session stood out at camp as being "most improved" player.

That weekend, we went to the Cape. Anna brought a friend, Kendra, and my young nephew Patrick joined us. Anna only talked to me at one point when she was mad at Kendra. Overall, she was struggling and did not want to swim, put a bathing suit on, or go paddleboarding.

On 8/12/19, Anna walked out of the house midday, when I asked her if she'd gone to CVS instead of the gym earlier in the day.

In August, there were a lot of meetings having to do with Anna's school IEP and placement, as well as discussions of her latest neuropsychology report.

The initial suggestion to consider the Walden School came from our education consultant, with backing from the neuropsychologist, Dr. Jeffries. He expressed concerns that a large local high school could potentially lead to difficulties. The Walden School specializes in providing trauma-informed residential school and treatment for females coping with trauma. It offered a nurturing environment for both living and learning.

He closed with the analysis that she was merely doing what allowed her to survive: "Ms. Becker's behaviors are a reflection of the type that were effective in helping her survive the environment in Ukraine and not a concerted, conscious effort on Ms. Becker's part to manipulate her parents or others."

With this recommendation, I had a call with the case worker from the Department of Mental Health. *But he totally disagreed,* repeatedly saying that it is not good for kids to be taken from their home, it might make her worse off. I understood, but unless he could lend us a small army, it would be difficult.

The bottom line is that this could have been a major turning point in creating a treatment plan that supported Anna in the right way, but the Department of Mental Health thought different. Not only did they criticize and deny important aspects of the report, such as the BPD diagnosis, in my view, and the need for DBT-informed family treatment, the recommendation for a single member of the treatment team identified as the team leader, and the caution that enrolling her in a public high school at that time would result in significant problems that could lead to disciplinary actions, such as suspension or expulsion, but none of the Department of Mental Health team members or clinicians or the program clinicians where Anna was ultimately placed *ever mentioned BPD* despite me having gone through hoops, trying to have them take advantage of a session with Dr. Jeffries where we could discuss the findings as a team.

CHAPTER 34

Dumbfounded

None of us can go back and start a new beginning, but all of
us can start a new day and make a new ending.
—Lisa Lieberman-Wang

8/16/19 – On the afternoon of August 16, Anna and I were at the library. After an hour and a half to two hours there, she asked to walk home so she could get some fresh air. Could she?

I was a little concerned but said, "Just be home in thirty minutes." She was (not) at home when I arrived, but coincidentally, I got a call from a friend who said she saw her walking in a direction away from home, on the other side of the library. She was "running" again.

Eventually, officers found her at a baseball field.

Unfortunately, she was aggressive, so they had to handcuff ("section") her and took her to the local hospital near our home. The term "sectioned" refers to the rules around a person with a mental health disorder to be detained for a certain period due to risk to themselves or others.

On August 19, she was transferred by ambulance to Bay Point Behavioral Health in southeastern Massachusetts. Mark did the intake. While she was there, we had many conversations with Anna, mostly involving her requests for medication to sleep vs. melatonin.

After several days at Bay Point Behavioral Health, Anna called me to let me know that she'd signed a three-day contract and would be discharged that Friday.

On Thursday I attended a pre-discharge meeting. The psychiatrist met with us first, alone. He said she was "a rockstar'" at the hospital.

What did he mean? I asked and explained that this is how she typically presents in a hospital—it's basically fun and games for her, with little work (is it that she likes getting attention? Having people treat her with kid gloves? Getting to complain about her home life?). I brought up Anna's attachment to me and the need for therapy.

He said, "Well, you can't 'see' attachment."

I didn't say it out loud, but to myself I said: Do you want a bet? *I can "see" attachment.*

It was prevalent in all the ways Anna had been pushing the boundaries, having outbursts, and showing passive-aggressive behavior, especially over the past six months. Also, even though I repeatedly brought up her borderline-personality-disorder diagnosis and the potential safety issues for my daughter and my family, the doctor and other staff brushed it off.

Her appearance and manner in the hospital trumped the reality that Anna exhibited at home, school, and in community environments.

After the psychiatrist spoke to us, the social worker went to get Anna and bring her in. At that point she was full of complaints about the hospital experience. We discussed the discharge plan, and I mentioned that we could take some time on the weekend to go school shopping. Suddenly, her demeanor turned inside out, and she said she liked it better at the hospital. "I'm not ready to go home."

However, frustrated and angry she felt with the staff, it was less than at home, and she liked hanging out with the kids.

The team encouraged her to stick to the plan of discharge on Friday, but she was firmly against it now. We all sent her to get better, she said, and she was not better, so she would stay. It was as if she were in charge, she knew best, which, though in part true because this was about her, was a matter of whatever direction she was currently fluctuating in, it seemed.

Knowing that nothing was going to change over the weekend, I reminded Anna that she had the high-school orientation on Monday afternoon, so going home as late as Monday would be tricky. She held firm. Nothing changed, so I stood up and prepared to leave. To me, it was her loss and another missed opportunity for us to do some school shopping or in other ways prepare for a new school year and a new school—a big transition.

I tried to remain optimistic. But as I mentioned Dr. Jeffries was convinced a big high school was going to be too much. It could be setting her up for failure. Mark and I agreed.

My phone rang Monday morning, "You need to pick me up! I have the school orientation today!" I was used to situations like this, so I said, "I will be there at 2:30" . . . Click. Another thing I was used to. When I arrived at Bay Point, they had me sit in the waiting room. After about thirty minutes, I asked if she was almost ready. They said they would check. After another ten minutes, they told me I could go in. They walked me back to the nurses' station, where a chaotic scene was underway, with a lot of kids around the desk. I asked a nurse if she could tell me what happened, and she recounted that Anna had created a scene on top of the desk, then begun damaging property, and attempted to assault staff.

During this exchange, Anna was coming up the hallway, swearing and yelling, "They #@%%# drugged me! They shot me up!" A staff member took us to a locker area to collect her belongings. While she was looking for her locker and belongings, I asked the staff what caused this uproar, and they explained that before lunch she had been sitting on top of the nurse's station, and nobody told her to get down. After lunch, she did it again, but this time was told to get down.

Being Anna, she refused. Grabbing at the lighting on the wall, she attempted to rip it down. When the staff tried to intervene, she became physically abusive, so they gave her a tranquilizer shot in her arm.

As we were walking out of the large room the psychiatrist was passing by. I rushed toward him "Doctor!" . . . Anna is supposed to attend a high school orientation this afternoon?" He looked at *me* furiously and said, "Take her!"

Did she cause the scene at the hospital because she was anxious about going to a two-hour school orientation? Was she no longer interested in going to the local high school after she won her six-week campaign demanding that we must let her go there? Was she mad that she did not get her way and sit on the nurse's station desk after lunch, but she was allowed to before lunch? Did she create havoc because she would be walking out the door within an hour anyway? What could they do?

Well, the psych doctor showed her, didn't he?

Then he got me in the middle by telling me to take her to the orientation. Quite frankly, although my gut said *don't go* for the obvious reasons, I agreed with him—*if she can cause all that trouble*, I thought, *then she should splash some water on her face and attend the orientation.*

We left—but the sedative would kick in soon. I was more than a little bit put out by that.

I still had a gut sense she should not go; she was too riled up *and was starting to look sleepy.* Also, I was frustrated, so tired of days like this. But the doctor said she should go, so I took her.

At the school, ten minutes late, I said she was a little "off" because she'd been given a sedative at the hospital. The gentleman in the office took a few seconds to register what I was saying; he gave me a funny look, as if thinking he did not hear me correctly. By this point, such outrageous situations had become somewhat mundane for me: "Oh, just dropping my daughter off at school after being tranquilized." But it was not the case for the gentleman in the office. I was going home to let my dog out, I told him, and would be in the parking lot after that.

I was glad I conveyed the absurdity by saying matter-of-factly that the psychiatrist had told me to bring her to the orientation, straight from the hospital, drugged. The Department of Mental Health clinician, whom I considered the weakest link in the team chain, called the hospital without my knowledge to confirm that the doctor had really said that. I found this out when I called about additional discharge paperwork. He did not question me again.

I was just pulling into my driveway when the school principal called. He said, "I have your daughter in my office. Can you please come back and see me?"

I said, "Sure, I'll be right there." This time, I did not rush.

When I arrived, the office personnel greeted me and walked me into the principal's office. Anna was slouched down on the chair, half asleep. The principal told me she was too tired to attend.

I said, "Okay, I will take her home, but the psychiatrist at the hospital she was just discharged from told me to bring her here. That's why she's here. This is not her typical self."

"I can see that," he said, looking at her falling asleep in the chair.

My words came out before I could catch them. The complication of trying to explain anything to anyone not in our immediate family, close friends, and healthcare providers was daunting. *Oh, excuse me, Mr. Principal, my daughter loves me so much that she acts out because she is scared I will leave her; she has difficulty with others because. . .*

Even that group did not understand anywhere near the full extent. I did not go on to explain that what I meant was *she is a bright, young woman, who for the better part of three years, just here in the U.S., has been going through a very difficult time. Not to mention the time before she even came here.*

The school, *his* school, did not understand any of this. I knew it wasn't the right time to question the team's decision to place her at Madison High because we had been fruitlessly skeptical of that decision for months, and the school administration still insisted they could accommodate her.

I should have also added that *if I had followed my gut, and not the psychiatrist that called her a rockstar just four days ago,* who told me I should bring her because she caused a lot of mayhem on his watch, that we would be home right now, she could be in bed, and I could be doing my other job just like he was doing his.

The same afternoon, I received a call from the team chair of the Pupil Personnel Services at Madison High. Because Anna had been in the hospital, she would need a reentry meeting, he explained, but it could not be scheduled until Thursday a.m. Before meeting that requirement, Anna could not start class. I expressed my dissatisfaction, but ultimately, I felt I had no choice, so I agreed that we would attend the meeting on Thursday a.m.

When we got home that afternoon, I got Anna settled in bed. She ended up missing our family-therapy session at the house with Alex that night. It pained me to have a session when we were not all there. Without Anna's participation, it was a colossal waste of time.

CHAPTER 35

Sympathetic

I was once afraid of people saying, "Who does she think she is?" Now I have the courage to stand and say, "This is who I am."

—Oprah Winfrey

On Thursday morning, I walked into the local public high school's reentry meeting with Anna. What a surprise awaited me: eight to ten people sat around a large, square table, all looking my way. To my recollection, but I'm not 100 percent sure, Anna joined from the beginning. At this point, her friends were not calling, she wasn't curling up with the dog or me anymore, she was a big shot at the hospital, pushing boundaries and ultimately angering the head psychiatrist. Nevertheless, at this reentry meeting I explained that Anna was a smart, loving, young woman, eager to learn and attend high school, but that she had been struggling mentally and emotionally.

The team appeared compassionate. They expressed their interest in supporting Anna and explained how they could do it. They had a program at the school where Anna could spend time in a classroom with a therapeutically trained teacher. Anna could choose to attend all her mainstream classes, or she could determine what schedule worked best for her. It would be up to her. The guidance counselor also enumerated ways she could support Anna and said she could see her whenever Anna needed to talk or get support.

With the Labor Day holiday upon us, we were all heading to the Cape. This proved to be a well-timed break after the chaotic hospital stays and the abrupt start to school.

This was what she wanted. Madison High at last. It was what she'd fought for.

Reflecting on that time, I think part of her insistence on going to the local Madison High may have been a reaction to her thinking we forced her to go to Aquinas and wouldn't "allow" her to choose her own high school.

She doesn't like to be told what to do. I get it. Some kids don't, and some adults don't. But this thinking was only in her own mind. We introduced her to schools, and she chose Aquinas. I realize now that they were all-girls schools, but many in our area are segregated this way. Anna was thrilled about going. A friend of Anna's mom asked me to have Anna talk to her daughter because it was her second choice, behind a co-ed school. In parallel, she wanted to be "normal," with groups of friends, places to "hang out," and sports and activities to burn off energy.

If I think about her life from age five to ten, it makes sense that being institutionalized in an orphanage 24/7 would probably make you very tired of rules and people telling you what to do.

The complicated part was that, due to her trauma, which we still had little insight into—but something must have happened to her, beyond, hypothetically, the betrayal by her mother—and the way her brain functioned, she had difficulty processing the reality that she was a minor, with parents (us) who loved her but had to impose basic rules and boundaries, as all parents do.

Massachusetts, by law, requires minors to attend school. Anna was compelled to rebel against things like this. The sad part was that until about a year prior to the start of tenth grade, she was so excited about learning and the opportunity and promise of going to college.

Shortly after she started at the public high school, Anna told us she liked being in the Achieve Program; she had great support there. The head of the program poured her heart and soul into her job, and the results were evident as things were going well. The school nurse was also extremely supportive. The same was true with the counselor, although I believe there may have been an incident where Anna became frustrated because the counselor was busy and could not see her.

The most concerning aspect was at home she said she did not like the other students—they weren't the same as her friends from before. This was awful to hear because even through the challenges of the past year, Anna had always been social, eager to spend time with friends. And the feeling was always mutual on the part of her friends when she was in elementary school.

Mark and I felt terrible for her. It was exactly what Dr. Jeffries warned against. How far-seeing he had been. This was a big school, no matter how small and intimate her program was.

One bright spot was that I received a call from the school to let me know that Anna wanted to try out for soccer. They asked if I could bring cleats, gym shorts, and a T-shirt up to the school. I was excited, so during lunch I went to a small sports store and got the cleats and shorts–grabbing a T-shirt from home. I dropped it off at school. A few days later came Anna's first game. I was over the moon excited, and I could not wait to watch her from the bleachers just like old times. I hoped this could provide some grounding for her to find her "place" at the school and build a community.

The game turned out to be a bit heartbreaking for me, and I was not sure how it was for her. The coach was a substitute, and Anna was sent out early in the game. I was anticipating seeing her race for the ball, block players, kick the ball straight into the net, and raise both arms in celebration! *This is not what I saw.* I saw a lost deer. Circling and moving about with no formal direction.

I could *feel* the confusion. I felt my own heart ache for her. The only saving grace was when I saw her after the game, and I said "great game," she smiled. It truly was a great game because she put herself out there; she tried her best, but her mind did not give her body and her confidence much of a chance.

After the so-so start, things began to deteriorate. It began with phone calls home, nurses' visits, Anna absent from classes, perhaps simply still in bed, not getting up for school. After-school time was messy. Having the Department of Mental Health team in our lives, visiting our home, continued to be interruptive, with little to no visible progress. I felt like Anna and I were getting increasingly further apart. She was looking for what was missing in her life, and she thought Kevin, Anna's DMH case worker, Alex, or someone else was going to find it for her.

September 2019

This is another place you may want to skip ahead to the next chapter. It was a period of deceit, manipulation, and misconduct. All seemingly small, but it was adding up like "death from a million cuts."

On September 3, more minor issues sprang up. First, Anna did not take the late bus, as expected, so I went to pick her up. Driving circles around the school, I looked for her, visions of driving around town flooding back. She had me believing the late bus did not come, but a couple days later I realized it wasn't true. She was playing games with me.

The next day, she asked Mark for forty dollars for school lunch. I questioned it because she was on the lunch plan and had money in her account. We found out later that she was buying a vape pen from someone at school. That afternoon, she again did not take the late bus, so I called her at 4:00 p.m. to check in because I was getting worried. Anna said she felt like walking. I said, "That was not the plan. You are twenty minutes late for Melanie" (her therapeutic mentor). Arriving home, she said she'd called me twice. My phone had no record of the call. I no longer knew whether I could believe a word she said, which she knew.

The next evening, after a discussion with Mark, I told Anna she would lose her phone for twenty-four hours for not following the agreed-upon plan, not calling me, and being twenty minutes late for Melanie, whom she knew was coming at 4:30 p.m. Anna said no to this. I said yes. She said, "Well, I will just run away . . ." Mark came in during this exchange. She said she'd intended to run away earlier anyway, so now she would just do it tonight.

Mark calmly took the phone. Though I stayed in the room for another ten minutes, her anger didn't subside. And she would not talk other than making threats about running away in the middle of the night.

I called her Child Requiring Assistance (CRA) lawyer. Since she felt he was advocating in her best interest, I thought she might listen to him. At first, she aggressively refused to speak to him, slammed the door in my face, and clipped my finger. After a little while, however, she talked to him and wound up laughing, apparently in good spirits.

I learned that just like with any child, but particularly with someone with BPD, you must set clear, consistent boundaries to provide a sense of security and predictability. Also, it helps to encourage them to take responsibility for their actions to help teach them about the consequences of their behavior.[14]

The next day, Anna refused to get out of bed. I encouraged her, period-ically, until 10:00 a.m., then told her there was no time to waste and I would drive her to school. My son and I had an appointment at 1:00 p.m., and I could not leave her alone. But she then left the house, not to go to the car, but to walk carelessly down the street. I drove up to her and asked her to get in the car, but she refused. At this point, I simply called the police to ask for help.

---

[14]   Grouport Online Group Therapy, "Parenting Styles and Borderline Personality Disorder," https://www.grouptherapy.com/blog/borderline-personality-disorder-parenting-style#:~:text=Set%20Boundaries%3A%20Clear%2C%20consistent%20boundaries,the%20consequences%20of%20their%20behavior.

I can imagine that this may sound over the top, but they had said it was okay, and there was nothing else I could have done but let her roam around wherever she wanted. Reflecting on this moment, I wonder if maybe I should have let her wander. In some ways, I believe my chasing her around was feeding her fire, and I should have trusted the natural consequences of not going to school. The part that was difficult for me was that even though she was very bright and showed a real flair for independence, I didn't know if she appreciated that it could be dangerous if she ever tried to get a ride from a stranger, despite us talking about it a lot.

We arrived at school at about 11:00 a.m. Pick up or late bus? She said "neither" and refused to provide an answer. When I came at 2:30 p.m., she was just inside the large doors to the school, engaged in a lively conversation with the vice principal. She came out laughing, and he said she'd had a good day. I thought: *Well, that's good because you are totally disruptive to mine.* It was maddening.

On Tuesday I excused her from school for a physical appointment. She ignored me most of the appointment and, for some reason, became angry when the doctor/nurse gave her a "healthy hygiene and behavior" info sheet for fourteen-to-seventeen-year-olds. She was also frustrated, in the car, because the faulty headphones that she bought weren't working. This led to a major outburst when I was driving because I told her she couldn't borrow my headphones. We had made an agreement that when she came clean about how the forty dollars was spent, she could borrow my things again.

She started threatening that she was going to go crazy in school.

The ultimatum worked, and to avoid a situation at school, I gave her the headphones, knowing it wasn't what I wanted to do. I felt petty and stubborn too, but I was tired of the nonsense.

It was a chaotic week, with her walking out of family therapy on Wednesday for no apparent reason, then skipping a class at school, forcing the administrators to search for her. When they approached her, or so they reported it to me, she was defiant and threatened to flee school. It was the same circus, just a different venue. Many things seem small, but in aggregate things weren't working. She was still crying out that she was *not okay*.

I picked her up later that day and we went to CVS and the market. She stayed in the car, listening to music. Driving home, I asked her what happened at school. She said she didn't feel like going to math. I asked her what about the importance of others' time? And she said she didn't care. When we got home, I told her to leave her phone downstairs; she said no. She went up to her room, packed her backpack, and walked out.

Once again, I called the police to see if they would look for her and bring her home, so they did. The officer talked to her about respecting parents and stated that phones were a privilege. Anna told the police they should stop wasting their time on her. I wish I'd thought to ask the officer to take the phone with her, even if only as a joke. That light banter might have uplifted my mood a bit.

The next day, she and I met with the principal, adjustment counselor, Special Education director, assistant principal, and counseling intern to talk about the previous day's incident and to review the safety and coping plan, moving forward. I was used to all of this. I am sure you are too, by now, or in your own lives. My husband, the education consultant, and I all tried to let the high-school team know there was a reason we had received so many recommendations from psychiatric health professionals to provide Anna with a therapeutic education environment, where the program is focused on adolescents like Anna who have experienced significant trauma.

On September 16, I urgently emailed the high school's special education team chair, stating "an emergency meeting needed." The urgency stemmed from Anna's escalating behavior at school. We could not wait until October 11 for a meeting that we'd been requesting since mid-July. The chair assured me they would coordinate something sooner.

Then on September 23, our education lawyer contacted Mark. A meeting wasn't deemed necessary; Anna would be transitioned to a therapeutic high school. It was a moment of realization for us, recognizing that despite all of our efforts, this had been the catalyst needed to prompt them into a decision.

The unfortunate part was the Walden School wasn't part of the mix. It had never been on the table from the school district's perspective. Surprisingly or not so surprisingly, they kept this information hidden from us for months. They would tell us what therapeutic schools we could select from; Lakeside Learning Academy, they now told us, was the only school accepting intakes at the time.

It was frustrating to rehash all these incidents that could have been avoided. I see that now. I fully knew it then but had been heavily outvoted.

From the first joint conference call with the Kennedy-Parker Pediatric Hospital, Department of Mental Health representatives, our education consultant, the hospital psychiatrist and social worker, the Madison High School team chair, and Mark and me, we'd informed them that at the Walden School, a trauma-informed therapeutic residential school for females, we thought Anna would have the best chance to thrive. Their residential housing was more like a home, and there was a sports and activities programs that included "basketball, yoga, drama, neurofeedback (aka EEG biofeedback), and other unique interventions."

I know now that despite the therapeutic environment having a more specialized support structure, it was not a guarantee that things would be different. I brought up the difficulties of the summer (getting alcohol in a friend's home, running away, bottling up anger that burst out) to the head of the school district, but she dismissed them as not related to school.

On Friday, Anna told the Special Education (SPED) teacher she didn't want to go to soccer. Ms. Radcliffe informed the coach. I don't think she felt well enough emotionally to do much at all. She thought the school was going to answer her prayers. She was going to run with the big dogs, but she got there, and everyone was focused on school, sports, theatre, etc. She said, "Everyone switched up, like they were all different, and I was the same." I can imagine how scary this must have felt. A huge high school, so many kids, so many classes, all new. She also wanted to walk home. I said fine. When she came home that afternoon, I said we needed to talk about her upcoming dance. Before we even began talking, she was crying and punching her bedroom wall. I went up and told her to stop. "Was it about the dance?" I asked. And she screamed no—lunging toward me—but didn't touch me. I told her to stop because she was scaring me.

A little later, instead of going up to her room, I texted her that we should restart the weekend; she could do anything she wanted—just provided she gave me a little communication. We watched a show together thirty minutes later, and the rest of the weekend was calm.

On Monday, Anna's outlook turned negative. "I hate school. I hate everybody in the school. And I don't want to go," she said flatly. I tried to empathize—recognizing, I said, how overwhelming it must be. And she said, "Finally someone understands."

I said, "Anna, you know I understand, but you are having a hard time accepting support and trying to do anything about it."

That afternoon she skipped soccer practice. She did not tell the coach or call home. She did call her mentor and our family clinician from the in-home family services program to say she was at the library. After she talked to the clinician, he called me at 4:00 p.m. to tell me.

An hour later, she came home from mentoring like nothing had happened. When I asked why she didn't tell the coach or me about missing soccer, she said she was scared to tell us. I said that she knew I would have been fine with it—we'd never had a problem about missing a sport if she wasn't feeling well.

She said she wanted to call her CRA lawyer, so I said, "You can call him anytime." They talked, and she laughed. Afterwards, he wanted to talk to me. He said, "I know you had a rough day." I told him it didn't matter, I was fine, and things had been like this almost every day for seven months. We had a good talk, but I told him that I thought he was enabling my daughter, allowing her to split, turning me into the enemy, even when I was trying to provide appropriate parental boundaries to keep her and our family safe.

I said, "You can continue to do your job, but I need to save my family."

Mark called Kevin at DMH, to determine next steps for DMH to cover the residential portion of an appropriate placement for Anna, while our town's school district would cover the day program for a 45-day assessment at a therapeutic high school. The assessment was to determine her needs and eligibility for *attending* a therapeutic high school. How ironic.

On Tuesday, Anna refused to get up for school again, so I waited for her to get up and get ready and drove her there around 10:40 a.m. *Later that day, I found out that the* Department of Mental Health *denied the residential portion of the 45-day assessment—claiming that no such place existed. And they continued to assert she would be better at home.* Not in a treatment residence. We could request additional home-based support from them, they said.

The next day, when she refused to get up again, I left a message with the resource officer for help getting her to school, and then called the guidance counselor to fill her in, but at some point during the call Anna left the house and went to the town square. The resource officer picked her up there, bringing her to school at approximately 11:45 a.m.

On September 20, Anna was marked "Tardy, excused." The adjustment counselor promised her coffee and a muffin for breakfast as a reward for arriving at school on time. *Anna did get to school on time*, but skipped "academic support," claiming to me that the teacher was being rude. I was skeptical.

At approximately 5:00 p.m., Anna insisted that I take her to the Ulta makeup store for eyebrow pencils that she had a gift card for. I said we were not going anywhere right then, but that she could catch up on her chores the next day, and then we could go. Anna left the room abruptly. After a little while, I went to check on her. I noticed that she had an eyebrow pencil. I left the room. A couple minutes later, Anna began making loud noises that sounded like she was either punching the wall or pretending to. She started throwing things around the room, and I yelled "knock it off," but she didn't.

When the disruption still didn't stop, I went in and told her to pull herself together and stop immediately, then come down to carry on with the night. Anna came down a few minutes later. We did end up going to Ulta. I felt bad that she was so upset about her eyebrows, feeling self-conscious that they were so light. The rest of the weekend was calm without incident.

On Sunday, Mark found a vaping pen in her room, and there were three lighters in her school backpack. It was a time where we decided to pick our battles, so Mark just took them and threw them away without addressing it directly. She did admit later that she also steals a lot, and that the lighters were stolen. Her reasoning was that the people who own the stores should not care because they have so much.

Those days, I was working from home, and when Anna did not get out of bed to go to school, I didn't push her. If she ignored me, I would go to my home office and start working. I told myself that I was not going to worry about it, which was difficult. During these days, every half hour or so I would go up and say, "Anna, you need to get up and go to school." This seemed quite impotent, but it was the only tool I had. We had used all the tools in the toolbox and then some.

I would also tell her I would be calling the school to let them know the status of whether she would be attending or not; this was required. Typically, she got up soon after that. She would sit and have breakfast with coffee, making enough noise in the kitchen that I would know she was there. One time, I walked out and asked her if she needed a ride, but she took offense because I didn't ask her if she *wanted* one.

Another time in this same situation, I simply strolled out of my office and casually asked "Ready to go?" Obviously, this wasn't a better method; her response was an exasperated shout, "How else do you think I am going to get there!" and proceeded to run upstairs to her room and slam the door.

The next time this happened, I did not ask if she needed a ride. I asked her what her plans would be for getting to school. That must have been a dumb question because, at that point, she blew up at me about refusing her a ride and walked out of the house. I followed her in the car and pulled up next to her.

"Please, get in the car."

Nothing.

"I have to sign you in."

Nothing.

Now a change of route. She trotted across the street and through a backyard. I pictured one of those foot chases on TV, but I was not going to chase in that way; I was staying in my beloved 2008 Chevy Tahoe that was once my dad's. It enveloped me in love and warmth every day I was in it. I wish I had a decision tree sheet in my pocket for these types of situations.

I decided to pull over and called the police non-emergency line to see if they could help. The timing was perfect because at one point she popped out of the backyard to the main road, and there they were. Are you taking the ride to school with us or your mom? She walked straight to my car and got in. Well, that was easy. When I dropped her off, it was the typical scene, with an administrator high fiving her, praising her for coming. She ignored me when I said I would pick her up at the end of the day. She had an appointment with her mentor, Melanie.

As I continue to write I feel like these singular incidents could all be chalked up as teenage growing pains. But they weren't. As I mentioned, I had another teenager and it wasn't easy, but it was nothing like this. She was hurting and wrapped herself up with a heavy cloak. If I said black, she said white. I felt like she was constantly toying with me. I was a grown woman who was being emotionally mocked by my sixteen-year-old daughter. I was not feeling the love, and sadly I was not expressing it.

CHAPTER 36

Stormy

You need to spend time crawling alone through shadows to truly appreciate what it is to stand in the sun.

—Shaun Hick

On the morning of Monday, September 30, I was suited up in my favorite white golf pants and blue pullover, busy accounting for golf balls and tees before leaving to attend a golf tournament with a few longtime friends that I walk my dog with. I had taken the day off from work and let Anna know it was time to get up, but there wasn't a stir. We did not know that it would be another dark day.

Eventually, before I left, Mark went into the room and told her to get up. I followed. But she pulled the covers over her head while thrashing around and started shouting negative things about school and yelling that she hated all the students. Breathe, I told myself.

At that point, Mark took out his phone and started videotaping Anna while she was under the covers, screaming. He thought it was important for her school counselor to see the difficulty we had getting her off to school. In retrospect, it was probably not a good idea to videotape the incident, I knew.

That is, from the standpoint of how Anna might react. At that moment, lifting her head a bit from beneath the covers, Anna saw him. My god.

Not skipping a beat, she leapt out of the bed and charged rushing him, her head down. But she stubbed her toe on the corner of the baseboard, and he backed out into the hall. When, a second later, I got out of the room, I saw her pounding punches to his back, his neck, and his head while he sat, crouched over with his arms, trying to protect his head. She was striking hard. With force. I screamed, "STOP!"

But it took me a second to get to her and grab her clothing so I could yank her off him. I had her cornered next to a wall, but she was still enraged. I told Mark, "Call 911." *Was this the right decision?* Yes, it was. Could I have calmed her down? Probably not. I was nervous *and* angry, and the vision of the punches to the back of Mark's head and neck, *after a stroke*, will forever be ingrained in my mind. I PROMISED myself not to take any chances with the safety of my family, and this could have been an ultimate failure of mine.

Chaos ensued when the officers came. Mark was distraught, talking to one quietly; Anna was also distraught—agitated and yelling while she told another officer why she attacked Mark. From there, it was all about her toe, and she was demanding emergency services. I was in the hall between both scenes. When the officer who talked to Anna asked me what I would like them to do, I snapped, "She should go to school!" Later I realized she needed help, and that was not the right response. In the heat of the moment I'd found myself inundated with thoughts of Anna mocking my efforts to send her to the hospital, only for her to be sent home. I felt, in frustration, this was due to all the providers who refused to hear that an attack at home was a risk, that she had been constantly crying out because she could not manage her emotions, her anger. However, they could not see it.

The police officer saw the scene as I did. She knew that Anna was in a fight or flight mode, dangerous, unstable, unwell emotionally. It was the officer's decision to section her and have her taken to the hospital for a psychiatric evaluation.

I was left again feeling like, *what happened?* Not just this day, but looking back on the summer, it was as if we were on a train speeding so fast that it didn't make the sharp curve, it sped right off the tracks, crashing through our home, my head, and my heart.

CHAPTER 37

Outsider

"Parents can only give good advice or put them on the right paths, but the final forming of a person's character lies in their own hands."

—Anne Frank

October 2019

Anna was admitted to Brookside Psychiatric Hospital after a crisis-team assessment at a local Medical Center. The intake at Brookside was particularly irritating. Anna asked her DMH clinician, Alex, if he could support her during the process, so he and I made plans to meet there. Incompetent, dishonest, and sneaky in his role, Alex, I'd begun to realize, was playing games with me. I was not aware that he was going to meet with Anna first. I am not sure that he did, but something seemed fishy.

They had gotten into this habit during our family sessions at home. Anna wanted to control the session, to get his ear alone before it started, to split, and then ultimately not even participate in many of sessions, claiming one reason or another. Similar to other instances, we, or I should say I, was the only one accountable for therapy, meetings, rides to doctors or any event at all where a parent was needed. Once, when I wanted to go to a wake, I'd told Alex via text I was going to go to the wake and be just ten to fifteen minutes late for family therapy. I had never been late or missed a meeting. He gave me a long lecture via text. I was so irate that I did not go to the wake until the end of our session, our session that ran late. This was even after our first planned session when he could not make it due to car trouble. We offered to come to him in Boston and meet at a coffee shop, but he declined, and we had to reschedule. He missed a second session shortly after that.

Back to the hospital: I filled out the intake paperwork, and then Anna came in at the same time as Alex. They exchanged very jovial hellos. Neither one acknowledged me, and we were in a very small room, around a very small table. I looked at them in disbelief. Neither mentioned anything related to what Anna did to her dad, but rather they proceeded to be chummy, while she smirked and laughed as if at an inside joke, while ignoring me. My eyebrows lifted. This was outrageous. The way he conducted himself towards me was nothing short of disrespectful and utterly unprofessional.

As with the past hospitalizations, because she was now over sixteen, it was her right to petition to leave the hospital within three days. The only thing that would change this is if a formal commitment hearing were requested by the head psychiatrist. This is not typical for someone like Anna, but it did end up happening later in her stay.

Anna signed the three-day release, expressing her intent to leave the hospital after three days. Because she was a minor, she still needed our consent; if we didn't consent to the discharge, the hospital would be required to file a report with DCF. A 51A report is generated when DCF receives a report of alleged abuse and/or neglect of a child somewhere in Massachusetts. So not taking her would mean we would be reported for alleged abuse and/or neglect.

Walking out of the building, Alex and I quipped back and forth—he insisting it was safe to have Anna at home, under which circumstances the Department of Mental Health would continue to deny her residential placement. I looked at him like he'd lost his mind. And reminded him what she just did to her dad. *He could have been killed.*

Three days later, Anna became agitated that DCF was not coming to pick her up. The social worker at the hospital said at a meeting while I was there, "*It does not work like that when you have no place to go.*" After Anna left the meeting, she said she would need to file the report.

That night at about 8:00 p.m. the head of the hospital called. Mark and I were both in our kitchen having a late dinner. She let me know that Anna and another patient had "eloped" around 6:00 p.m. This is the technical term they use for escaping from locked hospital facilities. It also can refer to running away secretly without consent. At first, I panicked, envisioning Anna in the back seat of a speeding car barreling south to New York. Mark immediately thought that they would be involved in something near where the other girl lived.

That night, we began collaborating with police who were working on the elopement case in the town where the hospital was located. Neither one of us slept, so early the next morning Mark told me to sleep a little while he went to see what he could find out at the hospital. I couldn't sleep. At the hospital, he asked for phone records because one of the nurses told him another girl had made a phone call shortly before the incident. The police said they talked to the boy who was called, and he admitted to receiving a call from the girl, but he denied having anything to do with their escape. He had not seen them, he said.

It turned out he was lying. Mark also learned that one of the girls had yelled, "We're getting picked up from our 'crip!'"

We spoke to the police multiple times that day to try to get them to go to the boy's house to look for the girls (in Saugus or Lynn). When they finally did, very late that night, the grandmother confirmed that two girls had been there the night before but left that morning.

The police located Anna and the other teen on Sunday and brought Anna to a local hospital in the area that she hadn't been to before. At the hospital, the first thing Anna said when she saw Mark was that she was not going to apologize for anything she did that weekend or anything she had done to him. He ignored it. She started complaining about being sick because she rode around in a car most of the weekend, partying.

Thankfully, Brookside had held her bed, so after the discharge she would be going there. Normally, if the crisis teams come in, they need to do a new search for a bed. We were grateful that she was going back to Brookside, where the psychiatrist, Dr. Hill and the hospital social worker seemed to have a very clear picture of the current situation.

The social worker encouraged me to visit, even though Anna was refusing family therapy and phone calls. I did, although at this time, it was the last thing I wanted to do. I was so tired of the violence, the unwillingness to accept treatment or take responsibility, and the utter disrespect, but I knew it was important. I knew she was not well, but every time I was in front of her, I felt like an emotional punching bag.

I recall visiting Anna at Brookside shortly after the elopement. She would not talk to me but would get upset if I picked up or read a magazine. When I stopped and tried to talk or ask a question about something mundane, she would end the meeting in frustration, saying she'd had enough, she didn't want to answer any questions. If I wanted to keep the peace, I couldn't talk and I couldn't be quiet. So, leaving was my best option.

Anna called me about ten minutes after I left to say someone else got chicken wings delivered. She wanted me to come back with some. *Something I would love to do in normal circumstances, but today, I was not going back.* I told her I would order them and have them delivered, which I did. Some may say "that's crazy, she did not deserve them." But at this point I never knew what the "right" thing was. She was in a terrible predicament, and it didn't seem to matter what I did on any given day. The next day the clock reset, bringing new hostility and new demands.

I spent the rest of the ride receiving phone calls from the delivery person and Anna, due to a delivery issue. I thought: *Wouldn't it have been so much nicer if she could have asked for something like this before I came, and we could share a meal together like in the past?* Unfortunately, this wasn't possible. In her mind, I was the front-line enemy, and there wasn't anything I could do or say to change that right now. Reuniting or reconciling with me in a genuine way was simply not in her ability or plans at this time.

One of the most telling days at Brookside was a meeting between the Brookside psychiatrist, the assigned social worker, the guardian ad litem, the Department of Mental Health caseworker, the DMH mentor, alongside Anna and me. Mark could not make it, nor could Anna's CRA lawyer.

That last attack on Mark had shell-shocked me; I didn't believe it was safe for Anna to come home. She had already had various incidents at Brookside after the elopement, such as barricading a staff member into an office and threatening to hurt them. Nothing was going to convince me that she was incapable of hurting us or someone else. Every time she did something and got away with it (at least legally), she seemed to up the ante, taking the bad and violent behavior up a notch.

At home the previous summer, especially during July, we'd had some sort of incident almost every day.

At one point, the Department of Mental Health case worker looked at me and said, "I know you feel guilty, I know Anna feels guilty . . ." I said, "Excuse me? I do not feel guilty. I have advocated for Anna each and every day, so no, I do not feel at all guilty." Anna was in the room but was dismissed after that. There were individual goodbyes and well wishes. The next minute, when everyone was settled again, the case worker looked at the psychiatrist and said, "Doctor, do you think it will be safe for them to have Anna at home?" The psychiatrist looked at him and said, "She is violent, physical, using drugs, not going to school, creating distance, extremely egotistical, egocentric, and there has been no movement to repair. No, they will not be safe with her at home." Everything stopped. The meeting was over.

After that, Anna still planned to sign another three-day release. However, the team determined it would be necessary to have "hearing to commit" because she was not ready to be discharged. There were critical differences of opinion on what a discharge would look like and where Anna would go. The hearing didn't result in Anna's commitment, but the judge pressed the

Department of Mental Health about what was holding them up in finding a suitable residential treatment program.

Anna was still expressing interest in going into foster care, believing more glamorous things would be in store for her there. The Department of Mental Health continued to say she should come home, while the psychiatrist and social worker contradicted this recommendation, saying we would not be safe. *We proposed a very promising sounding option involving a fourteen-day Adolescent Acute Residential Treatment (ART) step-down at McLean before coming home.* Anna's CRA lawyer and the court-appointed guardian ad litem, both of whom were involved in countless meetings with Mark and me as her CRA lawyer *tried to negotiate this step down to home.*

In our living room when we proposed the ART step-down, the CRA lawyer was confident that Anna would accept this proposal. I did not like having a middleman, but it was necessary. Anna may not have trusted him, but she would listen.

To make matters even more complicated, the Department of Mental Health case worker said there were no residential-type group homes or facilities like this in our area. We found out soon that his information was not true.

During this negotiation period, Mark and I engaged various current and prior therapists and professionals who had experience with Anna, her diagnoses, and the reality of the help she needed. This included her long-time current psychiatrist, her past psychologist, the staff at Brookside and at Palmer (where she had done a step-down outpatient program), and her previous therapist. They all recommended residential treatment. Mark requested letters from them to support our position that having her come home was untenable.

"Over this time her symptoms have escalated and now include symptoms consistent with Borderline Personality Disorder, Oppositional Defiant Disorder, and some symptoms of Conduct Disorder," one letter concluded. *It pointed out the danger of her assaults. And to our pleasure pointed out the extent to which we had done our best to help.*

To sum up, the conclusion of all the experts was that the symptoms could not be explained *by Attachment Disorder alone.*

Back at Brookside, Anna would not budge. Refusing our calls and the family meetings. She had zero buy-in into the Brookside program; her emotional distress was only increasing, and it was almost impossible for her to manage her emotions on an hour-to-hour basis. Meanwhile, she continued to talk to everyone about us—the accurate word is "bad mouth"—while stating, contradictorily, her right to come home and live in the house without boundaries or parental guidance. She was sixteen and a half.

She needed help.

At the same time, we were put in touch with a Professor of Psychiatry and Pediatrics at a prominent Boston medical school through the Department of Mental Health. Mark was there in person, and I was on the phone. The doctor talked to the Department of Mental Health case worker prior to meeting with us and again after.

He confirmed that the situation was difficult due to the aggression and other unsafe behaviors, adding that "the obvious emotional issues she is suffering from are leading her to be highly reactive and highly controlling." He noted how I expressed being "scared and how we are unable to set limits or negotiate effectively."

Due to Anna "crying out for help" (my words), the doctor was also worried that *"her behavior was her way of saying she needed a caring containment in a safe environment where we could do the reconnecting work."*

"I think it will take time and patient persistence for the relationship between A and her parents to be repaired. I also believe that Mr. and Ms. Becker do want to parent A and have her in their lives."

The doctor kindly offered to go to the hospital to meet with Anna if she was willing. This never came to fruition because the Department of Mental Health was soon to be mandated by the court system and the judge at the commitment hearing to stop dragging their feet and find a suitable residential treatment program. Shortly after, Baker House was finally brought up and discussed by the Department of Mental Health case worker.

McLean's SouthEast Adolescent Acute Residential Treatment (ART) Program seemed ideal, in our view. But not to Anna.

It would have entailed a two-week step down from McLean's to home. But Anna refused it because it felt like a trick to her: it was an offer from Mark and me, whom she didn't trust. Why we would not let her come *straight home to no boundaries, no rules*—the independence and freedom she was seeking—baffled her.

Anna felt bullied by the pressure that the case worker and her CRA lawyer put on her to go to Baker House; it was her only choice now, and she wanted *out* of the hospital. Who could blame her? She'd been living there *for almost six weeks*. She agreed to the move.

It's too bad that she did not understand that she could have come home *and had* the independence and freedom she wanted if she had been willing *and able* to follow some very simple boundaries. I realize now that she was offering all she was able, based on how she felt. Her emotions were on fire and she didn't trust that she could control her actions.

But as I reflect now, McLean could have been a pivotal turning point for us, exposing us to BPD experts and guiding us onto a new path forward.

Ultimately, Anna ended up at a group home and therapeutic program, with an additional Trauma-Focused Cognitive Behavior Therapy (TF-CBT) program. The program had the education tie in. It was a ten-minute drive from our house. We found out later that the case worker was very aware of this program. I have some ideas why he told us it didn't exist; you probably do too.

CHAPTER 38

Hopeful

You'll never find a rainbow if you're looking down.

—Charlie Chaplin

On November 14, 2019, Anna moved from Brookside Hospital to Baker House residential home, one town over from our home. The purpose of the move was to have her attend a residential treatment program and to give her a forty-five-day extended educational evaluation at Lakeside Learning Academy on the south shore of Massachusetts. A massive and scary transition for her, despite her attitude of coolness, covering the simmering pot.

Like the "middle of the road" between home and a hospital, Baker House resembled a home physically and comfort-wise, much more than a psych ward. It was a residence—but with trained staff as support (a small army that we did not have at home). It did not look or smell like a hospital (or the orphanage).

The residents had chores and helped prepare meals. There were rules and boundaries—if you broke them, you lost privileges. No negotiation. There was a built-in trauma-based program (TF-CBT) in addition to the group therapy, family therapy, and written program with stages to gain more independence:

> *Trauma-Focused Cognitive-Behavioral Therapy (TF-CBT) . . . uses cognitive behavioral principles and exposure techniques to address symptoms of post-traumatic stress following trauma exposure as well as symptoms of depression, behavior problems, and caregiver difficulties.*

Among the tools she would be working with were "coping skills" (e.g., relaxation, feelings identification, cognitive coping), gradual exposure . . . [and] cognitive processing of trauma-related thoughts and beliefs.

We could not parent Anna at home—she basically pushed all the boundaries because emotionally she was not feeling well.

At home I couldn't get her to school. I could keep her safe from meds (we had things locked, but you get the idea). I felt emotionally manipulated: I was anxious about what was going to happen next; the trained staff was not.

Here, Anna could not trick the staff into thinking she had ailments or needs she did not have to get meds except in the instances where somatic issues came up. They got to know her well. At least, initially, she couldn't hide out and get sympathy from the clinicians with stories or complaints. Later things changed a bit, but we will get there. If she did run or have incidents with the law, the police took into consideration that she was a resident at Baker House and had mental health issues.

At Baker House, she would have various privileges: the opportunity to work out at the local YMCA, learn meditation and many other relaxation activities, earn money through chores, and go out with other residents and staff for group entertainment. The individual Trauma-Focused Cognitive Behavior Therapy program (TF-CBT) *included a corresponding parent component*. We felt optimistic that with the right treatment she could begin to work with us to come home.

Before leaving Brookside, she had wanted to go off the mood-swing-and-epilepsy–control drug Lamotrigine (common brand name Lamictal°). I don't know why. To be in control? Most likely. This was understandable. She often said that she didn't know if the medication was making her feel better or feel worse. She didn't want to be told to take a medication if she was not sure if it was helping her, and she wanted to be part of the decision-making process often scouring the internet in search of silver bullets, the search for the magical cure.

At her request, Dr. Hill at Brookside progressively decreased her dose, reasoning that that would be better than her not taking it at all. He recommended that we work with her psychiatrist on next steps regarding medicine. I trusted Dr. Hill would discuss with Anna and potentially challenge some of her requests. I was comfortable, hovering on the edge of these discussions until called in.

I do know that shortly after moving to Baker House, Anna ran away multiple times and—on numerous occasions—was called out for being aggressive at school and at Baker House. After the dosage was decreased.

On 11/25/19, the day before Anna was to go to court for the CRA hearing, Anna eloped from the therapeutic school she just started four days earlier. Additionally, she caused havoc in the hallway and the stairwell and punched out ceiling tiles. She would have to pay for the damaged school property with the money she earned. It's not a coincidence that this happened the day preceding court.

One common constant theme was that some sort of chaos would preempt events like court meetings, school meetings, or even a home pass for Thanksgiving. The impending court meeting caused anxiety and stress that would be so intense (think about quadruple compared to someone with normal emotional regulation), that she may act out even if it caused a different or greater consequence, anything to stop her pain. With home passes and holidays, we saw the same; she may not have felt worthy of the event, or her unstable and intense emotions just thinking about the event caused her so much fear that she would end up sabotaging it in some way.

Sadly, the example of Thanksgiving is true and you will see later how sad it played out.

We could not have been more engaged at Baker House and, looking back, it was way too much. *There were very few ah-ha moments, very few hugs, and very few laughs. Maybe no laughs while we were within the walls of the house.* How did this happen? If Mark or I ever laughed, Anna would accuse us of making fun of her. She struggled with her sense of self and her self-image which caused her to be hypersensitive. I am surprised that I did not dread going as much as I dread thinking about it now. Not because I didn't want to spend time with Anna, but because it made my head spin. If I said black, she said white. I felt like I needed to play nice and not say a word about anything that may trigger her or make her uncomfortable. In addition, it was an exact replica of the *us vs. them* mentality we had to contend with that was pervasive when we worked with the Department of Mental Health and our family at home. I was still the bad guy.

Even though Anna was giving Mark or me the cold shoulder, we continued to visit her, staying as engaged as possible. We thought it was just a matter of time before something changed and a light bulb would go off in her head—*if I just follow this program, I will be home before the summer.* Unfortunately, that is not how her brain was working; she was only thinking about how she could possibly survive in this environment and at school on a day-to-day basis.

The day before Thanksgiving, I dropped off a gingerbread house from a friend for Anna to decorate. The next day, Thanksgiving, Mark and I brought a Thanksgiving meal. Anna did not want to have it with us but agreed to sit at the dining table with us and talk. She did not seem interested in engaging with us and expressed anger afterwards because she said that we didn't *talk to her*, we only *talked about general things*. To me this was maddening, and I always felt stuck between a rock and a hard place if I said anything, or if I did not.

Prior to Thanksgiving I received a call, asking if I was interested in being the annual gala coordinator at my son's Catholic high school. I was just about to take some time off from consulting. My brain and nerves needed a rest. *Could I do this? Could I balance this with my responsibilities to Anna and my family? Yes,* I thought. *I could.*

I was still nervous on my first day, but I was brought to my new office. The first surprise was my name and title placard outside the door. *For me?* My boss walked me into my new office and showed me a beautiful lamp that was shining brightly inside. I smiled.

I was so happy, working with this amazing team to coordinate their annual fundraising gala. Hundreds of people would be attending. And I was able to hold my correspondence, phone calls, and visits to Anna to nights and weekends. I would have a peaceful lunch in my office and enjoy a peanut butter and jelly sandwich almost every day—another mom worked in the office and, who, like me, didn't want to mortify her high school senior by going to the cafeteria. Another respite in this warm, nurturing environment. Knowing Max was in the same building brought me additional comfort. I was surrounded by strong faith, spirituality, and love.

Each morning a prayer came over the intercom. I listened carefully and jotted down a few notes in my planner about the prayer. Being in this environment gave me a great sense of peace. Another incredible aspect of this job was the opportunity to work in a Catholic environment. It was here, at the school, that I felt like I deepened my spiritual connection to God.

The month of December was typical of the starts and stops.

In terms of earning privileges, the elopement from Lakeside Learning Academy, her school, in November had set her back; this upset her because she was demoted from Stage 2—thus, not allowed to go on walks by herself.

On 12/6/2019, at Baker House, she said she needed a walk—a staff member agreed, going with her. But during the walk, she took off running to a nearby shopping plaza. While there, she shoplifted and darted in and out of a wide multi-laned street with LOTS of traffic. For safety reasons, the staff member had to notify the police. As a family clinician (or the program director) recounted to me, Anna was deep into fight-or-flight. Later, after many attempts to get her to stop flailing, they had no choice but to put her on the ground and handcuff her. This vision, naturally, was very upsetting to me.

By ambulance, she was taken to the nearby medical center ER. By the time I got to the reception desk, she had calmed down a bit.

Why a hospital? She'd been less than five minutes from the group home. But the rule was that a resident who eloped would need a safety-assessment evaluation by a state crisis team member at a hospital.

In her room, I found her yelling to one of the nurses, demanding a form to fill out—shouting that the police had hurt her and she was going to sue. The nurse said bluntly, "There's no form like that." I felt bad that she had to go through this experience, but there was not a lot I could do. I did ask her why she ran away, and she said because it was not right to deny her walking-alone privileges, as she'd made Stage 2; having run away from school, she said, should have nothing to do with it.

Like a quiet intruder, I stayed in her room while she lay in bed with her sweatshirt hood covering her head and half her face until the crisis team came and she was cleared to go back to Baker House.

We were at family therapy the following week; later that week we had a treatment-plan meeting with the team. Those meetings were heavy for Anna; there were too many people. The Baker House team did as much as they could to make her comfortable, but what they should have done is scaled back the attendees. I had the feeling that some members of the team were fascinated with her case, but they did not add any value to the meeting. Both Baker House and the state mental health department program teams had multiple members attend, including both directors; it was overkill, for sure. *Why did Mark or I not speak up?* I am sure you are wondering. But I have to—hate to—admit, I was a wimpy mouse, and Mark probably thought because Baker House was running the meeting, they could invite whoever they wanted. The result was another day for Anna to be consumed with worry, if not fear.

One part of the treatment plan I had a hard time with was the language around our *family-relationship goal.*

I can say quite confidently that Anna did very little family-treatment work at Baker House. But because she was doing other types of programs, she often exclaimed, "I've done the work; it's *their* turn to do the work too"—meaning Mark and me.

I typically did not push back on much, for fear of escalation. But on this topic I asked Anna in a session, what we could do better: "What haven't we done?" Silence. If you think this question is familiar, yes, you have read it multiple times before. We could not get any answer.

The third week of December, Anna joined the family-therapy session, mentioning that she wanted a pass home.

I was a bit taken aback. "I'm not ready for that," I insisted— unfortunately—because I think if family therapy had been mandatory, it would have provided us more opportunity to talk and for me to express that I was not about to carry the tension, straight back home, I was feeling in the meetings. In hindsight it's easy to see that this is what I should have said in the meeting—I was not ready to relive that tension. The trauma seemed to have rolled off her, though I couldn't believe it had. The fact that she couldn't open up about it was part of her disease. But for us, it went deep.

I had little fear of her being violent, coming home on a pass, but felt, that by skipping the meetings or attending erratically, now one, not another, she was "playing" us. I had hoped attendance at family therapy would be a first step, or big step, toward repairing the relationships that got snapped when she attacked my husband. I needed, before she came home for a visit, that to happen as an act of good faith. That's how I looked at it, but she refused. With all the mother love in the world, who would not, I wonder, have had a difficult time agreeing to next steps under those circumstances? So we were at a stalemate. But I had no idea it was to last. Prolong itself. Be insurmountable.

I continued to push back because of these games, and *there was still not the slightest motion to repair the break with us.* None of this was helping. It only added tension to an already awkward and uncomfortable situation. But Anna continued to refuse to come, or she would come and not participate, and I had a difficult time agreeing to next steps when she didn't live up to the new "plan" we'd all agreed to—which was, we all show up. *And participate.*

The next day, I received a call from the guidance counselor at Lakeside Learning Academy to report that Anna had said some concerning things. I appreciated the heads-up, but intuited it was due to not getting the pass. As part of the treatment plan, we had scheduled a set time when Anna would call home. But she rarely did, and the director later explained in an email to us that Anna would feel better writing letters. You see how I am getting my information from an intermediary. It was a stark contrast from just a year earlier. With my own daughter!

Even though I love letters and Anna has written me beautiful ones, it was another decision that led to less face-to-face interaction. In addition, the "letters" ended up being a grand total of only one to each of us; we wrote back, and that was the end of the letter trail. I feel like I complain a lot about these things, but so many of these plans and ideas became fruitless.

On the evening of December 22, answering the phone, I could hear screaming in the background: shouting, "I have to go to the hospital! My stomach hurts!" "Is she vomiting or has she a fever?" I asked Tiffany, who called me. She said neither. I told the Baker House staff member, "We had the exact same circumstance on Christmas of 2018." And that at the ER, we were sent home right away with an enema. "The stomach pains," I explained to the staff person, "are due to eating too fast or eating too much." "Nothing more serious." "I suggest you have Anna put a warm cloth on her belly and rest." I did not hear back after that.

Prior to the Christmas holiday, we had a few discussions about plans and how to include Anna. We ended up deciding to all go out for a family dinner. Three days before Christmas, Anna said she did not want to go. "But why don't you come to the Group Home for a visit?" However, to us, it was so impersonal. We never really had any positive family experiences there. As usual I said, "Sure, honey. We will do that."

But not to Max. He was disappointed—uncomfortable going to the Group Home. Upon reflection I don't understand why I would not have offered to have the dinner at our home. Another miss.

I ended up asking Anna again if she would reconsider. No, she said. In the end, we took gifts to the house. The visit went fine, better than I had anticipated, and she seemed to like the gifts. She made us a nice handwritten Christmas card. We then all went to Starbucks for coffee.

The day after Christmas, Anna joined Mark and me at a portion of the family-therapy session—to talk about a pass to get a haircut. She wanted me to take her. I said I wanted to stay in walking distance of the Baker House. Anna said (rudely), "But I want to go somewhere like Boston." To me, at the time she sounded like Veruca Salt, the spoiled little girl from the movie *Willy Wonka & the Chocolate Factory*, who sang "I Want it Now!"

She went on to describe *everything she wanted and if she didn't get everything "NOW NOW NOW," she was going to scream.*

Mark perked up. "I can take you to the gym in Boston," he said, "if you want an outing," happy with the idea. "And then we can go to lunch."

Boston was twenty minutes away; he was truly excited she was interested in going to the gym with him.

To me, this outing struck a nerve because the year before she tricked him into going to Boston, to the gym and ostensibly to see his office. It was a ploy. While he was in the bathroom, she rifled through his desk and took back her cell phone that we'd taken away. But Mark was a positive guy. He had loads of unused hope. He reported later that during the afternoon, on the outing, he tried to talk to have a heart-to-heart about a few things, but she got angry. So he gave up. And much of the time passed in an awkward silence. But they both enjoyed a good workout, working up a sweat.

At family therapy, Anna again brought up her pressing desire for a haircut. "Okay, on Wednesday," I agreed. The unfortunate effect of her requests, made with such take-over insistence, was that we each wanted to get our way. I always felt pressure, bullied, deducing—as it seemed transparent—that she only wanted to see me now if I immediately did things for her. I mentioned before, I know this sounds like typical teen stuff, but it was not. It was more about her subconscious testing me: if I say yes, I love her; if I say no, I don't. Gifts = love. Yes = love.

Shortly after we left Baker House, something—I forget what—happened in the car. I told her to stop immediately. "I am not going to allow any of this, especially today."

She stopped, and we went and got her hair cut and styled. One of the stylist's dogs was in the shop, and they let Anna hold it on her lap. She looked happy. I snapped a picture and sent it to her school principal. She was thrilled and noted Anna's smile. After that we went to a local bagel shop. Here the idyll ended, with Anna annoyed by the woman who worked there.

The following week when I arrived at a meeting at her school, Anna was in the office, and someone inquired about the haircut. Anna replied that she would not drive with me alone because it was not safe *for me*. "Going to get a haircut was a bad idea," she said. I said I had fun. Anna then said, "You do not know how I feel."

She was usually right about this; I could not read her mind.

She said later that when I was driving, she had thought about doing something to me but did not because she wanted the haircut.

In these situations, I never called a bluff. She succeeded in scaring me if this was the intention. In the next session she complained that she was bored in school and not interested in reading, unlike her intense interest in it in the past. This was a real turnaround. Remember how she wanted to buy books before leaving Ukraine? And as soon as Anna learned English, she loved to go to the library and pick out books to read.

PART 8

2020

CHAPTER 39

Stuck

Calgon take me away!
— from a series of television advertisements for
Calgon, a brand of water softener and bath products

I struggle with trying to illustrate how many healthcare, educational, and other service providers I was involved with in 2019; similarly, in this next period, 2020. On a weekly basis it had to have been at least ten. That part didn't change. It was like an Army of Chaos! Feel free to skip right past the winter, spring, and summer of 2020. There are a few bright spots, but it is primarily chock full of unproductive family therapy, meetings galore, more failed attempts at plans, until Labor Day weekend—when the ante is upped, and everything goes awry.

An army of chaos indeed. Stepping back, was I on a hamster wheel? Was Anna? It seemed no amount of intervention could get us off. But wait! A call. On New Year's Day, 2020, Anna called. She wanted me to stop in at Baker House because—yes, again—she was having stomach issues. No sooner had I gotten in the car, on my way, than she let me know that she was going to Target with the group and would phone when she got back. I thought: *Great, maybe some shopping therapy will help.* She called a little after 6:00

217

p.m., when I was making dinner. She was "feeling better." I asked if, because I was making dinner, it would be okay if I came to see her after school the next day. She said yes. "You are sure?" I insisted. "Yes," she was sure.

Approximately ten to fifteen minutes later, Daniel (one of Anna's advocates until she fired him) called. Anna's pain was bad, he told me, and she wanted to go to the ER. I explained that I had just spoken to her and she was feeling better.

To try and settle her fears, I said as soon as I was done cooking dinner, I would come and see her. "Did she have a fever?" I asked Daniel. "No." "What about vomiting?" "No." But he said he would check her temperature.

At the group home, I found her not screaming as she was earlier. I explained why I was not taking her to the ER—reminding Anna what the doctor at Charles River Medical Center had said last year: that in the case of a stomachache, only a fever or vomiting warranted a trip to the ER. But *this was different*, she insisted, while also admitting that she'd eaten a lot of hot sauce. I told her I could make an appointment with her PCP. It took an hour to assure her she was not in a medical crisis.

Using the ER doctor's admonition to avoid an unnecessary ER visit was helpful. I also felt successful at validating her concerns—empathetically—trying to do things to help her feel better, but explaining what warrants a visit to the ER and what does not.

As an example of Anna's rebellious nature and disregard for our rules, when she was seventeen, at Baker House, she pierced her own nose with an earring. Yes, with an earring, not at a kiosk or Claire's at the mall. We had a family agreement that if the kids decided to get piercings (other than earlobes), or tattoos, it should not be before eighteen. I say agreement because both kids agreed to follow this rule. A few days after she pierced her own nose, I received a call from the group home; Anna, they told me, thought it was infected; she insisted on going to the doctor. I told them I would look at it during our next pass, that day or the next.

When I checked it out, I told her, matter-of-factly, that she had a zit next to the piercing—so she should put some alcohol on it and keep it clean.

What I wanted to say over and over was, "This is what happens when you do something really dumb." Wouldn't that be normal in most households? But this kind of thing, I could never say. It would be like gas on a fire.

Such situations were tricky because there was often a fine line between a valid health issue and perception, worry, hypochondria, and somatization.

I learned, by putting my mind to it—out of necessity—to differentiate between what was truly serious (consequently needed medical intervention) versus what was largely in her head . . . It was interesting to see professional staff at Baker House wrestling with these somatic issues. Finding them just as baffling to deal with.

Reflecting on what might be the root of Anna's somatic experience with stomachaches I need to take us all the way back to 2017 to when Anna was admitted to Kennedy-Parker Pediatric Hospital after the overdose. Anna and I were in the sensory room. I felt like I was inside a blue and bubbly lava lamp. She was worried. There was so much talk of how ingesting so many pills could cause damage to the stomach. She was still feeling ill and kept asking me, "Did I ruin my stomach?" I told her no.

She received emergency treatment and was medically cleared. She wasn't convinced. As I mentioned earlier, throughout that visit, her treatment team brought up increased somatic symptoms. This started the cycle of GI doctor visits, unexplained pain, and constipation.

Do you remember how in Chapters 20 and 29, I said that "somatization" is real . . . and is the expression of psychological or emotional factors that pop up as physical (somatic) symptoms"? The information below takes the discussion further and is from the website *Somatization—GoodTherapy*.[15] To return to the point, as it's very important:

Somatic symptoms are not fake or imaginary. People experiencing soma-tization are not pretending to be sick for personal gain either—that is called

---

[15]   GoodTherapy ©, Somatization, https://www.goodtherapy.org/learn-about-therapy/issues/somatization.

malingering. Somatic symptoms may not have an observable cause, but the pain and distress are real. Individuals with this issue deserve as much compassion as those with a physical diagnosis.

In Anna's case, we dealt with extreme physical symptoms, but they ended up (upon visiting the doctor or hospital) having *no physical explanation.* That is, they were somatic. On the other hand, her eating habits, such ingesting an excess amount of hot sauce, also explained some of the discomfort. There were less-severe physical symptoms, such as an itchy scalp, when she would exclaim, "I feel like I am going to go bald."

Also, sometimes after being out in the cold, she developed big red blotches on her skin. As I thought about the less-frequent but still-bothersome ailments Anna talked to me about, I looked for more information. The information I found on skin in the National Library of Medicine was remarkable: "The skin is the primary organ of attachment in early life and used for communication. Therefore, it may be 'vulnerable' to the development of somatization. The most common symptoms presented are pruritus, numbness, burning, soreness, and blotchiness."[16] Could this explain the red blotchiness, or maybe the itchy scalp?

I spent many a day with Anna at the dining room table, being a sounding board for things like this. On one particular day, complaining of a "dry, itchy scalp," she said, "It hurts too. I feel dizziness, pain from my heart down to my belly. My left side too. I'm getting lightheaded" (not due to her medication, she said). "I'm bumping into things; this isn't normal. Five times I bumped into things, just today. I drink water all day, but my mouth is dry, I could not concentrate in class today, and I cannot remember anything." At other times, she had insomnia, felt that her neck was swollen, felt cold in warm temperatures, and had tingly arms and legs. I didn't mind being a sounding board because I knew that if she was attended to and I showed empathy, she

---

[16] G. W. M. Millington, M. T. Shobajo, J. Wall, and M. Jafferany, "Somatization in Dermatology," *Skin Health and Disease* (2022) Sep 29;2(4):e164, https://doi.org/10.1002/ski2.164.

usually began to feel better and could move on in her day. It took patience and practice, but I felt like I could easily make her feel better.

I started personal therapy for myself in the fall of 2019. There was a transition earlier that year because when we started DBT, by requirement, Anna could see only a DBT therapist. I asked Anna's former talk therapist if she could initially, at the outset, meet with Mark and me a couple of times to help us sort through the next steps.

She agreed, and it was so productive that I asked her to continue to meet with me—that is, privately, alone. She said yes, which was *truly one of the best things that ever happened to me during this time*. It allowed me a space to talk openly with someone who had a lot of experience and history in adolescent mental health. She understood trauma, attachment issues, depression, anxiety, and BPD; also, she was knowledgeable in other areas such as somatic and disordered-eating patterns. She explained some of the more complex topics to me and guided me to my faith and God when I did not know where to turn. Her insights, I found, served me better than any other healthcare provider I worked with. Another benefit was that I no longer had to continuously talk about my feelings and personal relationships with my friends and family. I got tired of myself every time I did it—that instead of having fun with them, I was sucking the life out of them or making them feel bad for our situation. I still see my therapist every other week, and it allows me to, in some sense, compartmentalize—being present with my family and my friends, feeling more positive and confident.

CHAPTER 40

Fleeting

God knows our situation; He will not judge us as if we had
no difficulties to overcome. What matters is the sincerity
and perseverance of our will to overcome them.

—C. S. Lewis

Because this material takes me back to more trying times, and my mind
and heart race, it is hard for me to constantly keep the reader in mind.
I also often hesitate while writing because I worry how things sound, and
what judgment I will receive. This is my daughter, whom I love. *What will
people think when I can't rescue her from all of this or take her in my arms and
comfort her?* The truth is, I am a strong person. I consider myself very loving.
But I could hardly rescue myself. Prompts and additional content as I go
along rein me in, and I again begin to see the forest, not just the trees.

Friday 1/3/20

Anna had been at Baker House for only seven weeks. It felt much longer. It had been four weeks since the last incident, running through traffic and letting loose in the store.

For Anna, December was consumed by the requirement to process the reckless event, as well as testing the limits at the new school.

On the family front it could have been the first opportunity to nip the never-ending home-visit standoff in the bud, before it even started. I say: could have been. Unfortunately, I felt too frazzled. I had no reserves. I just could not put forth options based on enough sound thinking.

I mentioned this earlier, but I wonder if it would have helped if I'd openly acknowledged my fears and anxiety. Like being open in general, probably yes. Did they understand that I was still in a dimly lit place? Did they not remember all the nonsense layered with heartache that I have put up with over the last eight months? Obviously, I was not expressing that.

Not only was I still reeling from the summer and fall and now this latest event, but I had a virtual revolving door of providers, educators, and other professionals offering their point of view, requiring information, asking questions, and coordinating more meetings and calls. What had we gotten ourselves into, stepping gingerly down the "precarious path"? My calendar is typically busy, but this was a layer of complexity that was overwhelming.

One of the first big meetings Mark and I attended was a treatment team check-in meeting at Lakeside Learning Academy on January 3 (with Anna, the school principal, the adjustment counselor, the chair of personnel services from our local high school, Anna's Department of Mental Health program case manager, and our family clinician from Baker House). Yes, the list alone is intimidating. And they did sit around a long, long conference table. A young girl—a minor, sixteen years old—and a war chest, as it were, of experts to work with her, all with the best intentions and a lot of training.

The purpose was to go over the educational component of a treatment plan that consisted of seven goals ranging from strengthening family relationships, to showing positive academic performance and attendance by attending 70 percent of academic classes.

They spoke as if Anna were not in the room; I had gotten used to this. But had she?

As a couple of months passed, she skipped many of her classes: in science (it was "boring"), in math, etc. She went to English class sometimes and sometimes participated yet did not follow instructions. They turned to Anna and asked what her favorite class was. "None," she informed them. They then asked who her favorite teacher was. Again, "Nobody." She had none. They asked her what was working, and she perked up to say, "I like playing basketball during breaks."

She explained that she did not like the small class sizes, but when asked if she liked having the support system in place at the school, *she said yes.* They asked about whether hands-on activity was helpful, and she said no. And did she prefer working alone? *Yes.*

These meetings were tough. Mark and I went in with a positive attitude and smile to show Anna we were there for her. But rarely would Anna engage with us. In thinking back, *I am quite sure she never did.* Was she just feeling uncomfortable, even embarrassed? Or feeling overwhelmed in her own mind and body? I have no answer, but whatever it was, it appeared to be consistent. Speaking for myself, my role seemed to me only to be to attend and continue to work with the team. I felt inadequate during these meetings, though we all focused on what was best for Anna.

What I would have liked to see was an acknowledgement of the BPD diagnosis, sharing this information with Anna in a non-threatening way (certainly not in a forum like this), and engaging in some of the current proven BPD treatments such as DBT (mindfulness), specific support groups, meditation, and other books and documentation that would help Anna understand that she was not alone, and others have gotten better.

The very next Monday, Maureen, the Lakeside Learning Academy adjustment counselor reported a miniscule incident to me. It started as paper throwing, and Anna may have been hit in the head with the paper, so she was upset. The situation was diffused quickly, but Maureen thought it was a good idea to let us know.

That night Mark and I attended family therapy with Catherine, our family clinician at Baker House, and Anna. It was obvious that Anna was agitated because she came in dragging her feet, plopped in her seat, folded her arms, and looked down. Many times, she would also not want to sit at the meeting table but sat on a couch near the table. This was nothing but trying to take some control of the environment, and it was a battle I wasn't going to pick. When Catherine opened the meeting, Anna said she had gotten in a fight at school. Catherine spoke up: "What type of fight was it?" Anna backed off and then out of the blue said she didn't feel safe. Because of this, Anna declined a weekend pass.

Mmmm. *Something small happens at school; Anna frames it as a fight; she is challenged by Catherine, backs off, and says she is not safe and declines the weekend pass. What just happened?* Is Anna trying to create chaos in the meeting? Is she frustrated by the pushback? Who knows? It is also difficult to analyze because in family meetings, Anna is not often challenged. If Mark or I push back on anything, there is an outburst. And—meeting over. The meeting moved on, and Catherine asked Anna and us if we could plan for her to call us weekly at 5:45 p.m. on Wednesdays.

Anna agreed to this plan. I felt as though this was just another set-up to fail. It was clear, from her failed promises to do this over the past month, that she did not want to call us. Catherine talked to Mark and me about the importance of staying connected and how Anna continued to refuse our calls.

CHAPTER 41

Bewildered

Only do what your heart tells you.

—Princess Diana

As planned, on Wednesday evening, Anna made the call. Before any pleasantries she said *she wanted to go in late* for school the next day, and could I drive her? When I asked why, she said, "I don't like the school, and I don't like the people . . . I want to fight everyone." And "You made me lose all of my friends"—in reference to *not having a cell phone*. A story for later.

Just a couple days earlier she said she was not feeling safe with us—wanting to fight someone, not trusting herself because of what she might do. Not that that frightened me in this instance. I had to go to work, I told her, which was true. And that she *had* transportation to school.

She started threatening not to go. If she refused to go, I did not have to move mountains to figure out why and how to resolve the problem. This was easy: to me. She ended up hanging up on me. I was used to this too.

Catherine called me back to say she was going to drive her because Anna was asking her appropriately. If it had been during a time of slight repair in our relationship, and she had wanted me to drive her *on time* to spend time together or for me to see her route to school, I may have been able to rearrange my schedule.

Morning prayer—Church is not just a physical building.

1/9/20: After school, back at Baker House, she got caught with a vaping device after denying having anything. When confronted with what they found, Anna walked out of Baker House. A scenario I knew well from at home. Right down the street was a grocery store and a small strip mall with a TJ Maxx department store in the same shopping center she made a grand entrance in before. Based on what was reported to us, she went into TJ Maxx and stole several items, then hid in the bathroom. The staff, from Baker House, had eyes on her from the moment she left, and while she was in the bathroom, either a store representative or the group-home staff member called the police.

As the police tried to deescalate the situation, she became aggressive, so they called an ambulance. The EMTs were able to stabilize her and allowed her to go back to Baker House without going to the ER for a crisis-team evaluation. I was happy to have avoided another superfluous trip to the ER but noted to myself that by skipping the mandatory ER evaluation, Baker House broke their own rule. I sound more and more like a tattletale; I just get frustrated when I think of how the rules changed, especially for me.

This was typical behavior whenever Anna got caught doing something she wasn't supposed to do or when caught with something illegal. *As a defense mechanism, I believe, her instinct to be aggressive kicked in, causing a lot of chaos so the initial infraction would become gray or forgotten due to the outburst or inappropriate behavior.* It also occurred to me that when the truth was found out, her first instinct was to flee; when in a corner or apprehended, it was to fight.

This was like the summer before at home: she could not manage her emotional response, so she took off out the door.

Over the weekend, Anna refused our calls. On the second day, I told one of her advocates, Daniel, to tell Anna that I missed her and hoped she had a good night. This was genuine, despite not knowing if it had an effect, one way or another at the time. But later at the house, at school, or in an angry rant if I did not tell her I loved her when I left a session (good or bad), or at the end of a phone call (good or bad), she would talk about being rejected and how much I didn't care. These were typical symptoms of BPD: fear of rejection or believing a loved one doesn't care.

I could never really tell if Daniel was friend or foe; he was never very open or receptive to me. I did know: he was foe. I have a really hard time calling people out like this. But it didn't bother me in this context. I never did anything wrong to him. Most of it related to Anna's splitting, convincing people that Mark and I were the problem. I was used to it with the many staff at the group home, but a couple in particular. I could sense their hairy eyeballs, and sideway glances even over the phone. I knew they had a difficult job, so I still tried to do some nice things for them as a team, like dropping off some meals at Thanksgiving.

1/13/20 – The "plan" was for her to go to two specific classes on her schedule, but on Monday afternoon I received a call from the counselor at the school, explaining that Anna walked out again. She walked outside, and when redirected back in, she went to one class. There, in this classroom or another room, she stood on a table and broke several more ceiling tiles; the infractions were written up. At 3:00 p.m., she incurred a two-day emergency suspension.

In addition to the suspension, as a consequence for the infractions, Anna was not allowed to have any electronics during the school day, except for her MP3 music because music was her coping skill—one of the few she utilized. Music. Sounds great, but unfortunately, we felt that her hip-hop music was part of the problem. Yup, the dull parents we were.

Anna chose to listen to explicit rap and hip hop; if anything, it seemed to validate her feelings that speaking disrespectfully, swearing, and practicing violence was normal.

Also, she was also going to have to pay for the damage to the school tiles. I do not know if she did—we didn't—but I imagine she may have. Anna would often boast that she never had to fully follow through with anything like that, and when she was supposed to pay for damages at Baker House, she never had to complete the payments. This was a common theme.

Anna claimed victory if she got away with things without a consequence, not understanding that almost everything you do has a consequence, even if it is not apparent at the time. We had tried to impress on her that the best thing is to take accountability and learn from everything, even failure.

When we got to the group home for the therapy session that night, I was expecting Anna to be reeling from the emergency suspension—out of sorts—but she was not. Basically, ignoring me, she went about her business or fooled around and—it was probably nervous energy—giggled a bit.

Though we did not know it, one of the clinicians at Baker House, Erin, had already "worked it out" with Anna that it was not a good day for her to join the session. It made sense to me that Anna's mood, her animation in the kitchen, could be related to the fact that she did not have to participate.

It was at least the second time Anna had damaged property at school. If she was upset, or remorseful, why wouldn't she come to the family meeting and share that with us? But this is a pointless question. She never did. Not once. Why did I keep hoping—in fact, set my hopes here?

Erin also explained the timeline of the prior Thursday's events: they were even more disturbing than first thought. Anna had refused to follow the police officers' request and was aggressive to the point an ambulance had to be called. She ultimately gave back the shoplifted items before returning to Baker House safely with Erin. Just bringing an ambulance to the scene costs a lot of money—mainly insurance but also co-pays. This issue comes up later, concerning ER visits. I often had a hard time getting in touch with Anna's caregivers. But the hospitals always called me to collect the $500 co-pay.

Erin also said that Anna was now claiming to feel "abandoned" by us. Real or imagined abandonment is typical for anyone suffering from attachment disorder or BPD, and she may not have been able to connect the dots as to what it meant that we kept showing up, wanting to be with her— but that in almost every instance, she was the one who was not engaging in family work, was refusing passes, and was refusing—and not initiating— calls. We understood that she may have equated Baker House with the orphanage, in which case we (I) were her birth mother all over again, leaving her somewhere, never coming to take her home—all the while that she waited expectantly.

In fact, I felt that her blaming us was becoming tiring. I was always ready to hold her pain and even sadness, but blaming me, or us, was different. I learned that this was part of the normal pattern of fear of abandonment, even though she saw us every week. At the end of the meeting, we agreed to stay the course and support her in any way we could. At the time, she was angry that due to the school suspension, she could not process the last stage of her Individual Treatment Services ITS. It would be revisited again on Friday, and maybe she would get out of her current funk.

CHAPTER 42

Patient

The strongest of all warriors are these two—Time and
Patience.

—Leo Tolstoy, *War and Peace*

What do you do when nothing works?

I spent some time during that week trying to find a new
psychiatrist; Anna refused to see Dr. O'Shea anymore. Dr. O'Shea was the
psychiatrist who, prior to her formal diagnosis of BPD, first mentioned it;
he had an excellent handle on her history and her medications. The team
at Baker House supported her decision, even though I thought a new
psychiatrist may set her back. This was a complicated case for any doctor, and
the thought of a new psychiatrist getting to know Anna seemed daunting.

1/16/20

On Thursday, I attended the reentry meeting at Lakeside Learning Academy
with the school counselor, the principal, and our family clinician from the
group home. Anna was completely disrespectful at the outset—casting

insults—claiming she gets zero support at the school, refusing to answer direct questions, and starting to argue with the principal about what happened three days before, when she received the emergency suspension. Then she walked out of the room. It was the old story of her not taking accountability.

"She is still suspended," the principal said. "Because she cannot collaborate with us on a schedule, she can't stay at school today. Baker House needs to take you back. Come try again tomorrow.

This was a good decision because *if there was nothing in the consequence that bothered Anna, the disrespect, rebellion, and poor behavioral choices would continue.* The principal also said that if her behavior did not get better, *the school couldn't keep her.* I believe that when Anna faced a consequence like the one the school presented, she was able to regulate her actions and stop the bad behavior, or so I thought.

The above consequence mattered to her. She did not want to get kicked out of school. The principal explained that for the two days while Anna was out on suspension, there was peace at the school; the school needed to recapture that environment.

The next day, they had the reentry meeting but said I did not have to come in for it, *thank goodness.* I was tired of the *unnecessary time involved—* only to put myself in a position where I was ignored and could not speak up due to the fear of causing an escalation.

That afternoon, I spoke to Rachel, the Baker House director, to let her know I was expecting a call from Dr. Brandt, Anna's primary-care doctor that morning about Anna's meds. Things like this seemed small but took time out of my day. The group home did their share of the work, and we functioned as a team, but not without added stress and late work nights to keep up with what I needed to do in the office.

I know I am complaining again. When I decided to write this story, I wanted it to have a narrow focus: my story with my daughter. But, like millions of moms and dads or other types of caretakers, I had a whole life going on.

While talking to Rachel, I mentioned a Thai restaurant down the street from Baker House. Anna and I had ordered from there before. I was hoping maybe Anna would go there with me for a quick dinner around 4:30 or 5:00 p.m., just to try to stop the refusals to see me. Or I would be open to taking her to the Y for some weight exercises, or to a court for basketball.

I asked if Rachel could let her know that we would not have to talk about anything from the past week or two, but we could play a card game or something at the restaurant. Rachel was going to pass this information to Catherine, the Baker House family clinician.

CHAPTER 43

Inundated

Feeling lost, crazy, and desperate belongs to a good life as much as optimism, certainty and reason.

—Alain de Botton

D o you think I simply walked away? I couldn't.

Immediately derailing the Friday morning meeting at Lakeside Learning Academy, Maureen asked Anna to push for the twenty minutes of class time, despite the written time being fifteen to twenty minutes. Anna became argumentative. They had to reschedule for midway through the day. At the outset of the next discussion, Anna would not consent to making a schedule and left the room.

Why didn't we see that any type of schedule, even when Anna could have buy-in, created an impossible situation of rebellion and chaos? Because she was stuck. We were all stuck. The plans, the schedules, the meetings, the large team, the family therapy, the trauma program, the enablement, was failing. Failing Anna *and* failing our family.

The family clinician sent me an email to let me know she thought the ideas I talked to Rachel about for a pass were great. She also said she'd received a call from school today because Anna wanted to check in. Anna was splitting.

On the call, Anna was frustrated but in control of herself, reporting that she'd followed the schedule that she and Catherine created for her reentry to school and had pushed herself to attend more classes than we planned for. She felt frustrated that from her perspective, even though she was keeping her end of the bargain, the school was having a hard time accommodating her. Looking at the email reporting how Anna followed the schedule, it's markedly different than how Anna reported it.

If I think back to three days before this, my mind settles on noting that Anna told Erin she felt remorse for her actions at school. Erin consented to her not attending family therapy. But now, after being served a two-day emergency suspension and an extra day for insubordination, here she was, immediately arguing with the guidance counselor about the schedule. A schedule she created.

At the same time Anna was feeling overwhelmed, I was inundated in the process of updates, plans, meetings, schedules, doctor liaison, and more. I just counted fifteen people I had regular monthly corresponded with and seven to eight that I needed to manage each week.

Looking at the list, I thought: *Something's wrong here.* Certainly, it cries, "too many people!" But I can only imagine how it was for Anna. It must have been even more overwhelming, due to her tendency to split and cycle through treatment providers, educators, and caregivers when she did not get her way.

At the beginning at Lakeside Learning Academy, they bent over backwards for Anna. Later, due to her lack of engagement and progress despite the enormous amount of support she was receiving, they seemed to hold her more accountable.

On Friday afternoon, Catherine let me know that Anna did not want to go with me on Saturday, due to everything that happened during the week. These last-minute changes having been normalized, I just said we would try for Sunday.

CHAPTER 44

Connected

Listen to the sunset; see its pretty hue. When you see it, think of me, and I'll think of you.

—Oksana Rus

That Sunday, I met Anna at the group home down the street from the Thai restaurant, as mentioned. We walked there. Things went well. Anna talked about everything, but we mainly focused on how delicious the food was. She told me how she hates school, who she hates, how she doesn't care . . .

Anna loved Thai food as much as I did. This setting—excited about sharing food so we could enjoy more variety, selecting fried bananas as a dessert and sharing the thought: *What on earth will they taste like?* Picture an egg roll casing that was sweet, with a warm but fresh banana taste within it. They were delicious, we both agreed! I always opt for Thai food if given the opportunity, and I have been picking up take-out or getting delivery from this restaurant (which is coincidently right down the street from the group home) for over fifteen years. So, a bonus is the warm welcome, the prompt service, and the cheerful goodbye.

1/22/20 – On January 22, Mark was going to take Anna to school for family night. Having a conflict, I couldn't go. As it turned out, Anna did not feel well, and she also expressed that she would not feel safe with Mark. *The next day, Catherine from Baker House explained to me that Anna had an epiphany that she did not want to be bad and did want to earn privileges.*

She said Anna didn't want to look like a fool and didn't want to get arrested. The day after this, Anna kept her end of the bargain. She was supposed to phone and did, but I was on another call, and she did not leave a message. When I called back, Anna said that Baker House was making her do a pass on the weekend, and she asked if I would bring some of her makeup.

On January 25, Anna and I walked to Starbucks. She wanted to go shopping at Marshalls, but I said we could if we walked—a fifty-minute walk. So she decided to take a rain check.

For most of the time during this pass, Anna was sassy and disrespectful when talking about other people. For instance, she didn't like the police. I objected that the police and service professionals were out there to protect us. She continued to disagree, so I dropped it. I understood where her feeling came from, as she'd had traumatic incidents that led to them, but it was also difficult for me to listen to the negative comments like this, especially when I wholeheartedly disagreed.

In our family session on the twenty-seventh, we talked about our expectations that she follow the treatment plan. For Mark and me, it had taken a long time for us to get Catherine and Erin, the clinicians at Baker House, to understand *why giving Anna home passes was different from giving her community passes. In spite of being aware of violent attacks she'd instigated, they seemed oblivious to the possibility that she might—unless we first built-up trust, mended fences, as it were—suddenly erupt in one at our house.*

Anna wanted to be alone at home, in her bedroom; she didn't want to be watched and didn't want people *on* her, like at Baker House. She wanted to go to get away from people, she said. I completely understood. Though it wasn't paparazzi, she must have felt followed around, the center of too much unwelcome attention—even people taking photographs of her, though they were verbal and mental.

Mark and I explained that we wanted to discuss more difficult topics with Anna, and for Anna to learn "mindfulness skills" to interact without anger, aggression, swearing, and threats.

Anna came up with a safety plan for home visits. "I will use coping skills," she volunteered. "I will play basketball." I was skeptical.

"You have not shown us to date that you can do this," I said.

So, once again, we stressed that some work in therapy needed to start *before* we could plan for the home visit.

The difficult part was that I felt she wanted to come home *only* to get away from Baker House. Very true, she missed her bedroom, her former sanctuary. I knew that.

When Catherine asked what she wanted to do at home, she said "Sit in my room and play basketball."

If she wanted to sit in her room and play basketball, she might as well do that at Baker House and use the broken-down hoop in their driveway. Our home was once again our haven, our calm and peaceful place, and from February to September the previous year it was the opposite. I felt like my head was a metal ball inside a pinball machine.

Reflecting on this, I wish I had put my own traumatic feelings, bad memories, and fear aside and offered to have her come home for the pass. To make matters worse the Covid pandemic delayed the visit longer. Another miss. I was stuck because I wanted to feel a tiny bit good about it. It didn't have to be like the "good old days," with Anna and me snuggling on the couch, eating popcorn, or lying on her bed, talking about school, boys, or sports. But the old me still held that memory of her and I was still that mom, I felt.

On January 29, Anna did the check-in call and told me *she got resident of the week* for good behavior. I told her how super proud of her I was. The call was going well until I inadvertently, inattentively mentioned family therapy. At that point, Anna raised her voice, saying, "We cannot talk about family therapy on these calls." In my head, I was like: *Whatever.*

The next day Mark and I attended the "final meeting" for the "45-day Extended Evaluation."

A lot had happened in forty-five days . . .

If I look at all the forms, it is hard to read between the lines to determine the purpose of the extended evaluation and of the final meeting, but I know the outcome was to determine whether Anna could fit into a therapeutic educational environment that would be provided by our school district.

Based on our work with an education consultant and an education attorney, the school district had already agreed to conduct the assessment *while* Anna was in a therapeutic educational environment. They did not agree to the one we requested, but they gave us two or three options, and we found Lakeside Learning Academy to be the best among these.

Eleven people were in the meeting, a big meeting with a lot of paperwork—something like you would see in a board room with large glass windows to view the skyline, and where all the executives and specialists fly in from all over.

Overall, Mark and I were impressed with the quality of the assessments from our local high-school psychologist, the speech-language pathologist, the special education lead, and the reports from Lakeside Learning Academy and Baker House. The problem was, we've had a lot of this information, and there was no direct correlation between the reports and the treatment plan.

The psychological assessment done in June of the prior year as part of the (Individual Education Plan) IEP eligibility assessment was a thorough report. But with bland recommendations, nothing that Lakeside Learning Academy was not doing.

Here's an example: to reinforce good choices and continue therapeutic supports. OR here's one: to encourage her to try difficult tasks and see them through.

The takeaways of the Behavioral Assessment system for Children, third edition (BASC-3) were that Anna reported *at-risk scores* in a number of areas: Sensation Seeking, issues with Attention, and Hyperactivity. Also, a clinically significant score for Relations with Parents and Self-Esteem was in the at-risk classification. Our at-risk scores were in Depression Atypicality, Withdrawal, Leadership, and Functional Communication.

The most interesting were Anna's teachers (at the high school), who reported Hyperactivity, Aggression, Conduct Problems, Anxiety, Depression, Somatization, Attention Problems, Learning Problems, Atypicality, and Withdrawal.

All of Anna's Adaptive Skills fell in the at-risk-to-clinically significant range.

Listening to this and thinking that we were in a meeting to determine eligibility for Anna to be educated in a therapeutic environment was astounding. That is, how could there be any doubt?

An insight that came to me from the second psychological assessment conducted by the Madison High School's psychologist was that comparative results from the BASC-3 test showed Anna's perception of her life and her behavior were wildly different than the evaluation made by three of her teachers, and Mark's assessment and mine. The high school psychologist noted that she was dishonest "in her responses to her behavior in relation to reports from her parents. There is a disconnect between Anna's perception of her life and her behavior."

The next day, Friday, Anna made some concerning statements at school, having to do with feeling hopeless, empty, and wanting to die. At that time, she appeared to be in a frightened state. This happened in the fall of 2018 at Aquinas.

Later that day, Baker House called me to say Anna had stomach pains and was screaming at one of the clinicians—she needed to go to the hospital.

I explained laboriously what you already know. She refused to talk to me. Anna was in a state. *No one cared about her. Nobody believed her,* she said. She would run, she threatened, if the Baker House clinicians did not take her to the hospital.

I repeated my tired comment.

Later Friday evening Anna repeated the same complaint with Erin, who wasn't in the loop and called me.

This was the third time Anna had done this at Baker House. As I've reported elsewhere, the ER staff and her doctor had advised me that no matter how hard she insisted, if she did not have a fever and was not vomiting, she should rest and put a hot compress on her stomach. Overall, she should watch her diet, try not to skip meals, eliminate spicy foods or foods that were known to cause stomach problems (caffeine, chocolate). Her doctor said she should take MiraLAX daily and try to do some mindfulness exercises or meditation for the stress.

After giving Catherine this message, I felt such a relief. In the past I did not do a good job of holding the line; on the contrary, I would just rush there. Many times, it was some sort of cry for help, and as much as I wanted to be there for Anna, I learned that I could spend hours at hospitals or an urgent-care facility, only to be told it was for nothing. The next day, I called Baker House at 11:00 a.m. Anna was doing great.

On Sunday Anna and I went for a walk, had some tea, and then went to a small restaurant for soup. She was very pleasant, not seeming unusually down or physically ill. I kept things very light. She did say she was getting restless and very bored at Baker House. That was understandable, I told her, and that she should try her best to do things she enjoyed. My brother-in-law also stopped by the restaurant. The pass went well, and Anna was overly attentive to me at the beginning until we had finished our lunch.

CHAPTER 45

Resolute

Relax into the moment and let the universe do the driving.
If there was a secret to happiness in life, I'd say that was it.
                                        —Jed McKenna

For Anna to have an experienced psychiatrist—one who understood and recommended treatment (not just medication) and who understood and monitored medication—was important. As I mentioned earlier, *I was looking to find another psychiatrist because Anna fired the last one. A very good one.*

Unfortunately, the medication part of her care took on a life of its own, with so much focus on meds that little to no attention or time was focused on recommending or coordinating other types of treatment like breathing work, meditation, mindfulness exercises, yoga, art therapy, or exercise. Never mind support for DBT.

In early February, I got a referral to the Charles River Medical Center Child Psychiatry practice. The new psychiatrist assigned to us conducted an intake on Friday, January 24 and let me know they had approved a psychiatric-medicine evaluation. I took the first available appointment: Friday, March 27 at 2:00 p.m.

In March 2020, just prior to the first appointment with her new psychiatrist, the Covid epidemic broke out. Obviously, there were no other options at the time other than to conduct the appointment by videoconference, but it appeared very difficult to treat someone with such complex illnesses this way. I had the initial conversation/intake with Dr. Fitzpatrick and right away thought she was a great listener, compassionate, a good fit. On the first one or two calls, Anna said it was okay if I remained on the line. After that I would be on the scheduled calls for the first few minutes, but Anna started reaching out in between calls about meds, and things quickly got confusing between the clinical team at Baker House, Dr. Fitzpatrick, Anna, and Mark and me.

That week, Anna's probation officer checked in. Yes, though a minor, she had an assigned juvenile probation officer as part of the CRA. There were court dates to meet with the judge to determine if the CRA requirements were being met. She asked that I invite Anna's guardian ad litem to Wednesday's team meeting at Baker House. Both the probation officer and the guardian were anchors for me. With a much sounder understanding of Anna, they could enlighten us to specific trajectories if she didn't start conforming to some basic norms very soon.

On February 5, we did not receive the weekly check-in call, and it turned out that Anna said she got mixed up on the schedule. We made a new plan for Anna to call Mark on Friday around 5:45 p.m., but she did not call. Surely, she would call on Wednesday. But no, no call. Just writing this makes me wince.

To prepare for the home pass, Mark and I had our standard ask—that she engage *incrementally* in family-therapy sessions: a "good faith" gesture. To me, it would mean a lot. It would let me glimpse again the beautiful little girl I could count on, whose promises I could believe.

On February 13, Anna made more concerning statements in school, and I got a call right before our family session at 5:00 p.m.

Monday 2/13/20

Reflecting on Anna's statement "I have done the work and now it's *their* [our] turn to do the work too," I tried to ask myself how we could support Anna. *What specific things? Is there anything?*

I was open to listening to how we could have handled situations better, while still providing an appropriate parental response that let her know her if behavior wasn't okay and continued that there would be natural, specific consequences.

It would have been helpful to have had back-and-forth discussions about what Anna thought we could do better, but if asked, she still—never—came up with specifics. Overall, I know her grievances usually had to do—insignificant as it might sound—with the phone.

I have written about times when we could have done things differently or better. One would be going back to early March of 2019, when she was near crisis at home, and spiraling after I told her that I saw she was soliciting for drugs on SnapChat. I asked for her phone, and she said no. Was this really the most important thing at that time? No.

When I didn't push this (for a variety of reasons), she calmed down a bit, probably not feeling as backed into a corner. She was still out of sorts, but the explosion came after I told my husband everything when he got home. He went up, like any parent disciplinarian. That is when the full-on fear and anger set in. She went into a crisis. She had been in one for a few months, but at that moment she was alone. Nobody to talk to or yell at because this wasn't the way she coped. She couldn't connect to anyone else *without her phone.*

So she felt scared and trapped. I tried to talk to her about going to the hospital, but she refused. We got the police assistance to help us because now she was spiraling further emotionally.

I believe if we had let her keep the phone, calm down, get some rest so we could have a conversation about how she was feeling, why she needed drugs, how we could help her, this situation would have unfolded much different. Instead, she saw the police car outside. I ask myself now, WHY? She couldn't believe it. Thinking back, I know I could have handled this situation differently. I still trust that she needed professional help, but it could have happened in a way that did not put us at odds.

On 2/14/20, the day after family therapy, I wrote to Anna's school counselor to tell her we'd had a good session where Anna participated, engaging with us in a group. True, though, she was mad at the end and walked out because she seemed to be expecting a home pass. Yes, she was mad as a hornet, again.

The reality was that her treatment plan had many components, and a portion of it was the family-relations aspect, but that was not the focus. It probably should not have been. It was distracting and gave her opportunity for her much-desired control. Baker House had a very detailed program and process that focused on her behavior and emotional regulation and her ability to succeed in the therapeutic education setting. The family portion largely seemed to be pushed back to secondary, and then the few months before she turned eighteen, nonexistent. It shouldn't have had to, but it took me a long time to realize that the constant pushing for her to engage with us as a family and requiring her to do anything to show progress with us was simply for naught. All it did was waste time and have her continue to push us further away.

CHAPTER 46

Embarrassed

When you tolerate disrespectful people, you disrespect yourself.

—Wayne Gerard Trotman

The above quote struck deep. To turn the attention for a minute onto myself, I did feel I was disrespecting myself. It was a blow.

When we went to family therapy on Monday 2/10/20 to begin to discuss the simple goals we'd come up with, we also wrote a long list of things we would do in an attempt to find what might help her. Anna refused to participate. Again. No, you didn't lose your place in the book and start reading backwards. Yes, you've read this before. I wonder if, had Anna taken a couple of minutes to look at them, she would have realized they were pretty simple. The list is below but seeing it now, I am not sure what I was thinking. Nothing was working, and it embarrasses me that I did not just cry foul and say, "This whole charade needs to stop."

- Say hello and goodbye
- Acknowledge presence of Mom and Dad (by looking at them and making some eye contact)

- Active participation in family therapy
- Engagement in car for the first few minutes during rides to appointments

You would think some of the things above would be spontaneous, but Anna was guarded; a quick hug, kiss on the cheek, or a mere hello seemed to be stuck deep within her.

> *If Mom or Dad calls and asks for a callback, call back, and if you do not want to talk, let them know you do not want to talk at that time. Offer another time or day. It would also be helpful if the staff could let us know if a planned call is not going to happen.*

We rescheduled for Wednesday 2/12. Catherine and Erin explained that I am not an Uber driver, there should be a few pleasantries and a quick expression of how she was feeling before she asked if it was okay to put headphones on. We decided to put that advice into practice Friday, when I took her to her individual therapy, and it worked well. She talked about her disordered-eating issues (they were still present). Then she asked to put her headphones in, and I said sure. As a joke, I said, "Good night." And she smiled. I mentioned this earlier, and it always made her smile.

Looking back, I recognize that family therapy was a key point of tension and, for me, a sign that Anna wasn't ready or couldn't work on a relationship with us. Showing up and not participating is one thing (and a step in the right direction), but not attending multiple times in a row was not fair to anyone involved.

Team meetings were also disheartening. In retrospect, it's possible it would have been better if we did not attend. They typically had Anna come in at the end of these meetings after the team had all discussed an overview of their updates. As I mentioned earlier, by the time Anna was summoned, she was understandably frustrated and tired. She shut down, typically not acknowledging us or communicating directly with us in person, or later on Zoom, although as you can imagine, there were different dynamics on Zoom, talking under her breath, hiding out of the camera view, whispering to the clinician. I learned early that she preferred one-on-one meetings and discussions.

I always wondered if this was because of splitting, not having a third party, like a witness. Or something else. She often used other people to talk to us for her. From simple things like *her toothbrush head is frayed*, to bigger things like paperwork she wanted, there were few times that the certain clinicians and staff asked that she talk to us directly.

There was a time later this year during *all things the same* that Anna was brought to urgent care for a stomachache and given another enema kit to administer at group home. I offered to support her, and although also through a middleman, she agreed. It was also during Covid when the rule was that parents and caregivers could not be in the group home. But they would break another rule for this. We set up the same as last time, but I was masked up, and on a chair in the bathroom versus the floor, rocking the tunes. She was very nice to me, smiling, laughing as if we were back in 2018.

On February 16, Anna called in the morning to wish me a happy birthday. I was out so we played phone tag back and forth and then we spoke for a little bit. I told her I was visiting my mom in Florida. And asked if she wanted to celebrate together on the weekend; she said yes. I suggested bowling; she liked the idea. (She changed her mind later, but I was able to look forward to it for a week or so.) It was brief but a nice conversation.

Since that Monday was a holiday, we scheduled our next session for Tuesday that week. I joined by phone because I was still visiting my mom. We had what we thought was a breakthrough because Anna joined the meeting, even though she was angry about a phone call she had just had. Despite this, she opened and said something truly revealing: *that the reason she was angry (mostly with me) was that she felt she <u>had to act fake around us</u> and couldn't act how she wanted with us or at home. She said she couldn't be herself.*

"Who is that?" Catherine asked. "Who are you?"

"I don't know," Anna said. Kudos to her for caring to find out.

She said she wanted us to allow her to act like she does at Baker House—having a temper when she feels like it, swearing, making threats—because they do not make a big deal out of it. Catherine and Erin explained that Baker House is a safe place, where they are trained to know how to restrain people, so they are not scared of her threats because *usually they are just that.* And don't mean anything.

They then explained that it's different for parents—it's uncomfortable and scary. Anna said, "They want me to be perfect like my brother." I don't know how much she believed this—it didn't come up often.

We tried to convince her that we were proud of all her accomplishments, big or small, truly amazed by them. And did not mean to make her feel pressured to be perfect in any way. Anna went on to say she wanted to be just as she was: free to do bad things sometimes—that she might do drugs, and she was sometimes scared herself—not knowing what she might do, what she was capable of doing.

This more honest exchange gave Catherine and Erin a view into what we had been trying to explain. Anna felt entitled to be home, with no rules, no boundaries, and a belief that she could threaten and swear without consequences. These thoughts were not "flavor of the day" like some other more significant things like hating pizza one week and loving it the next. This was a theme that started way back in the fall of 2018. Was this part of her pathology? Part of her illness? Part of her intense fear? Was it her trying to say, "I have had too many rules and boundaries, I do not want to be good anymore!" "I want to be free!" The bottom line was that we were not a disrespectful, rule-breaking, law-breaking family, so to be at home with us, she would need to figure out how we could help her get the support, or how she was going to get it herself so she could begin to understand that life at home was not going to be this way.

CHAPTER 47

Dismay

Your time is limited, so don't waste it living someone else's life. Don't be trapped by dogma—which is living with the results of other people's thinking.

—Steve Jobs

S adly, it started to become apparent that Anna still had not bought into the educational aspect of school but thought just attending was the key because it was the piece of paper, the diploma, that mattered. This thinking was the opposite of how she used to feel when she was younger, excited to devour new information or learn a new language. She did extremely well on her MCAS exams and was happy about it when the results came out, but despite this, her teachers reported she'd had a lackluster week.

The end of February, the team at Baker House conducted room searches on many residents and found contraband in a resident's room, as well as a note written by Anna—asking for more orange pills. I am not exactly sure what this referred to. Perhaps some sort of benzodiazepine: Xanax, Adderall, Diazepam, or something similar. In a room search on Anna, the director found razors, which were prohibited. This annoyed Anna because she did not like to use the cream that removed hair on your legs. Due to the contraband and the note, they required Anna to do a drug test.

She refused but eventually relented, and it came back negative. Also, they removed all her belongings from her room and told her she would need to check them out one at a time. They let us know that they were working on further consequences for the behavior of the house as a whole and would send an email update. This was one thing the clinicians did very well. They balanced the information. They didn't need to tell us every time Anna swore or needed redirection, but they did tell us about all safety concerns such as drugs.

February 20. Mark, Max, and some friends of Max and I went to a ski mountain in New Hampshire. Mark got chills and had a fever (maybe early Covid) on Friday night. Anna asked that we come to Baker House for a family dinner on Sunday and asked if Mark could make salmon. I told her, "Yes, if he is feeling better." But he wasn't as of Sunday morning.

I offered to bring the food and we cook together. She said no, she liked "the way Dad makes it." I ended up cooking, and Mark was able to come at the last minute. There was a lot of tension during the dinner. Mark and I tried to make small talk, but Anna was mad if he talked about classes, or really anything. The following week at family therapy Anna was mad because I was taking notes, and when I mentioned meds, she blew up, swore, and left the meeting.

In a way, I appreciated this. Wasn't it better than holding it all in? I told her I had a right to take notes but that because it made her uncomfortable, I would stop.

A couple days later I received a call that Anna had eloped from Baker House after admitting she was taking other people's drugs. It was a Friday afternoon. I had met a friend after work for a drink and some appetizers around 4:30 p.m. Baker House was tracking her, they said. I told them to please keep me updated.

If you remember, during Anna's elopements, typically I would rush out of wherever I was. But at this point there was not a lot I could do, and

I was not going to do anything at that moment. About an hour later I left the restaurant. I called Baker House when I got to my car. They told me the staff had lost track of Anna, so they filed a missing persons report and then went home.

At 7:45 p.m., the call came from Barnes & Noble in the Prudential Mall in Boston. Anna did not want to go back to Baker House and asked if she could come home. I told her that was not an option right now, but to stay tight and Mark and I would come get her. She was not calling from a cell phone, so I asked her to call back in fifteen minutes to tell her exactly when we would be there, which she did.

When I got to B&N at 8:30 p.m.—you guessed it—Anna was not there. The store manager said she left after making a couple of phone calls. New Hampshire had been mentioned at one point, and Anna was asking someone if they could pick her up. We began scouring the mall. I contacted security, and several officers asked me a bunch of questions, like a SWAT team. They were very nice, but it appeared to be the highlight of their night.

I was frustrated, worried that she was off in a car, headed to some other state. Was this just an expression of her impetuous nature, so unlike mine?

To my surprise, a little while later, what did I see but a security officer walking a sassy-looking, pleased-with-herself attractive young woman toward us? Anna. By this time, it was 9:40 p.m. She did not appear angry, but later told us that nobody was going to keep her inside, where all she could do was stare at the walls. "Why didn't you wait for me?" I asked. But she became verbally aggressive right away, so I shut my lips tight.

Mark and I kept things light for the remainder of the ride to the hospital close by to the group home. The team at Baker House confirmed that due to the elopement, a formal evaluation from a hospital was required. I was used to it, but it was red tape that was a huge time suck and something that I loathed. I can't imagine Anna was thrilled.

By now it was almost 11:00 p.m. Anna laughed and joked with the nurse at the Medical Center Emergency Department. She said her having to come there was a joke. She cocked her head and gave me a disrespectful smirk when she said this. Anna admitted to the doctor that she had been taking other people's pills and that she smoked marijuana that day. She also explained to me that she ran out of pills a few days before she got drug-tested on Thursday and was shocked that the test did not pick anything up.

At the Medical Center, her urine tested positive for cannabis. And in her pockets were forty dollars in loose bills when the doctor checked. The reason I asked the doctor to check is that I had asked the nurse to check her pockets earlier, before Anna went into the bathroom, but she looked at me like there was something wrong with me and didn't make a move. By this point, I was used to that.

3/9/20. At family therapy Catherine talked about Anna protecting herself—so as not to feel guilty or bad—because it is difficult to be accountable. "She thinks she is bad . . . She feels judged." Thus, she acts defensive, Catherine explained.

As Catherine worked through this description of her motives, Anna had a full-blown panic attack. Saying she needed to go to the hospital, she went upstairs, and Erin, the other clinician, was able to calm her down. About ten minutes later she came back down to the meeting room to say goodbye. I was happy she had recovered and that she was able to come and say goodbye.

The following week at family therapy Anna was upset because she felt that her real friends don't stick around; she wished she could survive on her own. *This was the beginning of a period where she would often say that she wanted to be independent and her goals were a version of living with a friend in an apartment in New York, getting a job and having three dogs.* There was certainly nothing wrong with that, as far as it went.

She went on to say that she could not sit still, had mood swings, and got annoyed easily. She didn't like it that she always had to answer when people addressed her, and her memory was bad, she said; she didn't want to talk to anyone, she added; nor—because she did not want to get hurt by them— did she want to have friends.

She was very tired of her situation, I could tell. I always thought she would realize that the sooner our relations improved a bit, she could come home and do many of the things she missed. But was that backwards to her—outside her comprehension?

Unfortunately, she could only seem to envision a life on her own *without anyone watching over her or telling her what to do.* Again, was this her destiny? Did she want to show us that she could do life on her own? Could independence free her of herself? Maybe.

At this time the Covid pandemic turned the world upside down; nearly everything went into lockdown. Anna was due to have her first visit in Boston with her new psychiatrist. But we ended up having it over Zoom. I had already had a prior phone call with the doctor, letting her know, among other things, I was concerned about my daughter's propensity to physical outbursts and intense anger. I added background details, winding back to her arrival in the United States from Ukraine, a time in which, concluding that although the beginning had been difficult, we had enjoyed a close relationship, where we had lots of fun cooking, singing, and playing sports. I also mentioned that for four or five years after arriving in the United States, she did very well in school. I went on to talk about the BPD diagnosis and the work with Dr. O'Shea.

I told the new psychiatrist that back in 2013, newly arrived in the United States, she had two years of productive specialized trauma therapy focused on acute and complex trauma from events that took place in Ukraine, prior to her adoption, and the exposure/response prevention model was utilized for a Tic Disorder and OCD symptoms.

CHAPTER 48

Optimistic

Writing is not life, but I think that sometimes it can be a way back to life.

—Stephen King, *On Writing: A Memoir of the Craft*

April of 2020, Anna began seeing Dr. Fitzpatrick: the bright, friendly psychiatry fellow at Charles River Medical Center. We shared lots of notes with her, but when I sent her Anna's neuropsych, it was password protected. I followed up with the information, but now I am questioning if she ever read it. The assessment from the neuropsychologist was spot on, and the diagnosis was clear—borderline personality disorder and post-traumatic stress disorder.

The therapy with her new psychiatrist got off to a hopeful start. *She and Anna spoke about her memories from the orphanage, including the lack of adult interaction, the scarcity of food, and the verbal abuse. They touched on when, in seventh grade, Anna started to feel depressed and her memories around suicidal feelings and cutting. Anna articulated that she was looking for help with her out-of-control behaviors and negative moods, while sharing that it was difficult for her to be around other people. She was afraid to make friends and expected to be left or otherwise disappointed.* Her abandonment issues.

She said that lately she had low motivation and couldn't focus. When asked, supposing she had three wishes, what would they be, she said to make it through high school, have her own place, and become better at basketball.

After the first meeting with Dr. Fitzpatrick and some initial med changes, one of the clinicians let the doctor know that Anna was not experiencing side effects, but frustration that she had not felt immediate results. She said Anna had built up a sense of miraculous results from medication in her head and expected it to be the keystone to controlling her emotions. Anna, she added, struggled to understand that the medication plays a *supportive role*; ultimate control and understanding of her emotions and behaviors belongs to her.

I did not take on a new consulting or contract role until later in the year, but I was still involved in volunteer work. Less stressful, but still time consuming. From April through August I felt like, on the *one hand, I was watching everything play out with the new psychiatrist and the army that was trying to work with Anna, and, on the other, I was completely in the middle of a tornado of feelings and emotions coming from Anna that were so scattered it was hard to keep up with what was happening one day until the next.*

I had become the central coordinator of the plans, schedules, discussions, theories, medication discussions, updates. This would have been fine, but much of the correspondence and many of the discussions were done individually by phone or through email, and it would have been so much better if I could have had open communication with Anna.

I felt like a middle woman. No matter how hard we tried to engage with her directly, she refused. We had a few periods where she came to me, and I felt as though things were changing, but realized it was because she was at odds with some of the staff members that she had been close to and typically used them to tell Mark and me things that were not true about her availability or whereabouts. It was also apparent when she was at odds with a clinician, and she would seek out another one and attempt to have her needs met by them.

I believe part of the problem was that the sound advice from the neuropsych report—that there should be a central person, ideally the DBT therapist that Anna was seeing, who should be the main coordinator of the treatment plan—was not being followed. Quite frankly and unfortunately, however, the DBT therapist was a weak link in the program. Sadly, she failed to participate in any of the calls or meetings, leading to her work with Anna becoming exceedingly isolated.

In May we were still doing Zoom calls with Anna. It was not going well. Every meeting was different, but they were hardly ever smooth. There was a lot of blaming and a lot of complaining, along with whispering and hiding from the view of the camera. There was some opportunity to listen to Anna as she expressed herself more reasonably *about why she needed a phone.* Even this didn't go well because I told her I would buy her a phone so she could go on community walks and could check in, which was required, but I also said that I was not buying her the top-of-the-line fancy phone. She blew up, and the session was over.

As I didn't say it before, I will say it now: when I brought up BPD and asked why there wasn't focused treatment recommendations, and DBT as part of the treatment plan, the director at Baker House answered, "We treat behaviors, not diagnosis." Okay. But that doesn't seem to be working. Things were not okay. Witness a little assortment of comments that emerged intermittently during occasional rants:

> *"I am not sleeping. My mind is everywhere. It's all me and my problems. I am never going to let my wall down. I like things, not people. I am not mentally ill. I felt unsafe for three days, wanted to kill someone, stopped myself. Some things I don't regret and never will. My stomach hurts but nobody is trying to help me. Nobody can fix me. I don't feel like anyone is listening to me. I am antsy, bored. I like to get out of the house, but I don't want to go to school.*

I would call them clues, but the puzzle had been at least partially solved a long time ago. No matter how much she cried out for help, and no matter how much she confirmed symptoms that were clear-cut borderline symptoms, it would not be acknowledged, and the treatment would not be focused on this.

At one of the Zoom sessions, I read a list of times where Mark or I supported Anna. A very long list. It was emotional to read, and we could see it was emotional for her to hear. My goal was not to upset her, but to have her pause and listen, and yes, evoke some feeling. Some emotion. Enough was enough. I could not listen to one more complaint from her about how we didn't support her.

May–July

The long calls with Anna's new psychiatrist started in April and continued for the duration of the time that Dr. Fitzpatrick was at the practice. Anna was about to turn seventeen; there were lots of med changes around this time, and I never felt that Dr. Fitzpatrick had the full picture. On the other hand, she was very attentive and supportive in Anna's care.

In May the director and lead clinician started the Trauma-Focused Cognitive Behavioral Therapy (TF-CBT). The beginning seemed to go well with Anna, especially because not having been able to start the program earlier. Correspondingly, Mark and I had weekly classes. During these classes the director worked with us on various parenting strategies, effective expression and regulation techniques, and a couple additional course components until the sessions came to an abrupt halt, which I will detail later. It was apparent that the director possessed a thorough understanding of the material. Also, I had already listened to audiobooks, such as:

- *Reactive Attachment Disorder* (RAD): *The Essential Guide for Parents* by Keri Williams

- *Healing Developmental Trauma* by Laurence Heller and Aline Lapierre
- *Loving Someone with Borderline Personality Disorder* by Shari Y. Manning, PhD

To give you a taste, this is from Keri Williams' Amazon description:

Adopting or fostering a child with Reactive Attachment Disorder (RAD) is beyond challenging. They may have violent outbursts, engage in outlandish lying, steal, and hoard food. With histories of early childhood trauma, kids with RAD too often break even the most loving of caregivers. Many parents of these children feel utterly isolated as family, friends, and professionals minimize the struggles.

Reactive Attachment Disorder (RAD) – The Essential Guide for Parents comes from a parent who's in the trenches with you. Keri has lived the journey of raising a son with RAD and has navigated the mental health system for over a decade.

One of the most helpful things about the books back then was to find strategies to help support Anna. Later they were helpful to me. I listened on tape to moms or parents in similar situations. It helps to get rid of any questions that all of this was because of things I did or did not do. I also listened to survivor stories. This gave me hope. I did a lot of praying that something was going to click with Anna and it might only be a matter of time.

At this time, Mark and I saw more focused engagement on Zoom visit calls, and in family therapy. I reported back to the team that "These can be pleasant or unpleasant for Anna and/or us, but she does seem to be able to tolerate them better and is able to recognize and acknowledge some past behavior. Anna has called me several times to talk about her needs or feelings and she has talked about what she looks forward to in the future. This is something new and promising."

For Anna and me, things were on a permanent up and down. The less I said, the better. We were able to do passes—for example, a day to walk around Boston. She wanted new basketball sneakers, so we were going to buy a pair, then walk around the Seaport. At one point when we were about to cross the street, we did not have the "walk" signal. Anna went, anyway, because someone in a car motioned us to cross. There was a second lane of cars, so I grabbed her sleeve, pulling her back, and told the guy no—pointing to the other lane and the signal. Anna became furious with me because I grabbed her arm. It was a shame; the day had been going well. But we could not laugh it off and regroup.

We still walked to the North End and got some ice cream, but I couldn't get her to engage the same carefree way as earlier in the day.

I also had conversations with her when she seemed to be getting way ahead of things but was able to keep them light and move on to more positive topics. One thing that has been apparent is the general theme where she believes she has answers, and often they are just thoughts or assumptions. This happens when talking about health issues, about visits home or coming home, going out in the community, and medications. Most of the conversations or topics, she has repeated many times over the past couple of years in the same manner. She seems to forget the past ones, and I believe she does not have a recollection of them. This might be from the medication. It's hard to tell. I do know that prior to being on medication, her mind was sharp as a tack.

At Baker House around this time the clinicians were pointing to negativity, somatization, threats, impatience, aggressive communication; also, being challenged, unable to ground, making poor food choices, unstable mood cycle, cognitive triangle, irritated, mad about everything. School was tightening up, making her accountable, which was frustrating her. This sounds more like a train ready to go off the tracks.

At one point on a group hiking outing, she pushed a female staff member. Anna was beginning to go through a manic period, or mania.

From the clinicians' point of view, they felt like it was difficult to have a reasonable conversation: Anna was not hearing the answer she wanted, so she continued to seek out different parties to discuss the same thing. Catherine described it well. The gist was that having been taking meds for what seemed like forever, trying different types, Anna felt none of them were working the way she wanted or expected. She put her foot down, stating that if a medication did not give the results she expected," I am just not going to take it."

Also, it was around this time that she started to see things in black and white.

Anna received a glowing report from a couple of her teachers, and she received a slightly above-proficient score on the Science MCAS. This is something I noted because it was before she started taking Ritalin and Adderall, prescription medication stimulants that work in the brain, typically given in the case of ADHD.

On June 1, in family therapy via Zoom, Anna was still upset about Mark having said, the week before, that her attack had traumatized him.

In this session she said that after that she wanted to kill someone and wanted to be violent.

Catherine: "But you didn't."

Anna: "I would have if I was at home."

Both Mark and I knew that she said this out of anger, but it illustrated the main problem we were having. Her extreme unpredictability. When things seemed calm and we saw the bright spots, it was usually not *if* a shoe was going to drop, it was *when*. I tried to find patterns with months, seasons, the sun, and the moon. There were patterns of behavior, but it was very difficult to find the WHYs.

On June 11, 2020, at 9:42 a.m. RARE OCCURRENCE—

A sweet email arrived that may look like a breakthrough—with a cute cartoon with "I love you"; it makes my heart pang. But this is also an example of the complexity of her trauma and illness. Did she have ADHD? No. Did she get antsy and bored? Yes. Had she been seeking drugs (and alcohol) to make her feel better? Yes. To help lessen her internal pain? Yes. Did she con Dr. Fitzpatrick into prescribing Adderall? Probably. Could I have stopped it? Yes. Did I? No. Did I raise concerns? Yes, but I did not think I could challenge (more than I did) a psychiatrist at NEGH.

She had wanted an ADHD-type medication for her own self-proclaimed inattention for a long time. In an email she sent, she talked about anxiety, not attention, issues.

This was one of her first "normal" emails, or conversations if you can call it that, in a year and a half. Was she trying to get my approval, or was she trying to say, "See, I got it"? Or did she just feel like a cartoon would be an easy way to say, "I love you"? I don't know.

What I do know is that shortly after she went on Adderall and the Adderall XR, she had an extended period of manic-like symptoms. So much so that she was later diagnosed as bipolar. I am sure any DBT specialist could analyze and respond with sound, thoughtful answers to some of my questions in a matter of minutes.

The Adderall, she said in the email, had "made my anxiety a little better." She was just letting me know.

6/12/20

In late June, Anna called me, laughing about her behavior in school and how she was typically *late for every class*. She went on to ask me why she went on Lamictal in the first place. Talking loud and fast, she mentioned that she was lowering her dose because she wanted to go off it.

Taken aback, I told her I did not think it was a good idea. She kept asking why she was prescribed it in the first place, and I said it was a mood stabilizer. "I feel like it has been helpful to you over the past few years." Getting angry, she yelled, "You don't know how I feel!"

I backed off. Obviously, I didn't.

"You are right," I said. "I do not know how you feel, but I also have been here, observing how things have gone, and to me it seems like the one medication that has been consistently helpful."

The next day the family clinician from Baker House let us and her psychiatrist know that Anna refused her Lamictal that morning. It figured. If anything, I had hastened her decision. She didn't like to be told what to do, remember.

She explained that Anna said she was willing to take it that evening but wanted to "experiment" herself.

The rest of the summer continued with correspondence and appointments related to medications, her participation, progress, or lack of progress in the trauma-treatment program, our own weekly or biweekly meetings with the director for the parent portion of the trauma treatment program. I continued to update the guardian ad litem, I had calls with the counselor at the therapeutic school and weekly check-ins with a teacher at the school. And both Mark and I participated in treatment meetings.

With all the assessments plans, I wondered: *Is anyone assessing her motivation to follow any program or plan? What's in it for her? What is her motivation for reunification with us?*

CHAPTER 49

Disoriented

If something bad happens, I will start taking my meds again.

—Anna

Anna needed to rely on someone at all times. During this period, it was the director at Baker House. And she was going away the next week, over the Labor Day weekend. So, Anna and the director developed a coping plan. The director wrote it out with the staff and reviewed it with Anna. Ironically, she said that she looked forward to hearing how everything was going when she returned. Yes, things backfired.

On the Sunday of Labor Day weekend, I received a call from Daniel at Baker House. Anna had refused to stay in her room overnight, but instead spent a portion of the night in someone else's room (not allowed). She was getting written up for a violation. Thinking back, it all sounded a bit odd, but I didn't think about it too much. Did he know he was being played? That Anna was MIA in the early hours of the morning? More to come.

On Monday night, I received a call that Anna had been involved in an incident with a staff member. Then a phone call late in the night, summoning me to the hospital up the road from the group home to sign the consent to treat. The hospital staff told me they had to restrain and sedate Anna, so I should go home and wait until the crisis team came in.

It turned out that a couple nights before, on Saturday, she and another resident left the premises and spent the early-morning hours riding around in a car with two males, drinking alcohol. Later it came out that a staff member, frightened, under pressure from them, had let them go. But when she wanted to repeat the night out, he said no; the upshot was, she attempted to push him down the stairs at full force; he feared he was going to fall down the entire stairwell but was able to right himself a few steps down. And called 911. But while he was dialing from the staff office, Anna attacked—punching him three times in the face. He then fled to the parking lot to distance himself from her. A lengthy police report described in agonizing detail what followed: Anna being one of the "notables," as she pulled out a butter knife and charged toward the staff member while the police were talking to him. She spit on an officer and exclaimed, "I can't breathe" a number of times, for no apparent reason other than she was apprehended, again, and enraged.

It also made sense that choosing to go off her medication affected Anna's level of anger and rage.

As soon as a bed was found, Anna was transferred to Bay Point Behavioral Health. She had been here before.

What just happened? Was this the climax of Anna's frustration of not being free? Was this a well-crafted plan like her elopement from the locked down psychiatric hospital a year before? Was it seductive? Was it manipulative? Some people know, she knows, but we will probably never know.

Whatever it was, it was dangerous, and illegal.

One of these people was her CRA lawyer. He called her literally the day after she arrived and told her the Baker House wanted her back as soon as a safety plan was completed. Well, that may be the case, but prior to this *Anna believed safety plans were a joke, and she has never followed one.* What makes this different? Nothing.

She had major charges against her, so at some point someone needed to have the conversation and let her know that it was not okay to push someone down the stairs, to punch someone, to spit at anyone, especially a police officer, and to grab any type of knife and try to attack. Three counts of assault and battery was no joke. It looked scary to me on paper.

A field storm was created, just by the sheer number of people involved: Baker House director, two clinicians, a staff member (who was ultimately fired or resigned due to his actions on Saturday night), a Department of Mental Health case worker, the Department of Mental Health program director, a school counselor, a school liaison, a probation officer, the CRA lawyer, her guardian ad litem, hospital intake personnel, a hospital case worker, a hospital psychiatrist, and Mark and me.

Because this incident happened at Baker House, the director took the lead.

After the team-meeting call on 9/15/20, the director sent out a note to the team, explaining that before she went downstairs to go back to her office after the Zoom call, Anna reached out to them. She said she was calmer and apologetic, stating that she was upset with herself for reacting and how she didn't listen to anyone—*that she didn't seem able to*. Finally understanding the director's message, Anna said ultimately, and on her own accord, that she needed to trust her team and if they felt strongly the Lamictal would help, she would begin to increase to her last dose.

The director went on to say that Anna understood the expectations around being able to have conversations and work on repair with her team (parents, peers, Baker House, and clinical staff), as well as accountability, as part of her safety-planning for return.

They also discussed rescinding the three-day. I was able to frame it for her, considering the pending legal situation, as it being better that she was working with her team than against.

The Baker House director ended her note by thanking everyone in an email and expressing that it was a much quicker outcome and turn-around than she expected. She was hopeful—but not sure—Anna would hold to it.

But who do you think won out? The Anna who "hoped" she would hold to it?

I am sad to say no.

November 17—Family therapy—Anna said she is bad. A psychopath.

Later that week . . .

Bang! Bang! Bang! This was a sound that I used to be familiar with at our home. But it wasn't upstairs in my house; it was happening at Baker House.

Another incident.

It was on a Friday afternoon *after* Anna had a home visit, her first since mid-summer at the Cape, due to Covid and a very volatile late summer and fall. Despite her feeling of being a guest in her house, it was fun. We baked and played basketball outside. This was a week *before* she was due to come celebrate Thanksgiving with us and our extended family. About an hour after Anna got home from school, the trigger was a discussion about her not following the rules at Baker House. Things escalated, and she began banging on a window in her room. A number of times. Unable to calm herself down, she ultimately put her hands on, and pushed, the Baker House director while also verbally threatening her. Three separate times. As the director's head hit the wall behind her, someone called the police, and Anna was sectioned and taken to a hospital on the south shore. The crisis team told Baker House they were not comfortable with Anna coming back to Baker House at that time, it wasn't safe. The crisis team agreed that an in-patient psychiatric setting was needed, and at this point the crisis team was still looking for a bed at a behavioral health or psychiatric unit of a hospital or stand-alone facility.

12/1/20

It took over a week to find a bed, and in the interim the director sent a note to the teams, saying that she and I left a message with the director of mobile crisis because she wanted to have a back-up plan in the event that a bed was not found, and they would deem Anna no longer meeting the level of care. This meant that she was not at risk of being a danger to herself or others, and she would technically be released from the hospital. The problem was that when Anna was rolled into a hospital and initially got comfortable, there was a honeymoon period where she charmed nurses and doctors so much that many did not understand why she was there. At this new psychiatric hospital, she did just that.

After she was admitted, both Mark and I had several phone calls with Anna. On Saturday, she was appreciative of the support. I visited her several days later, finding her calm, although a bit frustrated. Overall, she was not expressing remorse.

Despite the incident that brought her in . . . *assaulting the director of a group home to the point where she needed medical attention for a concussion. . .,* she was able to get her hooks into the social worker, psychiatrist, and nursing staff. From them, she obtained meds that she had not been on and nicotine patches, saying she'd been vaping every day at school and was in withdrawal. She told the psychiatrist a long tale about how it was the director's fault that she was admitted to the hospital.

Because the "assaultee" was the Baker House director, the Department of Mental Health program case manager, a friend of the director's, partnered with her to have the necessary discussions with Anna. I was grateful to be able to step aside. I could not fight another battle with a psychiatrist who was being fooled, so it was important that the Department of Mental Health program caseworker and the Baker House director lead the coordination of the team and discussions.

Anna *wanted* to go back to Baker House after this incident, so they were firm about next steps: what they would need to see before this happened. As I mentioned, I was insignificant to the clinical process, despite feeling like I understood Anna at least as well as the clinicians.

The discussion with Anna started with the typical "he said, she said." Anna claimed the wounds were not that bad, and the director should not have intervened. If she hadn't, she would not have gotten hurt. Anna continued to have a hard time understanding that no type of physical aggression is okay—not against people, not against property. Anna still has a distorted view of meds and continued to claim that she didn't have any mental health needs. Once she was independent—just wait. She would show everyone that she could be fine. She admitted to wanting to control her meds because they were the only thing she had control over.

I called Anna on Friday evening, and she told the nurse she did not want to talk to me at that time. I said okay, thank you. The staff person asked if there was a message, and I said—meaning it—"Please tell her that I love her, and that I miss spending time with her."

I was hoping that one of these times, the words would penetrate and resonate in some deep way, especially as right then she seemed at odds with almost everyone else now. I did not want her to split, but I wondered if any nurses ever said, "So, your mom called and left the message that she misses you and loves you very much. *That must make you feel good.*"

The director wrote the team, apologizing for an unauthorized visit to the hospital, claiming a staff member had brought hygiene materials and together they visited with Anna.

In fact, they brought her an MP3 player, plain and simple. She called the group home and was still making significant threats to the director and staff: she "would do it again," but worse. She was not happy with her inability to split the staff and director, now that the director "had her number." This behavior had been going on for a year. Was the splitting allowed with us, but now not with staff?

269

This is a repeat of almost every other time she had used physical violence. The difference here is that she did it to the director.

But . . . did she push too far?

One thing I found interesting was the comment from the director: "I needed some personal space to regroup after all the direct threats she made towards me and to staff this weekend." I understood this and was glad she made it known. I was taken aback, though, because I never had an opportunity to do that when I could have used it in the past. When they said jump, I said how high?

Even before this plan was documented I lost interest. And even though it ended up in a zero-tolerance plan, last straw, the only description missing was under "Family Therapy." Empty, blank space. I pushed back, but the feedback I received was, "We left it blank so you can determine your own plan." What? No thank you.

CHAPTER 50

Observing

Why does everything have to have a point? Why does it all
have to be part of a plan? Sometimes it's best to let things
just grow naturally, like wildflowers.

—Clare Pooley, The Authenticity Project

Towards the end of Anna's stay in the hospital, Elizabeth, the director at
Baker House, reached out to us with the plan for her return to Baker
House. Anna would return on "Close Watch," to be reviewed every twenty-
four hours.

Around this time, in December, Mark and I had Covid We were
both sick, but it was more serious for him. While still in the hospital, on
December 19, I received a call where someone shouted, "Hey, where are you
at? You were supposed to come and pick me up!!!" I said, "I think you have
the wrong number; this is Anna's mom." I am not sure why I said that, but I
had just woken up and was confused at the time because I knew the number
came up as the hospital's. He yelled something again at me and hung up. I
called the hospital staff back to let them know what was going on. I let them
know that I thought that Anna was playing games having someone else call

me. I asked the nurse to please tell her that this was not okay. The nurse asked if I wanted to talk to her and I said "No, I do not want to talk to her right now."

I called on Christmas Eve or Christmas Day, but she would not take the call, so I dropped off some gifts. One was a little jacket with "New York" written on it. She returned my call to say thank you while I was on my way home. I wondered if I would have gotten the call if she didn't like the gifts. I didn't appreciate this negative attitude I had, but by now situations like this were transparent.

On December 28, Anna had a typical discharge, with everyone jumping through hoops to organize actions, medication requests, and transportation. Baker House sent me a message, explaining that they were short-staffed, requesting that Mark or I drive Anna from the hospital to Baker House, and if we couldn't, they might need to call for an ambulance. Mark brought her back to Baker House.

Before the discharge I saw that Anna was on some sort of social media and checked with the social worker about it. The response was, "All the patients on South 1 were given an Amazon tablet for Christmas; the tablet is hers to keep, so feel free to do what you please with it!" This is a perfect example of the type of potential manipulation that occurred often. I highly doubt that all the patients received the tablets, and if they did, it was obvious where it stemmed from.

When Anna got back to Baker House, a frustrating pattern that emerged was that the clinicians were constantly asking what we would like to do for the community passes on the weekends, despite Anna refusing them unless they involved shopping or in other ways purchasing material things. If I suggested a walk, a hike, or playing basketball, she would refuse.

By this point I was so tired of the pattern and the clinicians giving her the first right of refusal. I decided I would give it one more try before the weekend, so I sent a note to the Baker House director, saying that Mark and I would like to visit on Sunday around the usual time of 3:00 p.m. Could we use the basement to play some sort of dice or card game with Anna and try to get things back on track in a low-key way? We also wanted her to agree to the visit before the pass was finalized and to an activity we would be doing. The director wrote back that Anna had been a little overwhelmed that afternoon, a little up and down in mood. Now, she was reporting feeling as though a visit might be too much. When prompted further, Anna had reported feeling as though she was having difficulty holding it together just on her own; more expectations, she added, might push her over the edge. The director, though, wrote a pass, just in case, leaving it available for Sunday if she changed her mind. So, more of the same.

PART 9

2021

CHAPTER 51

Replaced

I want her to be safe. I want her to be mine.

—Jodi Picoult, *Keeping Faith*

January 2021

Yes, I wanted her to be mine. She had been. Then she wasn't. But I wasn't one of those people who want their child with them at all costs. If the cost was to be replaced, then so be it, if she became more stable and happier. Let's see if that develops, now that she's seventeen, on the verge of coming "of age." Not that I could imagine her out on her own. I couldn't, not for the life of me. But she could. And there had been success stories. Take the fictional Johnny Depp film in which "a mentally ill young woman finds her love in an eccentric man who models himself after Buster Keaton." Was such a long shot open to her? In the movie, the brother came around, becoming convinced the two could make a life together. What about here? What about in the case of my daughter?

In the beginning of 2021, Anna was seventeen and still living at Baker House. As of over a full year, she had been there, away from the home we made for her, when bringing her out of Ukraine.

As you know by now, I was "hung up" on trusting an equal emphasis would be put into the family work and family expectations. However, the contract included only one line, titled "Family Therapy." I've told you this. We had been stuck before, and it appeared a deep rut indeed, even as it all continued to go backwards.

In addition, the contract placed a heavy burden of responsibility on Anna: expectations of what she could and could not do—basically letting Anna know that since the incident with the director, from then on the rules would be followed formally, and if she did not follow them, specific action would result. Would she adhere to these rules, knowing it was, for them, the Last Straw? Yes, because it was simple: there were a few consequences. *Plus, no requirement to do family work.* She thought she only had to hold it together until she was eighteen, so I knew she could white-knuckle it till then.

I am not sure why I continued to press on for family therapy. I talked to my therapist about it at length. Was I still going along to get along? I don't know, but I do have a tendency to do that in order not to ruffle anyone's feathers or hurt anyone's feelings. As confident as I felt about Mark and me doing as much as we could to help our daughter, I am surprised we did not *take control of the situation and have everyone freeze in order to take a look at what we were doing.* Not to look at any plans or paperwork but look at the circus that we had created.

Finally—the light bulb went off in my head. Why do we continue to force the family work? Let's step aside. Could we *step aside?* Anna's brain was not fully developed; it was hardly developed. She would mature. *But right now,* I told myself, she *is resistant, preoccupied, and has a constant need of attention and validation. She is preoccupied with herself and her purpose in life. She needs to push me away. Push us away when we are together.*

I continued explaining to myself, at last: *There are so many negative relationships getting in the way. Especially the mother–daughter relationship. To her, this relationship is full of demons.*

I'd thought this for so long but had been torn: *If we don't, she claims we don't care, claims she feels abandoned. But that is inherent in the situation. Her birth mother, her family of origin, abandoned her. She is still longing for her; despite knowing that she is and always was unavailable. That instilled so much pain in her, so much fear, so much anger and rage. I gladly held her pain; she transferred that anger; she transferred the rage and even transferred some fear, all to me.*

Regardless of anything I do, we do as a family, we have become that family of origin that she cannot hold onto anymore; for herself, for her sanity, she needs to abandon us. This is out of her control and out of our control.

It will be very painful to let her go, difficult to bring her safely to what she wants. This is in God's hands. I can only begin to give it up to God. I cannot fight this losing battle, for Anna's sake. I will look for the light. There is light and a path for Anna. I need to trust that her needs are being met in some way.

Someday the pain will make sense. We do not have all of the answers.

Increasingly, she was expressing that she wanted to be independent and show everyone that she could live out on her own.

I still believed that if Anna didn't accept any treatment, there was very little chance of her surviving on her own and that, as a result, coming home would be less likely. In fact, not coming home now looked like it was a *fait accompli.*

Should I give up on the hopeless cause of insisting she attend meetings she was guaranteed to dig her heels in against and not attend? Yes, that is my conclusion.

Anna has a lot of reasons to want to live independently. For one, she was tired, she told me, of people telling her what to do. Tired of people "watching her." It was sad that she had to live under such a tight leash, I knew. Being contained in an orphanage at a young age and not being able to eat when you wanted, play when you wanted, be nurtured when you needed, or have a sense of "home" or "family" is traumatizing. Feelings of abandonment by her birth mother, her grandmother, and her stepsister deepened her trauma and harmed her sense of self. And it looked like, to her, I suppose, she had just exchanged one very limited environment, where she wasn't free, for another. And yet she had insisted on going outside Ukraine, wanting, even as a tiny child, as much freedom as possible—in a different culture. She came to the Land of the Free, and she wasn't free.

One of the major setbacks at this time (maybe just for me) was that a new mentor, Nadia, was assigned to support Anna. Initially I was excited. Anna's first mentor, Melanie—amazing in so many ways—was from the same state program. One of the many things that had been great about Melanie was that I felt comfortable with her decisions on how to support Anna. She created a mindfulness plan, which she shared with me and updated, through text or email with successes or concerns. This did not need to happen often because she understood Anna's needs and focused on her strengths as much as areas to work on. In such a comfortable, safe place, Anna could express herself and be supported, without having her negativity toward us validated. Anna loved to go with Melanie in her car and listen to music and take trips to Starbucks. This gave her a sense of freedom, almost like having a big sister.

Grounding. One day Anna came home with a worksheet on Grounding; her mentor worked with her on reviewing the principles. There was a blue sticky in it that had a few notes: "punch a pillow, and rip paper." Ripping paper was something that relieved tension for Anna, so it was a go-to coping skill at home.

Grounding techniques work by "grounding" you in the present moment and pulling you away from intrusive thoughts or feelings. Not only in the sense of having your "feet on the ground" but also you're having your "mind on the ground." There is a simple but fascinating article in Psychology Today online; When you turn your attention away from thoughts, memories, or worries, you can refocus on the present moment.[17]

I learned that I had been doing a form of "grounding" ever since our dog was a puppy, when I'd take her out to the woods or park for a walk in the

---

[17] Zamfira Parincu and Tchiki Davis, "What Are Grounding Techniques?" https://www.psychologytoday.com/us/blog/click-here-for-happiness/202208/what-are-grounding-techniques. The quote is from J. Fisher (1999), "The Work of Stabilization in Trauma Treatment," *Trauma Center Lecture Series*, Boston, Massachusetts.

morning. It's probably the reason I do not feel like I can start my day without my feet hitting the ground, in nature. Even though I am not barefoot, these grounding walks help me clear my head and increase my energy.

Early on, Anna showered me with beautiful notes, poems, and cards. One of my favorite possessions is a Mother's Day jar labeled "The reasons why I love you." I often open it and pull out a few of the sayings to read.

. . . You are lovely.

. . . You are gentle.

. . . You are beautiful.

. . . When I am sick you always give me my medicine.

. . . You make the best pancakes.

. . . You put me to bed every night.

I guess I was stuck because I couldn't get out of my mind the memory of those days, that relationship.

I had hoped Nadia would help Anna comprehend how difficult it is to be out on your own at eighteen.

As a mentor and role model, she seemed competent, and we looked forward to meeting her. She spoke about working with us closely, so we were excited about that as well. In our minds, we thought she could encourage Anna to participate in treatment and eventually come home with us instead of seeking independence and breaking ties with us. Unfortunately, the opposite happened.

Nadia seemed to reinforce Anna's notion that a lot of teens and young adults do not get along with their parents or moms. What I eventually realized was that she did not have any experience with the complicated nature of Anna's illnesses, any history of our past eight years as a family, or knowledge of the myriad treatment providers' plans and treatment plans already attempted. She also lacked a sophisticated understanding of the behaviors that stemmed from Anna's illness, as well as her disengagement in treatment.

Most confusing, she began to work with Anna to set goals that were solely focused on what Anna wanted. It also gave Anna another opportunity and another person to "divide and conquer," making herself look innocent and rational, while casting us as unreasonable and rigid. The initial meetings consisted of Anna joking with Nadia, offering her sweet potato fries, and whispering at times right in front of Mark and me as if we were the adversary.

I was used to being shut out like this, in similar circumstances, *but I also knew that Anna did it because she was given the latitude to. It would have been helpful for the mentor to nip it in the bud.*

In moments like these, the urge to protest surged within me—to demand an end to the games and disrespect. Yet Mark and I knew all too well that beneath Anna's tough but immature façade lay a layer of inner turmoil that she sought to hide through her behavior. So I held my tongue. *This time.* This was a tool I had postponed learning to utilize, never thinking that I would need to stand up for myself in front of my own family, which otherwise practiced respect towards each other. I began to learn when to communicate, how to communicate better, and when it was best to stay quiet.

Nadia supported and guided Anna through the process of getting access to subsidized transportation and worked with me on setting her up with state-funded healthcare and a state ID. This was all fine, but she pushed forward, seemingly with the primary, if not sole, goal of facilitating Anna's desire for independence, as if this were the solution to everything. *I became aware that I served one primary purpose for the mentor, to supply her with anything Anna needed to be independent.*

Regardless of how many times I talked to Nadia about my discomfort with what was going on, she proceeded to focus on Anna's agenda and allowed the house-divided dynamic to not only happen but to increase. She fed Anna's power, while diminishing any ability we had as parents to advocate for other options for her to consider. At one point, our family social worker at Baker House had planned to facilitate a discussion to go over Anna's background and family information during a family-therapy session with

Catherine. I thought it was a good idea. Also, much earlier, Dr. Sophia (her first amazing psychologist) said we should wait as long as possible to share this type of information with Anna. We took that advice and decided to wait.

In preparation for the family-therapy meeting, I FedExed confidential copies of the information to Nadia. I also submitted one document *by mistake*: Anna's original birth certificate. This was something we wanted to share *in person* even though it was null and void. In Ukraine when a child is adopted, a new *birth certificate* is created with the adoptive parent's details and any name alterations. In Ukraine a child's middle name is patronymic; they combine the father's first name with the suffix "vych" for a son, and "yivna" for a daughter.

After I realized I'd accidently sent the additional birth certificate, I called Nadia to let her know the mistake. She then told me she'd already given Anna a copy. I was taken aback, but she explained that when she let Anna know she had the information, Anna told her that I'd said it was okay to give her the information, so she did. I was beyond shocked and irate at this breach of trust. I lost a lot of confidence in Nadia that day. Afterwards, Anna, quite naturally curious about her birth mom, used the information to conduct a lot of web searches and became very upset. This was precisely the type of situation we'd wanted to handle with kid gloves.

Another thing I think became a major setback for family relations was that Joan S., the DBT therapist, was the only therapist who hardly involved us in Anna's treatment, and I saw little to no progress coming from the work that they were doing.

We did not ask for or require a lot, but what we typically hoped for was someone who helped bring us together and didn't allow the splitting (so prevalent at this point). At times, Anna fretted that she complained and complained and got no input from the DBT therapist. I cannot comment. But when I had a conversation with the therapist, which was rare, and only typically happened because I requested it, I did not get any constructive advice or feedback either.

Another major problem was determining who would have overall accountability for Anna's care. Her neuropsych recommendations had stated that there should be one person who managed the care of the team and, at the time, the best suited would be the DBT therapist. This has been a problem I continue to mention because this never came close to happening, and it resulted in a very fragmented implementation of the care plan. One valid issue was the fact that Anna was at a group home where there were three staff clinicians, one of which was our family clinician. Put succinctly, there were a LOT of people involved, and it was difficult to get everyone on the same page without a clear point person.

Anna was calling the shots, and she wanted independence to follow through with her desire to live on her own, supported by the state. At this point, I was still only being asked to give information to the new mentor so she could help Anna secure things like a state ID. I had to show up at the registry and do things that Anna wanted, but from the mentor's perspective Anna did not have to engage with me. She had a small outburst when it was time to pay the fee at the registry, and Anna said she didn't bring money. I offered to pay, and she refused the money, saying it should be the state who paid. The mentor ended up using her own money or her organization's credit card to pay the fee.

In May, on Mother's Day, I received a call. One of a very few over the past couple of years. But I was not surprised to hear her voice. It was late in the day. I was out, having a key made at the hardware store, so I stepped away from the counter and answered. "Happy Mother's Day," she said right away. "Thank you very much," I said but felt the irony and didn't go on. She doubtless had no idea how much she had hurt me, so I let the silence linger. That did it.

Because there were a few seconds of silence, in which I didn't speak, she got angry and hung up. I later learned she started shouting at the house about how I didn't talk to her and I didn't appreciate the call.

Could I have been more receptive? Sure. But I was tired. All her unpleasantness towards me sucked the life out of me; a pleasant "Hello" and a genuine thank-you were all I could muster up at the time.

The bottom line is that I hadn't given up on having a relationship with Anna, but I was aware that the train was hurtling out of the station, and as I determined earlier, I needed to stop insisting that she engage, and engage respectfully, while she was continuing to push me away, quite disrespectfully.

Anna's eighteenth birthday neared.

Shortly beforehand, the group home prepared a summary that stated that our daughter could not engage in a trauma-treatment program there, due to multiple elopements, shoplifting incidents, major assaults on staff and police, and several hospitalizations. It noted that we consistently attended the parents' portion of the program, but it was stopped when no progress was made with Anna. *"No Progress Was Made with Anna"*—sad words for us. *This was one of the main reasons she was there.*

For the entire time Anna was at Baker House, DBT was not mentioned by any members of the team despite the fact that Dr. Jeffries clearly recommended considering it, and despite Anna's work with a DBT therapist. If I mentioned DBT books, workbooks, or other resources to Nadia, it fell on deaf ears similar when I tried to talk to Anna about it and she would exclaim "I am not doing that. It didn't work!"

Weekly family meetings continued but the time was used for preparing her for her transition, away from us, and towards the independence she wanted.

At the end of June, on her eighteenth birthday, we brought some gifts and a cake to a family meeting because she had already said that she had plans. "Celebrating" this way felt as vibrant as the dimly lit basement we held the meeting in. I couldn't shake off the lingering emptiness it left with me after we left.

Turning eighteen, Anna had informed us that she could now prohibit us from talking to anyone on her behalf, including about her treatment— for example, at Baker House, the Department of Mental Health program case worker and team, and others. She was an adult now and could do adult things. We received the same phone call from the therapeutic school, no more contact.

Did they explain to her what excluding us really meant? Did they encourage her to have a conversation with us about it, or did she sign away and write us off? Yes, she did. A thread was broken.

She also signed similar forms so we could not talk to her psychiatrist, her PCP, or anyone else without her permission. We never received the permission. *Another thread was broken.*

We were effectively shut out.

Continued intermittently into August, the family meetings eventually ceased all together as preparations for Anna's transition to independent living were finalized. In late fall she relocated from Baker House to an apartment within the same city. The communication stopped. At least, most of it.

In September of 2021 I found respite. Rewarded with a new contracting role that included stellar bosses and remarkable teams, I dove in headfirst. The work was fascinating, and I was contributing to the team's success. To top it off, Lily, my faithful companion, claimed her cozy spot under my desk, adding a layer of warmth to my home office.

I was also coaching girls' ice hockey. Working with this bubbly but determined group of ten- and eleven-year-old girls, alongside extremely dedicated and kind assistant coaches, made the season enjoyable and fulfilling. As busy as it was, it filled a void of disappointment in my life and heart that was present at that time.

Around October, Anna moved into subsidized housing in the same town as the group home. Or so we understood.

She began texting us again before Thanksgiving, and our message was, "Let's do a couple of sessions with a professional, with the hopes of spending time over the Christmas holiday together." She was completely taken aback and angry about this. I should have known then to completely drop the idea that anything like this would be productive.

PART 10

2022

CHAPTER 52

$%$#@!

Only the man who goes through this darkness can hope to
make any further progress.

—Carl Jung, *Yoga and the West*

2022 February

Anna was now in "shadowland," as Jung put it, where she had been for
years. But now she was out on her own. *For the first time, we began a*
new year without a litany of appointments, team meetings, school incidents or
follow ups from hospitalizations. Anna had been "independent" since the previous
fall, and we had limited contact with her. We prayed that she was safe and hoped
that she had the support she wanted and needed to be happy.

But as the year went on, there were isolated incidents of chaos that let
us know that Anna was still struggling and unpredictable . . . *And ironically,*
not knowing what she was doing or where she was, while she still harbored angry
tendencies toward us, had the effect of making me feel more afraid than I had
in the past.

February 22.

When I am on a Zoom call, I don't pay much attention if I hear Thomas, the teenage boy next door, come into my house to take Lily for a walk. I was engaged on the call, camera on, but did pause for a second when I didn't hear him coax Lily out of her cozy, furry dog bed.

Instead, I heard—a bark? Where was she? Never had she barked at Thomas. It took me a second to excuse myself. I turned off my sound and video. *Who was that hooded, masked person I glimpsed exiting my house, running down the street?*

I was very confused. *Was it Thomas? Was he trying to catch up with his mom and their dog?* As I tried to put it together, it was not making a lot of sense, *Oh, camera. Check camera.* It should not have been a complete surprise when I saw a masked, hooded Anna. She had come to confront me, but why confront me when she can take away something that I cherish?

"911, what's your emergency? "

Yup, I was close to a panic attack. I could have called the non-emergency line to my local police department, but I needed to get help fast. I needed to get Lily rescued from this dangerous situation. So, it began: another afternoon of crime stoppers; Anna denying she took the dog until the police exposed the truth, and then her trying to negotiate the terms of the return including "no police present." Oh, okay, sure, Anna. You get to determine this.

Hours later, after struggling to get through my work due to feeling paralyzed, the rough-looking SUV with the license plate hanging off the front barreled into the dead end and landed at the foot of the driveway.

While I waited for the officer, I felt sick. I hadn't seen Anna in seven months and didn't know what state of mind she'd be in. My heart was pounding and my breathing heavy. I saw the SUV pull up close to the driveway, and I walked out when I saw the officers' truck come up and park a little bit behind them.

The doors of the SUV opened, and along with a blast of pot smoke, Anna and her friend that I recognized from social media came out with Lily. The driver was the friend's mom. Chaos ensued. Standing at the end of the driveway, Anna, wearing the same back sweatshirt as earlier with the hood over her head, relinquished Lily to me. The "new" her could not have been more different than the sweet little girl I held in my heart.

"You don't want to be my mom anymore! I still live here! This is still my dog! You don't want to be my mom anymore! Just tell me"—said in a rough, street-talk tone. Our home- security video camera caught the entire five-minute exchange, including another round of her trying to jump out of the car and come back to the house after the police officer got into his truck. My words were calm, saying we were here for her and we love her to the friend's mom; she heard me, trying along with the officer to calm Anna down. Anna screamed, "I AM CALM!"

I was quiet while she got in my face and continued to get everything she came to say earlier off her chest and out of her system. She was upset about the past Christmas and called me obscenities. Her friend struggled to persuade her to leave while she was still spurting out the obscenities directed at me. I stopped listening; I needed to get Lily in the house, away from the explosive scene and away from the people who put her in danger. The car pulled around to leave but suddenly stopped. The door opened, and the shouting continued. The officer commanded, "Do NOT get out of that car." He went to the window, and Anna proceeded to shout at him until he told her to stop.

A few minutes later he asked me about her things. I said we could arrange that via text.

Her text to Mark: "Tell your wife I am picking up my clothes tomorrow."

She texted me with a similar message a couple of times too. I didn't pay any attention. The day changed me, and our relationships, and not for the better.

We ended up packing up her things, and Mark brought them to her house the next evening, when she said she would be there. When she wasn't there, Mark texted her, and Anna told him to knock and leave it with the staff. Nobody answered the door, so he had to leave them on the front steps. Boxes of belongings, jewelry, makeup, and a bungee cord chair that she would melt into when we talked in her room. I didn't mind that Anna wanted her things, but it was sad to have her bedroom emptied. She took a lot of pride in keeping her bedroom clean and cozy, and even though she was out living independently, her room had remained intact the way she liked. This had given me a sense of promise that at some point she would be back home in her room. But that was then.

CHAPTER 53

Scared

No one ever told me that grief felt so like fear.

—C. S. Lewis, *A Grief Observed*

L ily was kidnapped.

I continued to receive a steady stream of bullying and threatening texts from Anna and from unknown callers. I took off my Apple watch and began turning my phone to silence most of the time. It was ringing while I was playing hockey, and it was disturbing. Many of the calls were incoherent, detached from reality, but they almost always had a menacing tone, with specific threats to "come get me," "I will get that dog", and other insults. I think she was trying to bait us into engaging with her, to vent her anger, and at the same time she wanted to stay close with me.

THURSDAY FEBRUARY 24, 2022—RUSSIA INVADED UKRAINE (the second major invasion)

Months later, I learned that on Monday, February 28, Anna did not show up for school. I am not sure if she was in the Friday before, the day after Russia invaded Ukraine. But February 28 was the end of high school for now, just three short months until graduation.

On Monday, February 28, 2022, the barrage of phone calls and texts began about whose dog it was, with Anna boasting she was not sorry for what she did.

"I am not staying on the phone for this, Anna."

"What are you going to do? Call the police?" I did not respond. There were more threats, and then the dreaded statement that she was going to come back and get the dog and "finish what she started with me."

"Stop threatening me and do not contact me if you are going to harass me. You do not live here."

Laughing, Anna said, "Why do I have the address on my ID?" I told her I was not going to hang up on her, but I was going to say goodbye now. In all these times I do not know why I couldn't just say, shout, or scream — *you left us*—you had a home here, you cut us out from your life, and you walked away! All my anger was inside. I always tried to protect her feelings her sensitivity, her insecurity, her pain, her anguish.

The threatening behavior continued through texts and calls. I received "No caller ID" calls at all hours of the day and night but did not answer. I didn't change my phone number because I've always had that same cell phone number and have hundreds of contacts.

I was nervous about leaving our dog home alone, so I did that as infrequently as I could. I beefed up the security system and I installed spotlights. If she was only trying to scare me, it worked. One day I received a call from a Boston exchange that looked familiar, so I picked up. "I'm coming to get you," a voice said. I'm coming now. Make sure you leave all your doors unlocked!" I panicked and called 911. Yes, like a scaredy cat. I regretted making the call because it was mandatory with a 911 call that the police department send an officer out.

When he arrived, however, the officer could not have been nicer. He assured me that they would be available to help us in any way they could, and we discussed additional safety measures. From that point on, we locked the door regardless of who was home. I am not sure if it was residual, due to the Covid period, or it was solely these incidents, but I began not wanting to leave the comfort and security of my home, my family, and Lily. Since then, I have only worked remotely.

During this time, as the harassing calls and texts continued, I would typically pass information to my attorney so he would have it in his records. I had retained one a while back because I wanted any protection that I could for me and my family. My son worried about me and I wanted to prevent any potential surprises due to loopholes in the system.

On Monday, I received a call from what sounded like a young man. There was a lot of commotion in the background, and he said, "I am calling about your daughter." I could hear him asking someone "what should I say?" Then, the same woman's voice from a previous call got on the phone and said the same obscenity she'd said previously.

Early the next morning (1:37 a.m.) I received a call from a name and number I did not recognize. I did not answer. They continued to call and play this unappreciated game.

Although the calls had stopped since Tuesday, I was still feeling periods of overwhelming anxiety, and I didn't believe the harassment would stop for good. I was right, the ominous calls continued for the better part of the year.

Based in part on her history of violence towards our family and the current harassment directed at me, it was recommended that I fill out an application with the court where she would not be allowed on the property and could not contact me. At least until the onslaught died down. Mark agreed this was the right thing to do, so I wrote an affidavit. As uncomfortable as it was writing it, I had no problem going to the court to file it because I needed this nonsense to stop, and I was not going to live my life in fear.

When I went to file the affidavit, I learned the judge would hear the petition upstairs. I wasn't expecting this, but I went into the courtroom and waited until I was called. When the clerk called my name, I swore to tell the truth. While I stood, feeling very uncomfortable and hot, the judge looked through the affidavit. I did not have to say anything. She asked for my home address and work address. Then, was there anything else I wanted to share with the court? I told her I was nervous about the dog, and she asked me what the dog's name was. I said "Lily," so without hesitation the judge wrote, "Stay away from the dog Lily."

This incident was the beginning of when I began to feel increasingly nervous at home. Because Anna was out there on her own and I could not reach out to her school or any health care providers, I did not know much about how she was feeling and what type of treatment she was receiving, if any. The threatening calls and texts had an unsettling effect on me. They suggested that she was still highly volatile and angry, with her previous text comment, "I wish I finish what I started with you," always in the back of my mind. Rather than seizing her independence, it meant she now had become an emotional presence that could torment me at any time.

Last text from Mark's phone a day or so before the break-in in May:

> *Anna, I was not ignoring you, but will not respond to your texts about Mom. Both Mom and I told you over the last year that we wanted to restart family therapy. If you want to do that, we will talk to the court and make that arrangement. Also, Mom had nothing to do with making the restraining order for a year. It was for two weeks but it automatically got extended in court when you did not show up for the date called for on your subpoena. Please do not send mean and disrespectful texts and expect me to respond.*

Mark understood that allowing Anna to "split" between us—pitting us against each other—was out of the question. We needed to be on the same page, so we both worked hard at it to minimize the tension that could easily arise.

Speaking of this, because this content is so dense, I could not veer off into how all of this affected our family life, our marriage, and our work lives. What we did do was come together, and we all did our best to manage any chaos that I could not shelter others from. I managed my newfound fear and increased anxiety with the same methods that I have mentioned before, through my loving family and friends, hockey, yoga, books, art, therapy, and so much more. There was a point where I had to turn to a small dose of anti-anxiety medication and decided it is what it is. It has helped. There was still so much chaos. My head was still cloudy, and with the introduction of fear I began to lose sight of who I was and where I was going.

CHAPTER 54

Angry

There are two things a person should never be angry at:
what they can help, and what they cannot.

—Plato

On Sunday of Memorial Day Weekend (May 29, 2022), Mark arrived home from Cape Cod to a few unusual things; the first was a light on upstairs when he pulled into the driveway. Inside the house on the way to the kitchen he noticed the glass door of the mini refrigerator was open. This was odd. The refrigerator held beer and cold drinks. After a couple of steps, he heard a crunching sound; he had stepped onto a sea of glass. Everywhere. A large rectangular cobblestone lay in the glass on the kitchen floor, pieces of the broken window, with glass shards still attached.

He followed dots of red blood circles leading from the kitchen to my office, and then upstairs to Anna's room and then to my walk-in closet. All my desk drawers had been left open. Mark called me to let me know what happened; he was going to call the police. The initial officers who came walked through everything and seemed to understand why Mark thought it was Anna that had broken in. Unfortunately, the intruder avoided the cameras outside, and I negligently had not turned on the alarm, which would have been triggered by motion in the house.

The officers told Mark the detective would be coming over and he could not go into the kitchen until after the detective's initial investigation. This was challenging because it was late, and Mark had not eaten dinner; he was exhausted. When the detective interviewed Mark, he did not seem to understand why my husband thought he knew who had broken into the house. To give some context, Mark showed him a series of threatening texts Anna had sent about "coming back" to finish what she started, and other threats related to getting Lily. After a long and frustrating conversation, the detective left, and Mark called me. He said the detective said there was no probable cause to question Anna about the incident. He said the police asked that when I returned home in the morning, I should look through my office and closet to see if anything was missing.

This episode heightened my anxiety for the rest of the night. I decided to get up very early to head back home. It was extremely unsettling to walk into the house and see the now maroon blood dot trails on the carpet. I went through my office and found that a few of my credit cards were missing. It was hard for me to tell what else might be missing. I did not like it that my desk had been rifled through. Most of our important paperwork and other items were secured in another location, so we were thankful that those things were still there. Overall, I just felt violated and a bit sick. I called a handyman down the road, who came over right away to secure and board up the window.

I also called a rug cleaning company. When I called the detective to let him know what had been taken, I asked him if he was going to speak to Anna. He again said there was no probable cause. I was perplexed since it seemed obvious.

I asked him why recent events, including stealing our dog, the slew of harassing calls, and an active restraining order, were not probable cause. He said, "There is an active restraining order?" I said, "Yes, my husband told you that last night." I told him this break-in was illegal, and it also violated the restraining order, and was not okay.

Over the next couple of days, I did not hear back from the detective, nor did he return my call. I decided to take a walk down the street where whoever broke into our house most likely came from. Right away at the bottom of the street, I found a gap in the ground where two large cobblestones were taken out from around a tree. I knocked on the door of the house that was closest and asked if they remembered hearing anything on Saturday night or if their camera may have caught anything. They told me their son manages it, and they would ask him to check. We did notice that because they were on a hill, it most likely would not have caught the area where the cobblestones were. I thanked them and left my number just in case. When I walked up the street, I noticed another ring camera.

I knocked on the door and a man came out. I explained the situation and asked if he remembered any activity on Saturday night. He had two small children, so he had noticed that there was some laughing and commotion outside his home.

When he went to the window, nobody was there. He looked on his phone to see if the activity was caught on his camera and, remarkably, it was. There were two people dressed head to toe in sweat suits with hoods. Punks. One had a backpack that appeared to be full. They stopped briefly so one could adjust the backpack for the other, and then they continued down the street, cackling. I easily recognized Anna as the one with the backpack.

I reached out to the detective about this video footage. He stated that he had already been in touch with Anna and called her in for a meeting. He went on to say that she admitted to the break-in and claimed that she was only looking for her personal things and her passport. I told him we had already given her everything she asked for and the only passport she had was a Ukrainian passport she had used to come to America.

In a very pouty tone he said, "Well, she doesn't have any money, and she is going to move to Atlanta and not cause you any more problems." I wanted to say, "Are you sure about that? No trouble?" I understood that the detective was trying to resolve the situation, and she was barely older than a minor, but the way he was talking sounded like he had become something of a friend to her and was trying to downplay how her actions felt violating to us.

I had the very familiar sense of how Anna charmed people like social workers and hospital staff. Due to her illness, this may not have been conscious, but it happened often. No need to waste time trying to defend myself. I told the detective that just because she didn't have any money did not make it okay to throw a cobblestone through our window and take things that did not belong to her.

I understand that people like this detective want to help kids get on the right track and not get harsh penalties, but his type of behavior was enabling. If there were not going to be any consequences, it emboldened her, and she typically would up the ante. What might she do next?

Later when I called the police station, I learned that Anna was going to be charged with the crime of breaking and entering at night and violating an active restraining order. Her arraignment would be that day.

I had so many mixed emotions. The thought of Anna being arraigned for breaking and entering was excruciating, on the one hand. But how would she ever learn? I knew she was ill, but because this was premeditated and reckless, I still felt she needed to be held accountable. I knew from the incidents at Baker House that she did not want to go to juvenile detention or jail, so her boldness surprised me. We had no desire for her to go to jail, not for a minute, but how could we let this slide? I had only to look at the boarded-up window and blood drops all over my carpets for a reminder. This was after I put my ransacked office back together. There were zero consequences for stealing the dog other than the eventual temporary restraining order for the harassment afterward. So she disregarded the court order completely, damaged property, stole credit cards and other items, and then whined to the police that she was looking for personal things. Did she ever think to ask? Apparently not. Mark was always available to her by text or phone and would have been happy to help.

CHAPTER 55

Defeated

It's like a boulder rolling down a hill—you can watch it and talk about it and scream and say Shit! but you can't stop it. It's just a question of where it's going to go.
—Tom Wolfe, *The Electric Kool-Aid Acid Test*

In June of 2022, Anna left for Atlanta—moving there with a friend and her family. She posted multiple clips on social media—most of them in what I took for punk behavior: giving the finger, playing vulgar music with a very young child in the video, having a gun in the video with the title "Fake Gun" . . . It looked real to me. Using vulgar language. Knowing that she was in another state, Georgia, I admit that I had a sense of relief, but I was worried about what could happen to her while she appeared to be a rebel on the run. Didn't she know her over-the-top videos could attract the wrong type of person?

In fact, before long they did. We did not like seeing her in this situation, but it was exactly what for the past couple of years she'd said she wanted. And we couldn't even attempt to help her or keep her safe at this point. In fact, we had no control whatsoever.

The harassing phone calls did not stop. Throughout July, both Mark and I received a lot of "No Caller ID" calls in the middle of the night. Menacing texts were also part of the ordeal. Because they were sent to me or sent to Mark using my name, most were in violation of the restraining order. Three days before a family wedding Anna began harassing Mark. Despite his attempts to calmly explain his availability, she continued to accuse him of disrespect and rudeness for not responding right away. In another message to Mark, she went so far as to urge him to convey a hurtful message to me: "Tell that #@$^& (me) to kill herself." He replied, "Anna—what you are doing is wrong and breaking the law. This is not okay. Please stop texting."

The weight of this on top of daily life was taking its toll, and the night of the wedding after Mark gave his toast, he had a "ministroke." It was as scary as any other—disoriented, he had short-term memory loss—but we were lucky. It was a TIA (Transient Ischemic Attack) which is a brief stroke-like attack. Off to the emergency room we went.

One night in August, Anna called Mark's phone ten times in a row; I finally answered. It was before Mark's planned heart surgery, and he was not feeling well. Hospitals were busy, and if you weren't on the verge of a heart attack, it was a long wait for heart surgery. It ended up being a guy on the phone who told me he was with Anna in the hospital. Apparently, she had gotten into a fight and broken her jaw. "Is she okay?" He said, "Yes." "Are you going to stay with her?" He said, "Yes." I heard some commotion. I sensed he wanted to say more. "Tell her how sorry we are and that we hope she heals fast. We will pray for her," I told him.

A second later, yelling at me about what a bad mother I was, Anna got on the phone. I was taken aback; she could talk with a broken jaw?

It was a tough phone call; I called her "sweetheart" right away, when I heard her voice and again at the end, when I told her I loved her. This was natural and something I missed.

CHAPTER 56

Tense

He that passes by, and meddles with strife belonging not to
him, is like one that takes a dog by the ears.

—Proverbs (26:17)

Unfortunately, Mark had complications after his heart surgery:
extensive bleeding, lung collapse, back to ICU, and then on the
recovery floor, the wound became infected. A couple days later we received
the devastating news that the infection was in his blood which resulted in
him being in the hospital a full month. While he was in ICU, the phone
calls continued, so we needed to alert the staff to make sure the ringer on
his phone was turned off. During October, I had a revolving routine that
involved working during the day at home, then going to the hospital at
night. The nurses often let me stay past visiting hours, so I did occasionally.
I still did not like being away from home too long, especially with Lily there
alone. I felt safer at night with Lily tucked as close into me as she could. She
liked to lie partly on me, which I loved.

There is no doubt that all this stress took its toll on Mark. For years in
his always-upbeat way, he was burning the candle at both ends, working long

hours and spending as much time with us at home as possible. It was hard for him to bike and exercise the way he used to and enjoyed so much. He did his best, though, to follow the doctor's advice on his diet, exercise, and overall self-care. During this time, I did not exercise much, but still walked the Lily, which I loved to do, and played hockey later at night.

CHAPTER 57

No Words

If only. Those must be the two saddest words in the world.
—Mercedes Lackey

On October 17, 2022, while Mark was still in the hospital fighting the raving infection, I received a call from the local police department asking if I thought my daughter could be in another state, but not Georgia. I was taken aback. "I thought she was still in Atlanta."

A few minutes later, I received a call from a county sheriff officer in Mississippi. They were in the throes of a live rescue operation. The officer sought to confirm Anna's identity and age with me.

Initially I thought she was picked up on outstanding warrants from skipping out of town after the harassment and the break-in. As I verified the information he requested, his words sank in: there was an active rescue from an unimaginable dangerous situation. "What?" I struggled to grasp the reality of the situation.

According to him, Anna had been lured into a vehicle in one state and transported to another. "How could this be? She would not do that!" I'd spent countless days, talking with her about the danger of just that sort of situation. Was she harmed? Assaulted? Drugged?

He was very vague about the details, and at the time did not use the word "trafficked," but I could tell they'd picked her up in a perilous position. I knew what being lured into a car meant. She was kidnapped. "Wait," I said. I started to explain our situation but cut to the chase: "She already has trauma; she is not well; she is extremely vulnerable." He assured me they were taking her to a safe place. There was a lot of commotion in the background. "Have to get off the phone," he said.

From the snippets of information I'd received, I was left to imagine the details. My mind was racing. What had Anna endured, and how did it happen? Between Mark's condition and Anna's, I felt paralyzed and helpless, grasping for anything I could do to help either situation. I called Mark; I should have waited until I saw him, but I needed to talk. He was devastated and angry. "She is safe," I assured him. "I hope to have more information tonight."

Later that day I called the county officer back on his cell phone. "I need more information, please." He gave me the number of the deputy and the sergeant working the case. Eventually reaching the sergeant, I implored him: "Where is my daughter and is she safe?" Because she was over eighteen, they were prohibited from divulging additional information. I tried to explain that *his* office called *me* first and asked for a lot of details. "This is *my* daughter." Was I going to be shut out from even knowing how she was, what terrible situation they'd found her in?

He said it was a harrowing rescue; they apprehended two suspects; one was still at large. "Is she still in danger?" No, he said; she was safe and had been taken to a support agency. I thanked him *profusely*. They saved her.

These stories of attempted trafficking typically don't end this way. Since I needed to do something, I got online. The first thing I did was try to track down the support agency she'd been taken to, but I couldn't pinpoint it. Then I researched trafficking. Admittingly, I didn't have more than a cursory understanding of how trafficking works, although I knew it was horrific. I called our local DA's office and left a message; they might have answers.

When I visited that evening, Mark hadn't improved. Sluggish and unusually quiet, on top of everything, he was being treated for low sodium.

I felt like I was only getting pieces of his health status while he was at the hospital because I was not at the daily rounds. Sending a message to the surgeon through the patient portal, I hoped to get some straight answers. The surgeon would call me the next morning. On the call he assured me that the heart surgery went perfectly. "His heart is strong." He was still concerned about the post-surgery complications, a lung collapse, and the complicated infection. Mark was far from out of the woods. Reassured, I thanked him.

October 21, 2022

It was still early, so I went onto social media and saw that Anna had posted a video. The bright white background caught my eye. It was a new setting. Through some other investigating, I knew she was at Maryann's. I let out a long sigh.

A few days later, I received a call back from the district attorney's office. The woman apologized for the delay; she had been away. She confirmed that Anna was back in the state. Also, that she had gone to court with her court-appointed lawyer to clear her warrants and reported that she'd been a victim of a crime in Mississippi. The judge cleared the warrants and let her go. There would still be a bench trial for her outstanding charges related to the break-in earlier in the year and violation of the restraining order.

Around this time, Anna called, asking me if I even cared about what happened to her. This was the first contact I'd been able to have since learning about the ordeal. I wanted to offer her compassion and express how worried I had been but was taken aback by her combative tone. "Of course I care! I was worried sick about you!"

Relaxing a little, she began to share details. A few. Offering only a glimpse into how torturous the ordeal had been. "Don't you think I need a mother right now!!?" she yelled.

I said, "Yes, yes, of course, and I am right here. I have always been right here for you . . . You don't deserve this. I'm very sorry it happened to you."

I wanted to rip the vile creatures apart. I didn't want to ask about the monsters that kidnapped her, a trigger for sure. I should have, though, only because I still wasn't clear what happened.

Then she launched into the charges against her—demanding that I tell her whether I would be at court. I was overwhelmed. I could only picture her crouched in the corner of some old run-down shack with a gun to her head.

I snapped out of it when she started blaming me for having to go to court. *Is this why she called? It couldn't be.*

She asked me again if I was going to be present, so I answered, "I will be there. You need to be there too. It's the only way we can work things out . . .

"I love you," I said, "but now I have to get off the call and get back to work." I didn't need to get off the call because of work. I just needed to get off the call. I was in a living nightmare and was feeling the guilt of not protecting my daughter. And feeling guilty for wanting to protect myself.

CHAPTER 58

Firm

Letting go doesn't mean that you don't care about someone
anymore. It's just realizing that the only person you really
have control over is yourself.

—Deborah Reber

Around Thanksgiving 2022, I realized from my daughter's social media
that she was still staying at the home of one of her former babysitters.
She was posting videos on social media that I am sure my former friend had
not seen. *Yet.* Her beautiful home looked like a nightclub, at the end of the
night. Bottles empty and mascara smeared.

In early December, I received another call from Anna. She'd gotten
kicked out of this house, she said, and wanted to come by our house. My
mind was racing, my heart pounding. I thought: *Maryann, who loves Anna
deeply, kicked her out??* I told her that she could not show up at the house, I
could not help her. It would also get her arrested. She was not allowed on the
property. I knew that the only place she could get help was from a hospital or
the police, so I told her to go to a hospital or the police, they would help get
her to a safe place and off the street. She asked me about the court charges,

and I told her "We cannot talk about that." *It was an awful, awful call. Was I really doing this? Yes, I was.*

I had to do this. She needed help that was far beyond me, although thinking about this, and her on the other end of the line, made my stomach sick with sadness.

PART 11

2023

CHAPTER 59

Worried

I feel like a different person, writing this book, like it was a dream, not a reality.

—Brigitte Becker

Was that me? Did I spend years knowing it was that? Letting my heart be led around? Not listening to my own assessment? There is one thing. It abided. My love for Anna. For my husband, my son, for Lily. And, at least, with all the others, they expressed their loved. They never stopped showing it. No matter what reaction seemed to be called for at different times, I loved Anna as well. My heart always would.

I never stopped being concerned about her well-being, but after the incident in Mississippi the prior fall, I was especially worried about her— as I saw the extremely inappropriate and risqué things she posted on social media. Many of the posts seemed like they were thinly veiled jabs directed at me, as when she wrote about being abandoned by her adopted parents or about getting revenge. In April of 2023, she mentioned a time "when my probation is over, and I can finally do shit." I do not know exactly what she meant by shit, but I cannot imagine it being anything good or lawful.

At the start of 2023, Mark was still recuperating from surgery. Except for glimpses of her life posted on social-media accounts, we still had minimal information about Anna. I found it hard to believe—after the kidnapping out of state—that she would still be posting promiscuous content accompanied by indecent rap music. I did some research here and talked to a couple of professionals. I learned that this is a complex issue, influenced by a variety of factors. One of them is that victims of trauma often experience a psychological phenomenon known as trauma bonding, where they develop a strong emotional attachment to their abuser. This can lead to a distorted perception of the abuse and may result in the victim continuing to engage in risky behaviors.

I do not think this was the case for Anna, but there is also something called *normalization*, in which after being in a scary situation, a victim may have a distorted perception of what is normal, acceptable behavior. That meant Anna might not recognize that posting risqué photos or engaging in dangerous behavior could put her in harmful situations. Another observation relevant here is that many survivors of a scary situation suffer from mental health issues, such as PTSD, depression, and anxiety—which can influence their behavior.

Early in January of 2023, I received a phone call from the district attorney's office, letting me know that Anna and her lawyer had come in and were ready to make a plea on the charges related to the break-in and the exhaustive list of harassment incidents. This was the outcome we had been hoping for, so I was happy it was going to be resolved. With a plea, Anna would receive probation but no jail time. The advocate asked if Mark and I could get on a Zoom call right away, which we did. The court process to accept the plea was uneventful, although it was the first time in a long while, or maybe ever, that I heard Anna take any responsibility for her torment, her breaking the law.

CHAPTER 60

Sad

At the endpoint there is nothing but being, no time but
the present.

—Rabbi Akiva Tatz

I started writing in February of 2023; it was the same month that I rushed
my sweet thirteen-year-old Fox terrier to the animal hospital due to
possible kidney failure. It was a false alarm, but the disease was progressing.
I had to change her diet and care routine to make sure she stayed as healthy
as possible.

During the summer I spent more time down on the Cape. My mom
visited for over two weeks in early August, and we just enjoyed our happy
place together. I started a small project in late August, which helped with
the end-of-summer transition. I also did not want to take forever to get my
thoughts out on paper because I was still feeling overwhelmingly anxious
in several settings. Writing helped me immensely. I am learning as I go, at
first more about how to open up my privacy locks and *share* a story, but
then also about how to *tell* a story. To share, to tell—I am learning every day.

Quickly. *Still a work in progress. But the floodgates opened, and there was so much there to say.*

On November 2, 2023, the prosecutor in Mississippi called me. She was looking for Anna. My heart started to pound (yes, still).

I briefly explained our current situation and informed her that Anna had prevented us from talking to anyone on her behalf when she turned eighteen, several years prior. I also told her that we remained hopeful that Anna would choose to bring us into her current therapy, as a step to reconciling. I gave her the new cell phone number I had for Anna, letting her know that if it did not work, I could get her address from my husband.

A few days later, with an easy opportunity to reach out, Mark sent a text, letting her know it would be great if she wanted us to come into one of the sessions. She explained that they were focusing on her trauma, and we could not do that because of the restraining order. He reminded her that would not be an issue and said we both wanted to reopen the doors when she was ready. It will be interesting to see what happens in the year and years to come.

I am glad that she is in therapy to process her trauma, and I trust God that she will begin to heal and accept the love that people want to give her.

PART 12

2024

CHAPTER 61

Spirited

Your emotions are only signals. And you get to decide how
you'll respond to them.

—Arthur C. Brooks, Build the Life You Want:
The Art and Science of Getting Happier

Vacationing in Hawaii—swimming with giant turtles—I am at peace. I
would love it if Anna were swimming with us. She would love it. But I
cut the thought short. Right now, she has her own life. I wish her the moon
and stars. But I also give her the space to reach for it, knowing I am "with
her" without being with her. Every step of the way. In my heart.

2/7/24

There is new construction—new tracks are being built. The beautiful train
may glide again, against the beautiful landscape of what we know as life.

"I think it would be a nice idea if you reach out to Anna and ask her if she
wants to FaceTime with you and Lily over the next couple of nights," I said
to Mark a few days before we planned to put our sweet Lily to rest. Right

away he understood and sent a text. His phone chimed within a minute with a couple lines of text after a big Yes!

Things were going well for her. I overheard her describe many positive changes in her life. For example, she has a large support team, including a social worker, therapist, and mentor. Anna was taking classes to get her GED (equivalent of a high school diploma). All amazing and I felt such heartfelt relief. *Good for her*, I thought. She said she is working on herself and doing trauma therapy. I have heard this before, but something was allowing her to progress, be accountable and motivated, so this called for celebration.

Part of the conversation focused on her work, her old job where the people were lazy, the manager was unprofessional, and how happy she was to be in a different branch of the company now. She went on to talk about her stomach problems, having multiple trips to the doctor. I immediately felt like we were in the dining room, and she was talking to me. I didn't cringe. I smiled. Something was working to drive her forward; she was "doing the work" on this more productive path.

2/8/24

I am flat on the floor, with one hand on my heart and one hand resting gently over Lily's kidneys, which are worn. I fall into a meditative state, connecting with her and wishing her comfort, while also trying to envision what it will be like when I cannot physically touch her. When I awake, I feel her beautiful warmth under my hand. I need to say goodbye, to lead her to her next life, to let her be free from any pain while I take on the pain as a gift to her. I take a picture of us, heaven looking down.

I hoped I would want to write something about Lily passing. She is worthy of an entire book; she is sweet, curious, funny, smart, lovable. She is part of our family, and her love will last beyond a lifetime.

2/10/24 – She sleeps . . .

2/22/24

Walking alone in the park, startled by my pocket buzzing . . . The district court number flashes on my caller ID. "I am calling about the restraining order that is in place. It will expire on March 8."

"Oh, yes, thank you," I say, anticipating and ready for the next question.

I preempted it. "You can let it expire; everything is getting better, thank you for all your office did to help me." I felt a shift; she sounded taken aback . . .

"Okay, it will expire. Thank you very much and I hope you have a nice day."

"Thank you. You too."

3/8/24

I texted Anna last night:

> *. . . I would love to hear from you when you are ready—or let me know if you would like me to reach out. Love, Mom*

In my dream, *she wrote back . . .*

Epilogue

I am still learning . . . how to take joy in all the people I am,
how to use all my selves in the service of what I believe,
how to accept when I fail and rejoice when I succeed.

—Audre Lorde

I hope by telling my story it will help other moms or families in similar situations. Reading books like this helped me when I was feeling confused, judged, and alone, as if in a desert, hit by so many things I wasn't equipped to deal with. Nobody is, during such periods. Then I said slowly, "I need to get my thoughts out of my head and onto paper." My head was full of them, rolling around, over and over, in my head day after day. I needed to release them, release my worry, my successes, my failures. It wasn't easy, but once I made the commitment, I could not turn back.

During the more challenging years, 2017–2021, my life felt like a windy, swirling, maelstrom that I was sucked into. It wasn't until late 2021 that I felt "spit back out" the first time. This only lasted a brief period before a new storm took hold.

I became overwhelmed with fear. I know it might sound ridiculous; I am a grown woman. But it happened. Everything was uncertain. Over the past couple of years, I was determined to conquer this fear. I was not sure exactly what happened to me, but I did not like it and I needed to find my whole self again. What I was also searching for was how and why I could feel some peace with this profound loss of our daughter—opened up my version of Pandora's box. We had wanted to open ourselves up to a child: give that child the love and attention everyone deserves. That's how this journey began. Everything looked bright. A precious young girl entered our life.

Another thing that may not be obvious in my story is that it was not all about examining Anna with a microscope or finding her a fascinating case. Almost all these people who helped—family, friends, professional—bent over backwards to guide, support, love, partner with, and give her the benefit of the doubt in times of trouble. The transformation in my life may not have been obvious either. I transitioned from a fulfilled, active role as a working mom, business owner, wife, dog mom, daughter, sister, aunt, and sister-in-law. I was engaged in various responsibilities: volunteering at schools, coaching hockey, being a friend, juggling multiple household tasks, finding fulfillment in a meaningful job, dedicating time to charity, and cherishing moments with loved ones, whether it was exploring Cape Cod, visiting family, savoring red wine, or enjoying leisurely nature walks with our dog.

And then everything changed drastically. With Mark, I focused tirelessly on saving our daughter, prioritizing her well-being. She was number 1. Anything else took a backseat, but I was fine with this, believing it would all be worth it once a semblance of normalcy returned. I had visions of all of us together and happy.

But normalcy didn't return.

Did we help her by rescuing her from the now war-torn Ukraine? I would like to say yes, but we will never know.

But we chose her. AND she chose us.

Did we help her by having her go to therapy upon arriving, based on clues about attachment issues and recommendations through the adoptions process? Yes. There is no doubt in my mind that Anna was able to open up to Dr. Sophia immediately; they spoke in Russian and worked through some much-needed trauma immediately. She had already been through her own war, at home and in the orphanage. The doctor helped us both understand initially the attachment theories, resulting in Anna and me having a very strong bond, for years. So strong that it may have been too much for her.

Due to the foundation and trust that was established, they worked through Anna's OCD issues quickly, and she was relieved from the stress and anxiety it was causing. One regret is not returning to Dr. Sophia when Anna continued to experience pain and suffering that was manifesting in different ways.

Did we help her when we enlisted a state organization that expanded like a hot-air balloon? Probably not, but this was not due to the effort from the clinicians at the residential home.

There were many factors that contributed to a never-ending cycle. The most identifiable is that trauma, adoption, and mental illness are all complicated, each in its own right; now add disordered attachment, PTSD, and BPD, and additional coexisting conditions. An army was needed, but it would need to be an army of specialists: in particular, specialists familiar with similar case after case. Specialists who understand how the roles of the adopted mother and father play out and are perceived from the child's point of view.

I know when we invited in the army of experts, with some not so expert, into our life and our home, it may have overwhelmed Anna as much as it did me. She was used to chaotic environments in Ukraine, but was she used to so many people being fascinated by her? Wanting her to share her deepest secrets with them? I don't think so. Many times, over the past few years, when I questioned what we could have done differently or better, it was a little hard to answer, but at the end of the day I was confident we did our best. We never gave up, and we never walked away.

It was an effort that may someday bring ALL our family back together. I continue to pray this will happen. If it never does, my cup is full: I will continue to celebrate the immense love we have for Anna, *the outbursts of love she's shown for me—taking a bigger place in my heart than the later rejections*—and the overwhelming love imparted upon all of us in times of need. I will never forget the kindness and understanding of so many people.

I am not a psychologist or a specialist in mental health. I am a mom who wanted to provide love to our daughter, and to give her a family to love and care for her. Not leave her without that in an orphanage. I miss holding her, touching her, and comforting her.

Our daughter is innocent, trying to survive.

The abandonment from Anna's birth mother appears to be the deepest wound of all to her—from which all else stems—that promise to return, never fulfilled. A wound maybe never to be reconciled. It is my firm belief that that wound left her unable to trust our love: *She believed she had to leave us before we left her.* (Not intentionally or consciously.) I couldn't change this.

Amid her rage against her birth mother, there was so much pressure on her to reconcile with me. How could that have been possible at this time? Anna wanted to come home and be with us as her family and her family dog, but her incredible fear about this only increased the need to keep pushing us ... me away.

She did not feel deserving. "Good enough." And she could not sit in this calm but immensely uncomfortable (for her) environment and share her feelings. She didn't believe anyone cared or would ever understand. I even saw indications that she felt she was bad, which pained me. The inability to communicate (or the defense mechanism of holding everything in) during her teen years became overwhelming. Painful emotions made it too difficult (and unsafe) for her to regulate her emotions and behavior, thus making it impossible to parent her at home. Once she was free, she could show us—"Look at me. Look what I have overcome. Look what I can do. Look what I have accomplished." The same thing she wanted to show her birth mom.

The disconnect was—we did not and would not abandon her. She didn't have anything to prove to us. Having your own "crib" from state funds is different from having a loving family to rely on for support while you grow and learn and ultimately take on those responsibilities for yourself. For me, so much damage was done.

I still think the only place that could have kept the trains on the tracks or changed the course for more promising results may have been Dr. Sophia, McLean 3East Adolescent DBT program, or the few other specialized programs with an array of experts in BPD and other adolescent illnesses. It is so complex, but there are specific treatments, and people with this debilitating illness are healing.

Someone asked me. "What if she writes her own story, sharing the relationship from her perspective?" My response? It would be truly wonderful. She is beyond talented and perhaps, as with me, writing could provide her with a sense of release and healing.

So, waking from the dream, I am finding myself again, my own sense of freedom. Looking forward to moving ahead, relishing time with my husband and son, Mom, and the rest of my family.

I feel like someone who was trapped underground—rescued by the people closest to me and by myself—breathing slowly again, out there in the world. Feeling the sun on my face, the wind in my hair. Wanting to share it with Anna, whole and healthy. Not giving up on her healing, as it's not an impossibility. But letting her try it on her own. Only—a flaw in that plan— she wound up kidnapped almost immediately after her own escape from the love and support that she could not cope with. Still, it won't help her to lose myself, as I did for a period. I pushed through and have returned as the strong, independent woman I know myself to be. Also, I think there must be purpose in all this. It will show itself. And if not, I do not look back in regret. The adoption gave us so much. A lifetime in a few short years before the illness presented.

I miss stroking Anna's temple and giving her "massages." This connected us in a special and loving way. When she left my care, *my touch*, this connection was severed and has not been replaced, may never be. This, I could not prevent.

Only time will tell how our story, with its ups and downs, its happy promises and rays of sunshine blighted at times by storms of this illness, unfolds in the years to come. I feel the blessings of having the beautiful Anna as my daughter—sad about the time lost that could have been spent with her—the life we could have given her. We would have handed her the moon. But it wasn't to be, at least not in a direct-line, linear sense. I feel, instead, the immense challenges she's had to face, the repercussions that, God willing, will lighten and bring healing and peace to her, first of all, and then—yes— to this relationship in the years ahead. Wherever you are, Anna, you are always in my heart. And will stay there. All this worry that I might leave, which intensified the issue in the first place . . . What a plight your birth mother laid out for you.

Takeaways for the rest of you out there in a similar situation

I learned that I can turn away from someone who is not kind to me.

. . . Even if it is my own daughter.

It was a battle for a loving relationship not to be won by me, yet. I believe it is due to the complexity of the illness.

This isn't the outcome I had hoped for. It's a truth that's challenging to confront, but it's my reality at this time.

Finally, I learned that I am only human, and faced with attack after attack I had to keep reminding myself that it was not her standing in front of me, making the threats to hurt me, stealing the dog, texting my husband to tell me to kill myself—was that the old Anna? No. New Anna? No. It was the illness rearing its head, taking her over.

Acknowledgments

I am _eternally grateful_ to the following people for supporting me through this writing journey:

My husband

My son

My mom

My sister

My family and extended family

My amazing friends and acquaintances

My sweet pup

Ellen

Virginia

M.E.

Margaret

Brett H.

Nicole

My summer friend

Lisa

Dianne

Walter

Don A.

Sally

My hockey team

My dog-walking group

Matt S.

My book club

Notes

_____

_____

_____

_____

_____

_____

_____

_____

_____

_____

_____

_____

_____

_____

_____

_____

_____

_____

_____

_____

_____

_____

_____

_____

Recommended Reading

DBT Skills Manual for Adolescents by Jill H. Rathus, Alec L. Miller, and Marsha M. Linehan

Borderline Personality Disorder in Adolescents, 2nd Edition: What to Do When Your Teen Has BPD: A Complete Guide for Families by Blaise A. Aguirre, M.D.

I Hate You—Don't Leave Me: Understanding the Borderline Personality by Jerold J. Kreisman, MD, and Hal Straus

Stop Walking on Eggshells: Taking Your Life Back When Someone You Care About Has Borderline Personality Disorder by Paul T. Mason, MS, and Randi Kreger, et al.

Stop Walking on Eggshells for Parents by Randi Kreger, Christine Adamec, MBA, Daniel S. Lobel, PhD, Foreword by Fran L. Porter, MA

Healing Developmental Trauma by Laurence Heller, PhD and Aline Lapierre, PsyD

Loving Someone with Borderline Personality Disorder by Shari Y. Manning, PhD

Borderline Personality Disorder for Dummies by Charles H. Elliott, PhD, and Laura L. Smith, PhD

Get Me Out of Here: My Recovery from Borderline Personality Disorder by Rachel Reiland

Twenty Things Adopted Kids Wish Their Adoptive Parents Knew by Sherrie Eldridge

When Your Daughter Has BPD by Daniel S. Lobel, PhD

Reactive Attachment Disorder (RAD): The Essential Guide for Parents by Keri Williams

But, He Spit in My Coffee by Keri Williams

Reset Your Day Meditations by MoveWith

I Hate Myself: Overcome Self-Hatred and **Realize Why You're Wrong About You, 1st Edition** by Blaise Aguirre, M.D. (Author), Jewel (Foreword)

National Education Alliance for Borderline Personality Disorder (NEABPD)
https://www.borderlinepersonalitydisorder.org

The NEABPD website offers a wealth of resources on Borderline Personality Disorder, including blog posts, publications, webinars, and family support programs.

National Alliance on Mental Illness (NAMI)
https://www.nami.org

NAMI provides extensive mental health resources, including blog posts, publications, webinars, and support programs for individuals and families dealing with mental health issues.

About the Author

B rigitte Becker started her career as a graphic designer in publishing and transitioned to business consulting in the technology field.

Passionate about sports from a young age, she has competed in sixteen marathons and coached youth ice hockey. Besides family time, her favorite things include socializing with friends, playing hockey, practicing yoga, walking, creating art, and listening to audiobooks. She is a published photographer.

Brigitte lives in a suburb outside of Boston, Massachusetts, with her husband, and has two children.

For more information, additional resources, or to contact Brigitte about speaking engagements, please visit letthewildflowersgrow.net or use the QR code below.

Thank you for reading my book!

Dear Reader,

Your feedback is invaluable to me, and I would love to hear your thoughts.

Please spare a moment to share your insights by leaving a review on Amazon or Goodreads.

Gratefully,
Brigitte